FIELDING'S CONVERSATION GUIDE TO EUROPE

American Traveler's Companion

A WORD AND PHRASE BOOK *in*

English
French
German
Italian
Portuguese
Spanish

by **Graydon S. DeLand**

Professor of Modern Languages, Florida State University

Fielding Publications,
in association with William Morrow & Company, Inc.
New York   1966

This book is dedicated
To My Teachers and Students
through the years.

First Paperback Printing, 1975

Printed in the United States of America.

Library of Congress Catalog Card Number
66–17187

ISBN 0-688-61185-0

THE PURPOSE OF THIS BOOK

This book has been made for American travelers and students. It should also prove valuable to those living abroad, to businessmen, and to the many who are today studying foreign languages 'on their own.' In many years of study, teaching and travel, the compiler and his consultants have felt that there is a need for such a book. Listed below are some of the things which they hope you will like about it.

FEATURES

1. **Accuracy and authority.** This is a book prepared by language specialists. Dr. DeLand holds the B.A. degree from Colgate University, and the M.A. and Ph.D. degrees from the University of Wisconsin. He has taught modern languages for forty-eight years at Brown, Colgate, Denison, Michigan and Wisconsin. Since 1948 he has been Professor of Spanish and Portuguese at Florida State University. The consultants have likewise all had long teaching experience, have traveled widely and are all members of the Department of Modern Languages at Florida State University.

2. **Alphabetical arrangement.** There is available no other similar book which features this for *both* words and phrases. The usual device of listing under 'categories' such as The Restaurant and The Train Trip only slows up the finding of the word or expression you want.

3. **Pronunciation aid.** The pronunciation of any foreign language is acquired mainly through imitation and practice. Some acquaintance with the pronunciation of the particular language in which the reader may be interested is of course desirable. The text is uncluttered by dubious, often imaginary 'pronunciation helps,' so often found in pocket dictionaries of this sort. However, stressed syllables (or, in some cases, the predominant vowel), have been placed in BOLD FACE to facilitate pronunciation. Occasionally, accurate syllabication has been sacrificed to make pronunciation of the word easier. Words which

show no syllable in bold face have no syllable that is particularly stressed.

4. Practical vocabulary and idiom. The author hopes that the approximately 5,000 entries will prove to be neither on the short side nor excessive. In compiling such a work, it has been as difficult to decide upon what to leave out as to what to include. A feature is the inclusion of many very usable words and phrases not to be found elsewhere.

5. Adequate spacing for good legibility. It is hoped that here, too, there has been an improvement upon all other books available to the student or traveler. The type is clear and the 'banked' arrangement of the entries should make for easy reference.

6. Spanish-Mexican and Portuguese-Brazilian terms. Most Spanish words and phrases are understood throughout the Spanish-speaking world. In the case of Portuguese, too, there is a universally understood and used vocabulary and idiom wherever the language is spoken. However, there are many differences to be encountered in the language of Spain and Portugal as found on this side of the Atlantic. Since so many Americans are now going to Latin America, especially to Mexico, an attempt has been made to indicate forms current there by the insertion of (Mex.). Similarly, forms heard in Brazil are shown by (Br.). Still other forms, found in the Americas generally, are shown by (Amer.).

NOTES REGARDING THE VOCABULARY

1. In French, each noun is either masculine (using "le" for "the") or feminine (using "la" for "the"). All plural nouns use "les" for "the." In the text *m* indicates masculine nouns, *f* feminine nouns; *pl* designates plural forms.

2. In German, nouns followed by the letter *m*, are masculine and require the article "der" for "the"; those followed by *f* are feminine and require "die" for "the"; those followed by *n* are neuter nouns and require "das" for "the." All plural nouns require "die" for "the" and are shown as *mpl* or *fpl*.

3. In all five of the foreign languages used, plural forms are indicated by *mpl* or *fpl*, except for a few nouns which have no singular form.

4. In Italian, Portuguese and Spanish, most nouns ending in -o are masculine and those ending in -a are feminine. The text shows by *m* or *f* all exceptions and for all nouns which end otherwise. Refer to the entry THE for exact forms.

5. In all five languages, the definite article is shown with the noun wherever especially required.

6. The part of speech (noun, preposition, adverb, etc.) generally has been indicated only where the word otherwise might prove confusing in use.

7. The infinitive is shown thus: verb + comma + to: (see, to)

8. Stress that part of each word shown in BOLD FACE.

List of abbreviations used

acc.	accusative case	med.	medical
adj.	adjective	(Mex.)	Mexican usage
adv.	adverb	mil.	military
(Amer.)	Spanish American usage	n	neuter gender
anat.	anatomy	(n.)	noun
bldg.	building	mus.	music
(Br.)	Brazilian usage	obj.	object
bus.	business term	part.	participle
chem.	chemical	phot.	photography
conj.	conjunction	pl	plural
dat.	dative case	p.p.	past participle
dem.	demonstrative	prep.	preposition
dir.	direct	prof.	profession
e.g.	for example	pron.	pronoun
elect.	electrical	punct.	punctuation
etc.	and so forth	rel.	relative
f	feminine gender	R.R.	railroad
gen.	genitive case	temp.	temperature
gram.	grammar	theat.	theatre
ind.	indirect object	transp.	transportation
inf.	infinitive	trav.	travel
m	masculine gender	univ.	university
math.	mathematics	vb.	verb
mech.	mechanics		

GOOD LUCK!
BONNE CHANCE!
VIEL GLÜCK!
BUONA FORTUNA!
BOA SORTE!
¡BUENA SUERTE!

English	*French*	*German*
a, an (with fem.)	une	eine
a, an (with masc.)	un	ein
a, an (with neut.)	—	ein
a few	quelques-**uns**	ein **paar**
à la carte	à la carte	nach der **Karte**
a little (a bit)	un peu (de)	ein bisschen
a week ago	il y a une se**maine**	vor einer **Woche**
a week from today	d'aujourd'hui en **huit**	heute in acht **Tagen**
a while	(pour) un **moment**	eine Weile
a while ago	il y a peu de **temps**	vor kurzem
abdomen	abdomen *m*	Bauch *m*
able, to be	pouvoir	können
able (capable)	capable	fähig
about (approx.)	envi**ron**; vers (hour)	ungefähr; **gegen** (hour)
about (concerning)	de	über
about to, to be	être sur le **point** de	im Be**griff** sein
above (overhead)	en **haut**	oben
above (higher than)	au-dessus de	über
abroad	à l'étran**ger**	im Ausland
abscess	abcès *m*	Abszess *m*
absence	absence *f*	Abwesenheit *f*
absent	absent	abwesend
accent (speech)	accent *m*	Aussprache *f*
accelerator	accéléra**teur** *m*	Gaspedal *n*
accept, to	accepter	annehmen
accident	accident *m*	Unfall *m*
accommodate (have room for), **to**	loger	unterbringen
accompany, to	accompa**gner**	begleiten
accomplish, to	accomplir	vollbringen
according to	d'après; selon	nach
accurate	exact	genau
accustom oneself to, to	s'habituer à	sich gewöhnen **an**
ache	mal *m*	Schmerz *m*
ache, to	avoir mal	schmerzen
acid	acide *m*	Säure *f*
acknowledge (admit)	reconnaître	anerkennen
acknowledge (receipt)	accuser récep**tion** de	bestätigen

Italian	*Portuguese*	*Spanish*
una, un'	uma	una
un, uno	um	un
—	—	—
alcuni	alguns	algunos
alla carta	a la carta	a la carta
un poco (di)	um pouco (de)	un poco (de)
una settimana fa	há uma semana	hace una semana
oggi a otto	daqui a uma semana	de hoy en ocho días
(per) breve tempo	(por) algum tempo	(por) un rato
poco fa	há pouco	hace un rato
addome *m*	abdome *m*	abdomen *m*
potere	poder	poder
capace	capaz	capaz
circa	mais ou menos	unos; cosa de; a eso de (hour)
circa; verso (hour)	acêrca de	acerca de
stare per	estar a ponto de	estar para
in alto	acima	encima
al di sopra di	acima de	encima de
all'estero	no estrangeiro	en el extranjero
ascesso	abcesso	absceso
assenza	ausência	ausencia
assente	ausente	ausente
accento	sotaque *m*	acento
acceleratore *m*	acelerador *m*	acelerador *m*
accettare	aceitar	aceptar
incidente *m*	acidente *m*	accidente *m*
accomodare	hospedar	hospedar
accompagnare	acompanhar	acompañar
compiere	cumprir	cumplir
secondo	segundo	según
accurato	exato	exacto
abituarsi a	acostumar-se a	acostumbrarse a
dolore *m*	dor *f*	dolor *m*
dolere	doer	doler
acido *m*	ácido	ácido
riconoscere	reconhecer	reconocer
accusare ricevuta di	acusar recebimento de	acusar recibo de

English	*French*	*German*
acquaintance, (friend)	connaissance *f*	Bekannte *m, f*
acquire, to	acquérir	erwerben
across (beyond)	au-delà de	jenseits
across (through)	à travers	über
act (deed)	acte *m*	Tat *f*
act (theatre)	acte *m*	Aufzug *m*; Akt *m*
actor	acteur *m*	Schauspieler *m*
actress	actrice *f*	Schauspielerin *f*
actual (real)	réel	wirklich
actually (in fact)	en effet	tatsächlich
add (include), to	ajouter	hinzufügen
add up, to	additionner	addieren
adding machine	machine *f* à calculer	Rechenmaschine *f*
address (P.O.)	adresse *f*	Anschrift *f*
address (speech)	discours *m*	Rede *f*
addressee	destinataire *m*	Empfänger *m*
adhesive tape	sparadrap *m*	Leukoplast *n*
adjective	adjectif *m*	Adjektiv *n*
adjoining	contigu	anliegend
admiral	amiral *m*	Admiral *m*
admire, to	admirer	bewundern
admission (right to enter)	entrée *f*	Eintritt *m*
admit (allow to enter)	laisser passer	her-, hinein lassen
admit (concede), to	reconnaître	zugeben
advantage	avantage *m*	Vorteil *m*
adventure	aventure *f*	Abenteuer *n*
adverb	adverbe *m*	Adverb *n*
advertise, to	faire de la publicité	Reklame machen
advertisement	annonce *f*	Anzeige *f*
advice	conseil *m*	Rat *m*
advise, to	conseiller	raten; beraten
aerial (antenna)	antenne *f*	Antenne *f*
affection (love)	affection *f*	Zuneigung *f*
affectionate	affectueux, -euse	zärtlich
afford (something), to	se permettre	sich leisten
afraid of, to be	avoir peur (de)	**Angst** haben (**vor**)

Italian	*Portuguese*	*Spanish*
conoscente *m, f*	conhecido	conocido
acquistare	adquirir	adquirir
al di là di	ao outro lado de	al otro lado de
attraverso	através de	a través de
atto	ato	acto
atto	ato	acto
attore *m*	ator *m*	actor *m*
attrice *f*	atriz *f*	actriz *f*
vero	verdadeiro	verdadero
veramente	realmente	en efecto
aggiungere	acrescentar	añadir
addizionare	somar	sumar
addizionatrice *f*	máquina de somar	máquina de sumar
indirizzo	direção *f*; enderêço (Br.)	señas *fpl*; dirección *f* (Amer.)
discorso	discurso	discurso
destinatario	destinatário	destinatario
nastro adesivo	adhesivo; esparadrapo	esparadrapo
aggettivo	adjetivo	adjetivo
contiguo	contíguo	contiguo
ammiraglio	almirante *m*	almirante *m*
ammirare	admirar	admirar
entrata	entrada	entrada
ammettere	deixar entrar	dar entrada
ammettere	conceder	conceder
vantaggio	vantagem *f*	ventaja
avventura	aventura	aventura
avverbio	advérbio	adverbio
fare della pubblicità	anunciar	anunciar
annunzio	anúncio	anuncio
consiglio	conselho	consejo
consigliare	aconselhar	aconsejar
antenna	antena	antena
affetto	carinho	cariño
affettuoso	carinhoso	cariñoso
permettersi	ter recursos para	permitirse
aver paura (di)	ter mêdo (de)	tener miedo (de)

English	*French*	*German*
Africa	l'Afrique *f*	Afrika *n*
African (adj.)	africain	afrikanisch
after (conj.)	après que	nachdem
after (prep.)	après	nach
after a while	tout à l'heure	nach einer Weile
after all...	enfin	doch
afternoon	après-midi *m*	Nachmittag *m*
aftershave lotion	eau *f* de Cologne	Rasierwasser *n*
afterward (later)	ensuite	nachher
again	encore	wieder
against, (up-)	contre	gegen
against (in opposition)	contre	wider
age	âge *m*	Alter *n*
agency (bus.)	l'agence *f*	Vertretung *f*
agent (representative)	agent *m*	Vertreter *m*
ago (e.g. two years—)	il y a—	vor—
agree (assent), to	consentir	beistimmen
agree (concur), to	convenir	übereinstimmen
agreeable (pleasant)	agréable	angenehm
agreed!	c'est entendu!	abgemacht!
ahead (forward)	en avant	vorwärts
ahead (in front)	devant	voraus
aid	aide *f*	Hilfe *f*
aid, to	aider	helfen
aim (purpose)	but *m*	Zweck *m*
air	air *m*	Luft *f*
air conditioning	climatisation *f*	Klimaanlage *f*
aircraft carrier	porte-avions *m*	Flugzeugträger *m*
air line	ligne *f* aérienne	Luftverkehrslinie *f*
air mail	poste *f* aérienne	Luftpost *f*
air-mattress	matelas *m* pneumatique	Luftmatratze *f*
airplane	avion *m*	Flugzeug *n*
airport	aéroport *m*	Flughafen *m*
air raid	raid *m* aérien	Luftangriff *m*

Italian	*Portuguese*	*Spanish*
l'Africa	África	el Africa
africano	africano	africano
dopo che	depois que	después que
dopo	depois de; após	después de
qualche tempo dopo	daí a pouco	poco después
dopo tutto	no fim de contas	en fin
pom**eriggio**	tarde *f*	tarde *f*
lozione *f* **dopobarba**	loção *f* de **barba**	loción *f* para después de afeitarse
dopo	depois	después
di nuovo	outra **vez**; de nôvo	otra vez
contro	contra	contra
contro	contra	contra
età	idade *f*	edad *f*
agenzia	agência	agencia
rappresen**tante** *m*	agente *m*	agente *m*
—fa	há—	**hace**—
acconsentire	assentir	asentir
essere d'accordo	estar de acordo	estar de acuerdo
gradevole	agradável	agradable
(siamo) d'ac**cordo**!	combinado!	¡de acuerdo!
avanti	adiante	adelante
davanti	diante	delante
aiuto	ajuda	ayuda
aiutare	ajudar	ayudar
scopo	propósito	propósito
aria	ar *m*	aire *m*
aria condizio**nata**	**ar** condicio**nado**	aire acondicionado; clima *m* (Mex.)
portaerei *f*	porta-aviões *m*	portaaviones *m*
línea aerea	linha aérea	línea aérea
posta aerea	correio aéreo	correo aéreo
materasso pneumatico	colchão de **ar**	colchón *m* de aire
aereo	avião	avión *m*
aeroporto	aeroporto	aeropuerto
incursione *f* aerea	reide *m* aéreo	incursión *f* aérea

English	French	German
English	*French*	*German*
aisle	passage *m*	Gang *m*
alarm clock	réveille-matin *m*	Wecker *m*
alcohol	alcool *m*	Alkohol *m*
ale (pale)	bière *f* blonde	helles **Bier** *n*
alike (similar)	pareil	gleich
alive	vivant	lebendig
all (every)	tout	jeder; alle
all (everything)	tout	alles
All aboard!	En voiture!	Einsteigen!
all day (long)	toute la journée	den ganzen **Tag**
all kinds of	toutes sortes de	allerlei
All right!	Très bien!	Gut!
allergy	allergie *f*	Aller**gie** *f*
allow, to	permettre	erlauben
Allow me...	Permettez-**moi**...	Erlauben Sie **mir**...
almond	amande *f*	Mandel *f*
almost	presque	beinahe; fast
alone	seul	allein
along (side)	le long de	ent**lang**; neben
aloud	à haute **voix**	laut
Alps, The	les Alpes *fpl*	die Alpen *fpl*
already	déjà	schon
also	aussi	auch
altar	autel *m*	Altar *m*
alternating current	courant *m* alternatif	Wechselstrom *m*
although	bien que	obgleich; ob**wohl**
aluminum	aluminium *m*	Aluminium *n*
always	toujours	immer
a.m.	du matin	morgens
ambassador	ambassa**deur** *m*	Botschafter *m*
ambulance	ambulance *f*	Krankenwagen *m*
America	l'Amérique *f*	Amerika *n*
American (adj.)	américain	amerikanisch
American plan	pension *f* complète	Vollpension *f*
amethyst	améthyste *f*	Amethyst *m*
ammunition	munitions *fpl*	Munition *f*
among	parmi	unter

Italian	*Portuguese*	*Spanish*
passaggio	passagem *f*	pasillo
sveglia	despertador *m*	despertador *m*
alcool *m*	álcool *m*	alcohol *m*
birra chiara	cerveja clara	cerveza clara
simile	parecido	semejante
vivo	vivo	vivo
ogni	todo	todo
tutto	tudo	todo
In carrozza!	Todos a bordo!	¡Señores viajeros al tren!; ¡Vámonos! (Mex.)
tutto il giorno	o dia inteiro	el día entero
ogni sorta di	tôda sorte de	toda clase de
Molto bene!	Muito bem!	¡Está bien!
allergia	alergia	alergia
permettere	deixar	dejar
Mi permetta...	Deixe-me...	Déjeme...
mandorla	amêndoa	almendra
quasi	quase	casi
solo	só; sòzinho	solo
lungo	ao longo de	a lo largo de
ad alta voce	em voz alta	en voz alta
le Alpi *fpl*	os Alpes *mpl*	los Alpes *mpl*
già	já	ya
anche	também	también
altare *m*	altar *m*	altar *m*
corrente *f* alternata	corrente *f* alternada	corriente *f* alterna
benchè	embora; ainda que	aunque
alluminio	alumínio	aluminio
sempre	sempre	siempre
del mattino	da manhã	de la mañana
ambasciatore *m*	embaixador *m*	embajador *m*
ambulanza	ambulância	ambulancia
l'America *f*	a América	América
americano	americano	americano
pensione *f* completa	pensão *f* completa	pensión *f* completa
ametista	ametista	amatista
munizione *fpl*	munição *f*	munición *f*
fra	entre	entre

English	*French*	*German*
amount	somme *f*	Betrag *m*
amusing	amusant	amüsant
anchor (n.)	ancre *f*	Anker *m*
anchovy	anchois *m*	Anchovis *f*
ancient	ancien	uralt
and	et	und
Andes, The	les Andes *fpl*	die Anden *fpl*
and so...	puis alors...	also...
and so on	et ainsi de suite	und so weiter
angel	ange *m*	Engel *m*
angry	fâché	zornig
angry with, to get	se fâcher contre	sich ärgern über
animal	animal *m*	Tier *n*
anise	anis *m*	Anis *m*
ankle	cheville *f*	Knöchel *m*
announce, to	annoncer	ankündigen
annual (adj.)	annuel	jährlich
another (different)	un autre	ein anderer *m*
another (one more)	encore un (e)	noch ein (etc.)
answer (n.)	réponse *f*	Antwort *f*
answer (a question)	répondre à	beantworten
ant	fourmi *f*	Ameise *f*
antibiotic	antibiotique *m*	Antibiotikum *n*
antidote	contrepoison *m*	Gegengift *n*
anti-freeze	antigel *m*	Frostschutz *m*
antique shop	chez l'antiquaire *m*	Antiquitätenladen *m*
Antwerp	Anvers	Antwerpen *n*
anxious, to be	désirer vivement	begierig sein
any (anyone)	n'importe quel	irgendein
any (quantity)	de(d'); du; de la(de l'); des	irgendwelche
anybody (whosoever)	n'importe qui	wer immer
anyhow (in any case)	de toute façon	jedenfalls
Anything else?	...Et avec ça?	Sonst noch etwas?
anywhere (whereso-ever)	n'importe où	wo immer
apartment (flat)	appartement *m*	Wohnung *f*
apartment house	immeuble *m*	Mietshaus *n*

Italian	*Portuguese*	*Spanish*
somma	quantidade *f*	cantidad *f*; importe *m*
divertente	engraçado	divertido
ancora	âncora	ancla
acciuga *f*	anchova	anchoa
antico	antigo	antiguo
e; ed	e	y; e
le Ande *fpl*	os Andes *mpl*	los Andes *mpl*
e così...	então; pois	de modo que...
e così via	e assim por diante	etcétera
angelo	anjo	ángel *m*
adirato	zangado	enojado
andare in collera	zangar-se com	enojarse con
animale *m*	animal *m*	animal *m*
anice *m*	anis *m*	anís *m*
caviglia	tornozelo	tobillo
annunziare	anunciar	anunciar
annuale	anual	anual
un altro	um outro	otro
un altro	outro	otro
risposta	resposta	respuesta
rispondere	responder	contestar
formica	formiga	hormiga
antibiotico	antibiótico	antibiótico
antidoto	antídoto	antídoto
anticongelante *m*	anticongelante *m*	anticongelante *m*
negozio di antichità	loja de antiguidades	tienda de antigüedades
Anversa	Antuérpia	Amberes
essere ansioso di	estar com vontade de	tener ganas de
qualsiasi	qualquer, quaisquer	cual(es) quier(a)
del, etc.	algo de	algo de
chiunque	qualquer pessoa	cualquier persona
in ogni caso	de qualquer modo	de todos modos
Nient' altro?	Mais alguma coisa?	¿Otra cosa?
in qualunque luogo	para qualquer parte	dondequiera
l'appartamento *m*	apartamento	piso; departamento
stabile *m* ad appartamenti	casa de apartamentos	casa de pisos; casa de departamentos

English	*French*	*German*
apparently	évidem**ment**	offenbar
appear (seem), to	paraître	scheinen
appetite	appétit *m*	Appetit *m*
appetizer	apéritif *m*	Vorspeise *f*
apple	pomme *f*	Apfel *m*
applesauce	compote *f* de **pommes**	Apfelmus *n*
appoint, to	nommer	ernennen
appointment (meeting)	rendez-**vous** *m*	Verabredung *f*
appreciate (be grateful for), to	reconn**aître**	sch**ätzen**
approach, to	s'approcher de	sich n**ä**hern
apricot	abricot *m*	Aprikose *f*
April	avril *m*	April *m*
apron	tablier *m*	Schürze *f*
Arabic (adj.)	arabe	arabisch
arcade	arcade *f*	Arkade *f*
architect	architecte *m*	Architekt *m*
Are there...?	Y a-t-il...?	Gibt es...?
Are you ready?	Êtes-vous **prêt?**	Sind Sie **fertig?**
area (region)	région *f*	Gebiet *n*
...aren't you?	...n'est-ce **pas?**	...nicht **wahr?**
Argentina	l'Argentine *f*	Argentinien *n*
Argentinian (adj.)	argentin	argentinisch
arm	bras *m*	Arm *m*
armchair	fauteuil *m*	Sessel *m*
army	armée *f*	Heer *n*
around (prep.)	autour de	um
arrange (plan), to	arranger	einrichten
arrest, to	arrêter	verhaften
arrival	arrivée *f*	Ankunft *f*
arrive, to	arriver	ankommen
arrow	flèche *f*	Pfeil *m*
art	art *m*	Kunst *f*
art gallery	galerie *f* d'**art**	Gemäldegalerie *f*
artery	artère *f*	Schlagader *f*
arthritis	arthrite *f*	Arthritis *f*
artichoke	artichaut *m*	Artischocke *f*
article (thing)	article *m*	Sache *f*

Italian	*Portuguese*	*Spanish*
apparentemente	aparentemente	por lo visto
sembrare	parecer	parecer
appetito	apetite *m*	apetito
aperitivo	acepipe *m*	aperitivo
mela	maçã	manzana
conserva di mele	compota de maçã	compota de manzana
nominare	nomear	nombrar
appuntamento	entrevista	cita
gradire	agradecer	agradecer
avvicinarsi a	acercar-se a	acercarse a
albicocca	damasco	albaricoque *m;* chabacano (Amer.)
aprile *m*	abril *m*	abril *m*
grembiale *m*	aventa *m*	delantal *m*
arabo	árabe	árabe
arcata	arcada	soportales *mpl*
architetto	arquiteto	arquitecto
Ci sono...?	Há...?	¿Hay...?
È pronto?	Está pronto?	¿Está listo?
regione *f*	região *f*	región *f*
...non è vero?	...não é?	...¿ (no es) verdad?
l'Argentina *f*	a Argentina	la Argentina
argentino	argentino	argentino
braccio (*pl* le braccia *f*)	braço	brazo
poltrona	cadeira de braços	sillón *m*
esercito	exército	ejército
intorno a	em redor de	alrededor de
ordinare	combinar; arranjar	arreglar
arrestare	prender	prender
arrivo	chegada	llegada
arrivare	chegar	llegar
freccia	flecha	flecha
arte *f*	arte *f*	arte *f*
galleria d'arte	galeria de arte	galería de arte
arteria	artéria	arteria
artrite *f*	artrite *f*	artritis *f*
carciofo	alcachôfra	alcachofa
oggetto	coisa	cosa

English	*French*	*German*
artist	artiste *m, f*	Künstler *m*
as (since)	puisque	da
as (in the same way)	comme	wie
as...as	aussi...que	so...wie
as for (prep.) (me)	quant à (moi)	was (mich) betrifft
as many...as	autant de...que	so viele...wie
as much (money) as	autant (d'argent) que	so viel (Geld) wie
as soon as (conj.)	aussitôt que; dès que	sobald
as soon as possible	le plus tôt possible	so bald wie möglich
as though	comme si	als ob
As you wish	Comme vous voudrez	Wie Sie wollen
ash tray	cendrier *m*	Aschenbecher *m*
ashamed (be), to	avoir honte	sich schämen
Asia	l'Asie *f*	Asien *n*
Asiatic (adj.)	asiatique	asiatisch
ask (a question), to	poser une question	eine Frage stellen
ask about, to	s'informer sur	fragen nach
ask for (request), to	demander	bitten um
asleep	endormi	(e.g.er schläft)
asparagus	asperges *fpl*	Spargel *m*
aspirin	aspirine *f*	Aspirin *n*
assist, to	aider	beistehen
assistance	aide *f*	Beistand *m*
at (a price of)	à	für
at (in)	à	bei; in
at all costs	à tout prix	um jeden Preis
at daybreak	au point du jour	bei Tagesanbruch
at first	d'abord	zuerst
at home	à la maison	zu Hause
at last	enfin	zuletzt
at least	au moins	wenigstens
at midnight	à minuit	um Mitternacht
at night	la nuit	in der Nacht
at noon	à midi	am Mittag

Italian	*Portuguese*	*Spanish*
artista *m, f*	artista *m, f*	artista *m, f*
poichè	pois que	puesto que
come	como	como
tanto...quanto	tão...como; tão... quanto (Br.)	tan...como
quanto a (me)	quanto a (mim)	en cuanto a (mí)
tanti...quanti	tantos...quanto	tantos...como
tanto (denaro) quanto	tanto (dinheiro) quanto	tanto (dinero) como
appena (che)	assim que; logo que	en cuanto
al più presto possibile	o mais breve possível	cuanto antes
come se	como se	como si
Come desidera	Como desejar	Como Ud. guste
portacenere *m*	cinzeiro	cenicero
vergognarsi	envergonhar-se	avergonzarse
l'Asia *f*	a Ásia	Asia
asiatico	asiático	asiático
domandare	perguntar	preguntar
informarsi di	perguntar por	preguntar por
chiedere	pedir	pedir
addormentato	adormecido	dormido
asparago *m*	espargo	espárrago
aspirina	aspirina	aspirina
assistere	ajudar	ayudar
assistenza	ajuda	ayuda
a	a	a
in	em	en
ad ogni costo	a todo preço	a toda costa
all'alba	ao amanhecer	al amanecer
al principio	a princípio	al principio
in casa	em casa	en casa
finalmente	finalmente	al fin
almeno	pelo menos	al menos
a mezzanotte	à meia-noite	a medianoche
di notte	à noite	por la noche
a mezzogiorno	ao meio-dia	a mediodía

English	*French*	*German*
at—o'clock	à...heure(s)	um...Uhr
at once	tout de suite	gleich
at present	en ce moment	gegenwärtig
at school	dans l'école *f*	in der Schule
at that time	à ce moment-là	damals
at the beginning	au commencement	am Anfang
at the home of	chez	bei
at the latest	au plus tard	spätestens
at the most	tout au plus	höchstens
at times	parfois	zuweilen
At what time?	À quelle heure?	Um wieviel Uhr?
At your service	À votre service	Zu Ihren Diensten
Athens	Athènes *f*	Athen *n*
Atlantic	l'Atlantique *m*	Atlantischer Ozean *m*
atmosphere	atmosphère *f*	Atmosphäre *f*
atom bomb (n.)	bombe *f* atomique	Atombombe *f*
attaché	attaché *m*	Attaché *m*
attack, to	attaquer	angreifen
attempt, to	tenter	versuchen
attend (be present at)	assister à	beiwohnen
attic	grenier *m*	Dachboden *m*
audience	auditoire *m*	Publikum *n*
auditor (class)	auditeur *m*	Zuhörer *m*
auditorium	salle *f*	Hörsaal *m*
August	août *m*	August *m*
aunt	tante *f*	Tante *f*
Australia	l'Australie *f*	Australien *n*
Australian (adj.)	australien	australisch
Austria	l'Autriche *f*	Österreich *n*
Austrian (adj.)	autrichien	österreichisch
author	auteur *m*	Schriftsteller *m*
automobile	auto(mobile) *f*	Auto *n*
autumn	automne *m*	Herbst *m*
available	disponible	verfügbar
avenue	avenue *f*	Allee *f*
aviator	aviateur *m*	Flieger *m*
avocado	poire *f* d'avocat	Avocatobirne *f*
avoid, to	éviter	vermeiden

Italian	*Portuguese*	*Spanish*
alla, alle...	à(s)...hora(s)	a la(s)...
subito	imediatamente	en seguida
attualmente	atualmente	actualmente
a scuola	na escola	en la escuela
a quel momento	àquêle tempo	en aquella época
in principio	a princípio	al principio
a casa di; da...	em casa de	en casa de
al più tardi	no mais tardar	a más tardar
al più	quando muito	a lo más
alle volte	às vêzes	a veces
A che ora?	À que horas?	¿A qué hora?
Al vostro servizio	Às(suas) ordens	A sus órdenes
Atene *f*	Atenas	Atenas
l'Atlantico *m*	o Atlântico	el Atlántico
ambiente *m*	ambiente *m*	ambiente *m*
bomba atomica	bomba atômica	bomba atómica
addetto	adido	agregado
attaccare	atacar	atacar
tentare	tentar	procurar
assistere a	assistir a	asistir a
soffitta	sótão	desván *m*; buhardilla
uditorio *m*	auditório	auditorio
uditore *m*	ouvinte *m*	oyente *m*
sala	sala	salón *m* de actos
agosto	agôsto	agosto
zia	tia	tía
l'Australia	a Austrália	Australia
australiano	australiano	australiano
l'Austria	a Áustria	Austria
austriaco	austríaco	austríaco
autore *m*	autor *m*	autor *m*
automobile *f*; macchina	automóvel *m*	auto(móvil) *m*; coche *m*
autunno *m*	outono	otoño
disponibile	disponível	disponible
viale *m*	avenida	avenida
aviatore *m*	aviador *m*	aviador *m*
avocado	abacate *m*	aguacate *m*
evitare	evitar	evitar

English	*French*	*German*
awake (adj.)	éveillé	wach
away (absent)	absent	weg
ax(e)	hache *f*	Axt *f*
axle	essieu *m*	Achse *f*
Azores, The	les Açores *fpl*	die Azoren *pl*
baby	bébé *m*	Baby *n*; Saügling *m*
bachelor	célibataire *m*	Junggeselle *m*
back (anat.)	dos *m*	Rücken *m*
back, to be	être de retour	zurück sein
backache	mal *m* au dos	Rückenschmerzen *mpl*
back seat	siège *m* arrière	Rücksitz *m*
backwards	en arrière	rückwärts
bacon	bacon *m;* lard *m*	Speck *m*
bacon and eggs	oeufs *mpl* au bacon	Eier mit Speck
bad (evil)	mauvais	schlimm
badly	mal	schlecht
bag (purse)	sac *m* à main	Handtasche *f*
bag (sack)	sac *m*	Sack *m*
baggage	bagages *mpl*	Gepäck *n*
baggage car	fourgon *m*	Gepäckwagen *m*
baggage check	bulletin *m* de bagages	Gepäckschein *m*
baggage inspection	visite *f* de la douane	Gepäckkontrolle *f*
baggage label	étiquette *f*	Etikett *n*
baggage rack	filet *m*	Gepäcknetz *n*
baggage room	consigne *f*	Gepäckraum *m*
bake (be cooking), to	cuire (au four)	backen
baked	(cuit) au four	gebacken
baker	boulanger *m*	Bäcker *m*
bakery	boulangerie *f*	Bäckerei *f*
baking powder	levure *f*	Backpulver *n*
balcony (bldg.)	balcon *m*	Balkon *m*
balcony (theat.)	galerie *f*	Galerie *f*
bald	chauve	kahl
ball (sphere)	balle *f*	Ball *m*
ballpoint pen	stylo *m* à bille	Kugelschreiber *m*
banana	banane *f*	Banane *f*
bandage	bandage *m*	Verband *m*
bandage, to	bander	verbinden

Italian	*Portuguese*	*Spanish*
sveglio	acordado; **desperto**	despierto
assente	ausente	ausente
ascia	machado	el hacha *f*
assale *m*	eixo	eje *m*
le Azzorre *fpl*	as Açôres *fpl*	las Azores *fpl*
bambino; **bimbo**	criancinha; bebê *m*	criatura; **nene** *m*
celibe *m*	solteiro	soltero
dorso	as costas	espalda
essere di ritorno	estar de volta	estar de vuelta
mal *m* di schiena	dor *f* nas costas	dolor *m* de espalda
sedile posteriore	assento de **trás**	asiento trasero
indietro	para **trás**	hacia atrás
pancetta	toucinho	tocino
uova con pancetta	toucinho com ovos	tocino con **huevos**
cattivo	mau (*f* má)	malo
male	mal	mal
borsa	bôlsa	bolsa
sacco	saco	saco
bagagli *mpl*	bagagem *f*	equipaje *m*
bagagliaio	furgão	furgón *m*
scontrino dei bagagli	senha; talão (Br.)	talón *m*; contraseña
ispezione *f* dei bagagli	inspeção *f* de bagagem	registro del equipaje
etichetta	etiquêta	etiqueta
rete *f*; reticella	rêde *f*; portamala (Br.)	red *f*
deposito (di) bagagli	depósito de bagagens	sala de equipajes
cuocere (al forno)	cozer ao forno	cocer (en **horno**)
al forno	cozido ao **forno**	cocido
panettiere *m*	padeiro	panadero
panetteria *f*	padaria	panadería
lievito in polvere	fermento em **pô**	polvo para hornear
balcone *m*	sacada; balcão	balcón *m*
galleria	balcão de teatro	galería
calvo	careca; calvo	calvo
palla	bola	pelota
penna a sfera; biro	birome *m*	bolígrafo
banana	banana	plátano; banana
benda	ligadura; atadura (Br.)	venda
bendare	ligar; pôr a atadura	vendar

English	*French*	*German*
bank (bus.)	banque *f*	Bank *f*
bank (shore)	rive *f*	Ufer *n*
banker	banquier *m*	Bankier *m*
banquet	banquet *m*	Bankett *n*
baptize, to	baptiser	taufen
bar (tavern)	bar *m*	Bar *f*
barber	coiffeur *m*	Friseur *m*
barbershop	salon *m* de **coiffure**	Friseursalon *m*
bargain	occasion *f*	Gelegenheitskauf *m*
bargain, to	marchan**der**	feilschen
bargain sale	soldes *mpl*	Ausverkauf *m*
bark, to	aboyer	bellen
barley	orge *f*	Gerste *f*
barracks	caserne *f*	Kaserne *f*
barrel	tonneau *m*	Fass *n*
baseball	base-ball *m*	Baseball *m*
Basel (Basle)	Bâle *f*	Basel *n*
basement	sous-sol *m*	Keller *m*
basket	panier *m*	Korb *m*
basketball	basket(ball) *m*	Korbball *m*
bath	bain *m*	Bad *n*
bath mat	descente *f* de **bain**	Badematte *f*
bath towel	serviette *f* de **bain**	Badetuch *n*
bathe (take a bath), to	prendre un **bain**	baden
bathing cap	bonnet *m* de **bain**	Bademütze *f*
bathing suit	costume *m* de **bain**; maillot *m*	Badeanzug *m*
bathing trunks	caleçon *m* de **bain**	Badehose *f*
bathrobe	peignoir *m* (de bain)	Bademantel *m*
bathroom	salle *f* de **bain**	Badezimmer *n*
bathtub	baignoire *f*	Badewanne *f*
battery (storage)	accumulateur *m*; batterie *f*	Akkumulator *m*; Batterie *f*
battle (n.)	bataille *f*	Schlacht *f*
bay (inlet)	baie *f*	Bucht *f*

Italian	*Portuguese*	*Spanish*
banca, banco	banco	banco
riva	ribeira	ribera
banchiere *m*	banqueiro	banquero
banchetto	banquete *m*	banquete *m*
battezzare	batizar	bautizar
bar *m*; birreria	bar *m*	bar *m*; cantina
barbiere *m*	barbeiro	barbero; peluquero
bottega del barbiere	barbearia	peluquería; barbería
occasione *f*	pechincha	ganga
trattare; mercanteggiare	regatear; pechinchar	regatear
liquidazione *f*	liquidação *f*	venta; barata (Mex.)
abbaiare	latir; ladrar	ladrar
orzo	cevada	cebada
caserma	caserna	caserna; cuartel *m*
barile *m*	barril *m*	barril *m*
baseball *m*	basebol *m*	béisbol *m*
Basilea *f*	Basiléia	Basilea
sottosuolo	porão	sótano
paniere *m*; cestino	cêsto	cesta
pallacanestro	basquetebol *m*	basquetbol *m*
bagno	banho	baño
stoino da bagno	esteira de banho	estera de baño
asciugamano da bagno	toalha de banho	toalla de baño
fare un bagno	banhar-se	bañarse
cuffia da bagno	touca de banho	gorro de baño
costume *m* da bagno	fato de banho; roupa de banho (Br.)	traje *m* de baño
mutandine *fpl* da bagno	calções *mpl* de banho	calzón *m* de baño
accappatoio	roupão de banho	bata de baño
(stanza da) bagno	quarto de banho; banheiro (Br.)	cuarto de baño
vasca (da bagno)	banheira	baño; bañera; tina (Mex.)
accumulatore *m*; batteria	bateria; acumulador *m*	acumulador *m*; batería
battaglia	batalha	batalla
baia	baía	bahía

English	*French*	*German*
be (location), to	être	sein
be (exist), to	être	sein
beach	plage *f*	Strand *m*
bead (jewelry)	perle *f* (de collier)	Perle *f*
bean	haricot *m*	Bohne *f*
bear (animal)	ours *m*	Bär *m*
beard	barbe *f*	Bart *m*
bearing (mech.)	coussinet *m*	Lager *n*
beat (defeat), to	vaincre	besiegen
beat (thrash), to	battre	schlagen
beautiful	beau, belle	schön
beauty	beauté *f*	Schönheit *f*
beauty parlor	salon *m* de beauté	Friseursalon *m*
because	parce que; car	weil
because of	à cause de	wegen (with gen.)
become, to	devenir	werden
become acquainted, to	faire la connaissance de	kennenlernen
bed	lit *m*	Bett *n*
bed linen	linge *m* de lit	Bettwäsche *f*
bedbug	punaise *f*	Wanze *f*
bedpan	bassin *m* de nuit	Stechbecken *n*
bedroom	chambre *f* à coucher	Schlafzimmer *n*
bedside table	table *f* de chevet	Nachttisch *m*
bedspread	couvre-lit *m*	Bettdecke *f*
bee	abeille *f*	Biene *f*
beef	boeuf *m*	Rindfleisch *n*
beefsteak	bifteck *m*	Beefsteak *n*
been (p.p.)	été	gewesen (sein)
beer	bière *f*	Bier *n*
beet	betterave *f*	rote Rübe *f*
before (conj.)	avant que	bevor; ehe
before (earlier)	plus tôt	früher
before (earlier than)	avant de	vor
before (in front of)	devant	vor
beforehand	d'avance	(im) voraus
beg (entreat), to	supplier	bitten

Italian	*Portuguese*	*Spanish*
stare	estar; ficar	estar; quedar
essere	ser	ser
spiaggia	praia	playa
grano	conta	cuenta
fagiolo	feijão *m*	haba; frijol *m*
orso	urso	oso
barba	barba	barba
cuscinetto a sfere	chumaceira	cojinete *m*
vincere	vencer	vencer
battere	bater	pegar
bello	belo; formoso (Br.)	hermoso; bello
bellezza	beleza	belleza
salone *m* di bellezza	salão *m* de beleza	salón *m* de belleza
perchè	porque	porque
a causa di	por causa de	a causa de
divenire	tornar-se	hacerse
imparare a conoscere	travar conhecimento com	venir a conocer
letto	cama	cama
biancheria da letto	roupa de cama	ropa de cama
cimice *f*	percevejo	chinche *f*
padella	comadre *f*; aparadeira	silleta
camera (da letto)	quarto de cama; quarto de dormir	dormitorio; alcoba; recámara (Mex.)
comodino	mesa de cabeceira	mesilla
coperta	colcha	sobrecama
ape *f*	abelha	abeja
manzo	bife *m*	carne *f* de vaca; carne de res (Amer.)
bistecca	bife *m*	biftec *m*; filete (Mex.)
stato	sido; estado	sido; estado
birra	cerveja	cerveza
barbabietola	beterraba	remolacha; betabel *m* (Mex.)
prima che	antes que	antes que
prima	antes	antes
prima di	antes de	antes de
davanti a	diante de	delante de
in anticipo	de antemão	de antemano
supplicare	rogar	rogar

English	*French*	*German*
beggar	mendiant *m*	Bettler *m*
begin, to	commencer	anfangen
beginning	commencement *m*	Anfang *m*
behave, to	se conduire	sich benehmen
behind (adv.)	en arrière	hinten
behind (prep.)	derrière	hinter (dat. or acc.)
Belgian (adj.)	belge	belgisch
Belgium	la Belgique	Belgien *n*
believe, to	croire	glauben
bell	cloche *f*	Glocke *f*
bell (door-)	sonnette *f*	Türklingel *f*
bellboy	chasseur *m*	Page *m*
belly	ventre *m*	Bauch *m*
belong to, to	appartenir à	gehören (zu)
belongings	effets *mpl* personnels	Sachen *fpl*
below (adv.)	en bas	unten
below (prep.)	au-dessous de	unter
belt (to wear)	ceinture *f*	Gürtel *m*
bend (to make—), to	plier	biegen
bent (curved)	courbé	gebogen
beret	béret *m*	Baskenmütze *f*
Berlin	Berlin *m*	Berlin *n*
berry	baie *f*	Beere *f*
berth (train)	couchette *f*	Schlafwagenbett *n*
berth (ship)	couchette *f*	Kabine *f*
beside (next to)	à côté de	neben
besides (moreover)	de plus	ausserdem
besides (prep.)	outre	ausser (dat.)
best (adj.)	meilleur	beste
bet	pari *m*	Wette *f*
bet, to	parier	wetten
better (adj.)	meilleur	besser
better (adv.)	mieux	besser
between	entre	zwischen
beyond	au-delà de	jenseits
bib	bavette *f*	Lätzchen *n*
bible	Bible *f*	Bibel *f*
bicycle	bicyclette *f*	Fahrrad *n*; Rad *n*

Italian	*Portuguese*	*Spanish*
mendicante *m*	mendigo	mendigo
cominciare	começar	empezar
principio	princípio	principio
comportarsi	comportar-se	(com)portarse
dietro	atrás	detrás
dietro a	atrás de	detrás de
belga	belga	belga
il Belgio	a Bélgica	Bélgica
credere	crer; acreditar	creer
campana	campainha	campanilla
campanello	campainha	timbre *m*
ragazzo	garôto (Br.)	botones *m*
ventre *m*	ventre *m*	vientre *m*
appartenere a	pertencer a	pertenecer a
roba	coisas *fpl*; pertences *mpl*	efectos *mpl*
di sotto	abaixo	abajo
sotto	debaixo de	debajo de
cintura	cinto	cinturón *m*
piegare	dobrar	doblar
curvo	curvado	encorvado
berretto	boina	boina
Berlino *m*	Berlim	Berlín
bacca	baga	baya
cuccetta	cama; leito (Br.)	cama
cuccetta	beliche *m*	litera
accanto a	ao lado de	al lado de
inoltre	além disso	además
inoltre	além de	además de
migliore	melhor	mejor
scommessa	aposta	apuesta
scommettere	apostar	apostar
migliore	melhor	mejor
meglio	melhor	mejor
fra; tra	entre	entre
oltre; al di là di	além de	más allá de
bavaglino	babadouro; bibe *m* (Br.)	babador *m*; babero
Bibbia	Bíblia	Biblia
bicicletta	bicicleta	bicicleta

English	*French*	*German*
big	grand	gross
bigger	plus **grand**	grösser
bill (note)	billet *m*	Geldschein *m*
bill (invoice)	facture *f*	Rechnung *f*
billfold	portefeuille *m*	Brieftasche *f*
bill of fare	menu *m*	Speisekarte *f*
bill of sale	contrat *m* de **vente**	Verkaufsschein *m*
bind (tie), to	lier	binden
bind (books), to	relier	einbinden
binding (books)	reliure *f*	Einband *m*
binoculars	jumelles *fpl*	Fernglas *n*
bird	oiseau *m*	Vogel *m*
birth	naissance *f*	Geburt *f*
birth certificate	acte *m* de nai**ss**ance	Geburtsurkunde *f*
birthday	anniversaire *m*	Geburtstag *m*
birthplace	lieu *m* de nai**ss**ance	Geburtsort *m*
bishop	évêque *m*	Bischof *m*
bit (small part)	morceau *m*	Bisschen *n*
bite (sting) (n.)	piqûre *f*	Stich *m*
bite, to	mordre	beissen
bitter	amer	bitter
black	noir	schwarz
blackberry	mûre *f*	Brombeere *f*
blackboard	tableau *m* **noir**	Wandtafel *f*
black coffee	café *m* **noir**	schwarzer Kaffee *m*
bladder	vessie *f*	Harnblase *f*
blade (razor-)	lame *f* de ra**soir**	Rasierklinge *f*
blame	faute *f*	Schuld *f*
blame, to	blâmer	tadeln
blanket	couverture *f*	(Bett)decke *f*
bleach, to	blanchir	bleichen
bleed, to	saigner	bluten
bless, to	bénir	segnen
blind (adj.)	aveugle	blind
blister (n.)	ampoule *f*	Blase *f*
block (city)	rue *f*; îlot *m*	Strassen *fpl*

Italian	*Portuguese*	*Spanish*
grande	grande	grande
più grande	maior	más grande
biglietto	nota	billete *m*
fattura	fatura	factura
portafoglio	carteira	billetera
lista	menu *m*; lista	lista
atto di vendita	contrato de venda	carta de venta
legare	atar	atar
rilegare	encadernar	encuadernar
rilegatura	encadernação *f*	encuadernación *f*
binocolo	binóculo	gemelos *mpl*
uccello	pássaro	pájaro
nascita	nascimento	nacimiento
certificato di nascita	certidão de idade	partida de nacimiento
compléanno	aniversário	cumpleaños *m*
luogo di nascita	local *m* do nascimento	lugar *m* de nacimiento
vescovo	bispo	obispo
pezzetto	bocado	poquito
morso	picada	picadura
mordere	morder	morder
amaro	amargo	amargo
nero	prêto (*f* preta)	negro
mora di rovo	amora preta	zarzamora
lavagna	quadro negro	pizarra; pizarrón (Amer.)
caffè *m* nero	café só	café solo
vescica	bexiga	vejiga
lama da rasoio	lâmina de gilete	hoja de afeitar
colpa	culpa	culpa
incolpare	culpar	culpar
coperta	cobertor *m*	manta; cobija (Mex.)
imbiancare	branquear; corar (Br.)	blanquear
sanguinare	sangrar	sangrar
benedire	benzer	bendecir
cieco	cego	ciego
vescichetta	empôla; bôlha (Br.)	ampolla
isolato *m*	quadra; quarteirão	manzana; cuadra (Amer.)

English	French	German
blond	blond	blond
blood	sang *m*	Blut *n*
blood pressure	tension *f* artérielle	Blutdruck *m*
blotting paper	(papier) buvard *m*	Löschpapier *n*
blouse	chemisier *m*	Bluse *f*
blow, to	souffler	blasen
blow one's nose, to	se moucher	sich schneuzen
blowout (n.)	crevaison *f*	Reifenpanne *f*
blue	bleu	blau
blush, to	rougir	erröten
boarding-house	pension *f*	Pension *f*
boat	bateau *m*	Boot *n*
bobby pin	épingle *f* à cheveux	Haarklemme *f*
body (anat.)	corps *m*	Körper *m*
body (auto)	carrosserie *f*	Karosserie *f*
boil (med.)	furoncle *m*	Furunkel *m*
boil (cook), to	cuire	kochen
boiled (eggs)	à la coque	gekochte
boiled potatoes	pommes *fpl* de terre bouillées	Salzkartoffeln *fpl*
boiled water	eau *f* bouillie	gekochtes Wasser
boiling water	eau *f* bouillante	kochendes Wasser
Bolivia	la Bolivie	Bolivia *n*
Bolivian (adj.)	bolivien	bolivianisch
bolt (lock)	verrou *m*	Riegel *m*
bolt (with nut)	boulon *m*	Bolzen *m*
bomb (n.)	bombe *f*	Bombe *f*
bomb, to	bombarder	bombardieren
bond (debt)	obligation *f*	Schuldschein *m*
bone	os *m*	Knochen *m*
book	livre *m*	Buch *n*
book of matches	pochette *f* d'allumettes	Streichholzheftchen *n*
Book passage for me...	Vous pouvez m'inscrire pour la traversée...	Merken Sie mich für diese Reise vor
bookcase	bibliothèque *f*	Bücherregal *n*
bookend	serre-livres *m*	Bücherstütze *f*
bookstore	librairie *f*	Buchhandlung *f*
boot (shoe)	botte *f*	Stiefel *m*

Italian	*Portuguese*	*Spanish*
biondo	loiro; louro (Br.)	rubio; güero (Mex.)
sangue *m*	sangue *m*	sangre *f*
pressione *f* del sangue	pressão *f* arterial	tensión *f* (sanguínea)
carta assorbente	mata-borrão *m*	papel *m* secante
blusa; camicetta	blusa	blusa
soffiare	soprar	soplar
soffiarsi il naso	assoar o nariz	sonarse
scoppio	ruptura de pneu	reventón *m*; llanta tronada (Mex.)
azzurro; blu	azul	azul
arrossire	ruborizar-se	ruborizarse
pensione *f*	pensão *f*	pensión *f*
battello	barco	barco; buque *m*
molletta	bobete *m*; grampo de cabelo	gancho; horquilla
corpo	corpo	cuerpo
carrozzeria	carroçaria	carrocería
foruncolo	furúnculo	furúnculo; divieso
cucinare	cozer	cocer; hervir
sode; alla coque	cozidos	pasados por agua
patate *fpl* bollite	batatas cozidas	patatas cocidas
acqua bollita	água fervida	agua hervida
acqua bollente	água fervente	agua hirviente
la Bolivia	a Bolívia	Bolivia
boliviano	boliviano	boliviano
catenaccio	fecho	cerrojo
bullone *m*	perno	perno
bomba	bomba	bomba
bombardare	bombardear	bombardear
obbligazione *f*	obrigação *f*	bono
osso *m* (*pl* le ossa)	osso	hueso
libro	livro	libro
scatoletta di fiammiferi	carteirinha de fósforos	cuardernito de fósforos
Può prenotarmi per la traversata...	Reserve-me passagem para...	Resérveme pasaje en...
scaffale *m*; libreria	estante *f*	estante *m* (para libros)
reggilibro	suporte *m* de livros	sujetalibros *m*
libreria	livraria	librería
stivale *m*	bota	bota

English	*French*	*German*
bootblack	cireur *m*	Schuhputzer *m*
Bordeaux	Bordeaux *m*	Bordeaux *n*
border (frontier)	frontière *f*	Grenze *f*
bored, to be	s'ennuyer	sich langweilen
boric acid	acide *m* borique	Borsäure *f*
born, to be	naître	geboren sein
borrow, to	emprunter	borgen
bosom	sein *m*	Busen *m*
boss (master)	patron *m*	Chef *m*
botanical garden	jardin *m* botanique	botanische (r) Garten *m*
both (adj.)	les deux	beide
both...and	et...et	sowohl...als auch
bother (annoy), to	ennuyer	stören
bottle	bouteille *f*	Flasche *f*
bottom	fond *m*	Boden *m*
bought (p.p.)	acheté	gekauft
bound for...	en route pour	nach...bestimmt
boundary	limite *f*	Grenze *f*
bouquet	bouquet *m*	Strauss *m*
bow (of ship)	proue *f*	Bug *m*
bow-tie	papillon *m*	Fliege *f*
bowels	intestins *mpl*	Gedärme *mpl*
bowl (dish)	bol *m*	Schüssel *f*
box (large)	boîte *f*	Kasten *m*
box (small)	boîte *f*	Schachtel *f*
box (theat.)	loge *f*	Loge *f*
box office	bureau *m* de location	Theaterkasse *f*
boy	garçon *m*	Junge *m*
bracelet	bracelet *m*	Armband *n*
brain (anat.)	cerveau *m*	Gehirn *n*
brains (food)	cervelles *fpl*	Bregen *m*
brake (mech.)	frein *m*	Bremse *f*
branch	branche *f*	Zweig *m*
branch office	succursale *f*	Filiale *f*

Italian	*Portuguese*	*Spanish*
lustrascarpe *m*	engraxate *m*	limpiabotas *m*; lustrabotas (Amer.)
Bordeaux	Bordéus	Burdeos
frontiera	fronteira	frontera
annoiarsi	aborrecer-se	aburrirse
acido *m* borico	ácido bórico	ácido bórico
nascere	nascer	nacer
prendere a prestito	tomar emprestado	pedir prestado
seno	seio	seno
padrone *m*	patrão	amo; patrón *m* (Mex.)
orto *m* botanico	jardim *m* botânico	jardin *m* botánico
tutti e due	ambos	ambos
tanto...come	não só...mas também	tanto...como
molestare	molestar	molestar
bottiglia	garrafa	botella
fondo	fundo	fondo
comprato	comprado	comprado
diretto a	rumo a	con rumbo a
limite *m*	limite *m*	límite *m*
mazzo	ramalhete *m*	ramillete *m*
prora	proa	proa
cravatta a farfalla	gravata-borboleta	corbata de lazo
intestini *mpl*	intestinos	intestinos
scodella	taça grande; tijela	escudilla; tazón *m*
scatola; cassa	caixa	caja
scatolina	caixinha	cajita
palco	camarote *m*	palco
botteghino	bilheteira; bilheteria (Br.)	taquilla; boletería (Mex.)
ragazzo	rapaz *m*; môço	muchacho; chico; chamaco (Mex.)
braccialetto	pulseira; bracelete *m*	pulsera; brazalete *m* (Mex.)
cervello	cérebro	cerebro
cervelli	miolos *mpl*	sesos *mpl*
freno	travão; freio (Br.)	freno
ramo	ramo	rama
succursale *f*	sucursal *f*; filial *f* (Br.)	sucursal *f*

English	*French*	*German*
brand (of goods)	marque *f*	Marke *f*
brand-new	tout neuf	nagelneu
brandy	eau-de-vie *f*	Branntwein *m*
brass	laiton *m*	Messing *n*
brassiere	soutien-**gorge** *m*	Büstenhalter *m*
brave	brave	tapfer
brazier (for heat)	brasero *m*	Kohlenpfanne *f*
Brazil	le Brésil *m*	Brasilien *n*
Brazilian (adj.)	brésilien	brasilianisch
bread	pain *m*	Brot *n*
bread and butter	du pain et du **beurre**	Brot und **Butter**
break (come apart), to	se casser	brechen
break (make small), to	casser	zerbrechen
breakdown (auto)	panne *f*	Panne *f*
breakfast	petit déjeuner *m*	Frühstück *n*
breakfast, to have	déjeuner	frühstücken
breakwater	brise-**lames** *m*	Wellenbrecher *m*
breast	sein *m*	Brust *f*
breast (of fowl)	poitrine *f*	Brust *f*
breath	haleine *f*	Atem *m*
breathe, to	respirer	atmen
bribe, to	suborner	bestechen
brick	brique *f*	Backstein *m*
bride	mariée *f*	Braut *f*
bridegroom	marié *m*	Bräutigam *m*
bridge	pont *m*	Brücke *f*
briefcase	serviette *f*	(Akten) Mappe *f*
bright (shining)	brillant	hell
brilliant (remarkable)	brillant	glänzend
bring, to	apporter	bringen
Bring me...	Apportez-**moi**...	Bringen Sie mir...
British (adj.)	britannique	britisch
broad	large	breit
broadcast, to	diffuser	senden
broadcasting-station	poste *m* de radiodiffu-sion	Rundfunkstation *f*
broccoli	brocoli *m*	Broccoli *m*
broil, to	griller	braten; rösten

Italian	*Portuguese*	*Spanish*
marca	marca	marca
nuovo di zecca	nôvo em fôlha	nuevecito
acquavite *m*	aguardente *m*	aguardiente *m*
ottone *m*	latão	latón '*m*
reggipetto	soutien *m*	sostén *m*
coraggioso	valente	valiente
braciere *m*	braseiro	brasero
il Brasile *m*	o Brasil	el Brasil
brasiliano	brasileiro	brasileño
pane *m*	pão	pan *m*
pane e burro	pão e manteiga	pan y mantequilla
rompersi	quebrar-se	romperse
rompere	quebrar	romper
panna, guasto	avaria; pane *f*	panne; avería *f*
(prima) colazione *f*	pequeno almôço; café da manhã (Br.)	desayuno
far colazione	almoçar	desayunar(se)
tagliamare *m*	corta-mar *m*	rompeolas *m*
petto; seno	peito; seio	pecho; seno
petto	peito	pechuga
respiro	alento	aliento
respirare	respirar	respirar
corrompere	subornar	sobornar
mattone *m*	tijolo	ladrillo
sposa	noiva	novia
sposo	noivo	novio
ponte *m*	ponte *f*	puente *m*
portafoglio; cartella	pasta	cartera; portafolios *m*
brillante	brilhante	brillante
brillante	brilhante	brillante
portare	trazer	traer
Mi porti...	Traga-me...	¡Tráigame...!
britannico	britânico	británico
largo	largo	ancho
trasmettere per **radio**	irradiar	radiodifun**dir**
stazione *f* **radio**-trasmittente	radiodifusora; emissora	emisora
broccoli *mpl*	brócolos *mpl*	bróculi *m*
arrostire *m*	assar (na grelha)	asar (a la parrilla)

English	*French*	*German*
broken (p.p.)	cassé	zerbrochen
broker (bus.)	courtier *m*	Makler *m*
bronchitis	bronchite *f*	Bronchitis *f*
bronze	bronze *m*	Bronze *f*
brooch	broche *f*	Brosche *f*
broom	balai *m*	Besen *m*
broth	consommé *m*	Fleischbrühe *f*
brother	frère *m*	Bruder *m*
brother-in-law	beau-frère *m*	Schwager *m*
brought (p.p.)	apporté	gebracht
brown	brun; marron	braun
brown sugar	cassonade *f*	braune Zucker *m*
bruise (n.)	meurtrissure *f*	Quetschung *f*
brunette	brun	brünett
brush	brosse *f*	Bürste *f*
brush, to	brosser	bürsten
Brussels	Bruxelles	Brüssel *n*
Brussels sprouts	choux *mpl* de Bruxelles	Rosenkohl *m*
buckle	boucle *f*	Schnalle *f*
buckwheat	sarrasin *m*	Buchweizen *m*
budget (n.)	budget *m*	Budget *n*
bug	insecte *m*	Ungeziefer *n*
build, to	bâtir	bauen
building	bâtiment *m*	Gebäude *n*
bulb (elect.)	ampoule *f*	(Glüh)birne *f*
bull	taureau *m*	Stier *m*
bullet	balle *f*	Kugel *f*
bullfight	course *f* de taureaux	Stierkampf *m*
bullfighter	toréador *m*	Stierkämpfer *m*
bullring	arène *f*	Stierkampfarena *f*
bumper (auto)	pare-chocs *m*	Stossstange *f*
bunch (grapes)	grappe *f* de raisin	Weintraube *f*
bundle	paquet *m*	Paket *n*
buoy (n.)	bouée *f*	Boje *f*
bureau (chest)	commode *f*	Kommode *f*
bureau (office)	bureau *m*	Büro *n*

Italian	*Portuguese*	*Spanish*
rotto	quebrado	rompido; roto
sensale *m*; agente *m* di cambio	corretor *m*	corredor *m*
bronchite *f*	bronquite *f*	bronquitis *f*
bronzo	bronze *m*	bronce *m*
spilla	broche *m*	broche *m*; prendedor *m*
scopa; granata	vassoura	escoba
brodo	caldo	caldo
fratello	irmão	hermano
cognato	cunhado	cuñado
portato	trazido	traído
marrone	marrom	marrón; pardo; café (Amer.)
zucchero greggio	açúcar *m* mascavinho	azúcar *m* terciado
ammaccatura	machucado	cardenal *m*
bruno	moreno; trigueiro	moreno
spazzola	escôva	cepillo
spazzolare	escovar	cepillar
Bruxelles *f*	Bruxelas	Bruselas
cavolini (di Bruxelles)	couve *f* de Bruxelas	coles *fpl* de Bruselas
fibbia	fivela	hebilla
grano saraceno	trigo sarraceno	alforfón *m*
bilancio	orçamento	presupuesto
insetto *m*	inseto	bicho
costruire	construir	construir
edifizio *m*	edifício; prédio	edificio
lampadina	lâmpada	bombilla
toro	touro; toiro	toro
pallottola	bala	bala
corrida di tori	corrida de touros	corrida de toros
torero	toureiro	torero
arena per corride	praça de touros	plaza de toros
paraurti *m*	pára-choque *m*	parachoques *m*; defensa (Mex.)
grappolo d'uva	cacho	racimo de uvas
pacco	pacote *m*	paquete *m*
boa; gavitello	bóia	boya
cassettone *m*	cômoda	cómoda
ufficio *m*	secretária	oficina

English	*French*	*German*
burglar	cambrioleur *m*	Einbrecher *m*
burn	brûlure *f*	Brandwunde *f*
burn, to	brûler	verbrennen
bury, to	enterrer	begraben
bus	autobus *m*; autocar *m*	Bus *m*
bus stop	arrêt *m* d'autobus	Haltestelle *f*
busy	occupé	besetzt (line); beschäftigt (person)
but (and yet)	mais	aber
but (if not)	sinon	ausser
but (on the contrary)	mais	sondern
butcher (n.)	boucher *m*	Fleischer *m*
butter	beurre *m*	Butter *f*
buttermilk	petit-lait *m*	Buttermilch *f*
butterfly	papillon *m*	Schmetterling *m*
button (n.)	bouton *m*	Knopf *m*
buttonhole	boutonnière *f*	Knopfloch *n*
buy, to	acheter	kaufen
buy (a ticket), to	prendre un billet	eine Karte *f* lösen
buyer	acheteur *m*	Käufer *m*
by air mail	par avion	mit Luftpost
by all means	sans faute	unbedingt
by boat	par bateau	mit dem Schiff
by bus	par autobus	mit dem Autobus
by car	par auto	mit dem Auto
by chance	par hasard	zufällig
by day	pendant la journée	am Tage
by heart	par coeur	auswendig
by next (week)	avant la (semaine) prochaine	bis nächste (Woche)
by night	de nuit	in der Nacht
by no means	nullement	keineswegs
by ordinary mail	par poste ordinaire	mit gewöhnlicher Post
by plane	par avion	mit dem Flugzeug
by return mail	par retour du courrier	mit wendender Post
by sight	de vue	dem Aussehen nach
by the way	à propos	übrigens
by tomorrow	d'ici à demain	bis morgen

Italian	*Portuguese*	*Spanish*
ladro	ladrão	ladrón *m*
bruciatura	queimadura	quemadura
bruciare	queimar	quemar
seppellire	enterrar	enterrar
autobus *m*; corriera	autocarro; ônibus (Br.)	autobús *m*; camión *m* (Mex.)
fermata	paragem *f*; ponto	parada
occupato	ocupado	ocupado
ma	mas	pero
se non	senão	si no
però	mas	sino (que)
macellaio	açougueiro	carnicero
burro	manteiga	mantequilla; manteca
siero di latte	leitelho	suero de mantequilla
farfalla	borboleta	mariposa
bottone *m*	botão	botón *m*
occhiello *m*	casa do botão	ojal *m*
comprare	comprar	comprar
comprare un biglietto	comprar passagem *f*	sacar un billete *m*
compratore *m*	comprador *m*	comprador *m*
per via aerea	por avião	por avión
senza fallo	sem falta	sin falta
in piroscafo	por navio	en vapor
in autobus	de ônibus	en autobús
in automobile	de automóvel	en coche
per caso	por acaso	por casualidad
di giorno	de dia	de día
a memoria	de cor	de memoria
non più tardi di...	para...	para...
di notte	de noite	de noche
in nessun modo	de nenhum modo; absolutamente (Br.)	de ningún modo
per via ordinaria	por porte ordinário	por correo ordinario
in aeroplano	de avião	en avión
a giro di posta	pela volta do correio	a vuelta de correo
di vista	de vista	de vista
a proposito	a propósito	a propósito
per domani	amanhã	para mañana

English	*French*	*German*
by train	par le **train**	mit dem **Zug**
by way of (via)	par	über
cab	taxi *m*	Taxi *n*
cabbage	chou *m*	Kohl *m*
cabin (ship)	cabine *f*	Kabine *f*
cable, to	câbler	kabeln
cablegram	câblo**gramme** *m*	Kabel**gramm** *n*
cage (n.)	cage *f*	Käfig *m*
Cairo	Le **Caire** *m*	Kairo *n*
cake (dessert)	gâteau *m*	Kuchen *m*
cake of soap	pain *m* de **savon**	Stück *n* Seife
calendar	calendrier *m*	Kalender *m*
calf (animal)	veau *m*	Kalb *n*
calf (anat.)	mollet *m*	Wade *f*
calf's liver	foie *m* de **veau**	Kalbsleber *f*
call (summon), to	appeler	rufen
call (name), to	appeler	nennen
Call me at...please	Voulez-vous bien m'appel**er** à...	Wecken Sie mich bitte um...
called, to be	s'appeler	heissen
calling card	carte *f* de **visite**	Visitenkarte *f*
callus (med.)	durillon *m*	Hornhaut *f*
calm (adj.)	calme	ruhig
calmly	tranquille**ment**	ruhig
Cambodia	Le Cambodge *m*	Kambodscha *n*
camel	chameau *m*	Kamel *n*
camera	appareil *m*	Kamera *f*
camera shop	magasin *m* d'articles photogra**phiques**	Photohandlung *f*
can (be able)	pouvoir	können
can (tin-)	boîte *f*	Büchse *f*
can opener	ouvre-**boîtes** *m*	Büchsenöffner *m*
Can you...?	Pouvez-**vous**...?	Können Sie...?
Can you direct me to...?	Pouvez-vous m'indiquer la route pour...?	Wie kommt man nach...?
Canada	le Cana**da**	Kanada *n*
Canadian (adj.)	canadien	kanadisch

Italian	*Portuguese*	*Spanish*
in **treno**	de **trem**; pela estrada de ferro (Br.)	en **tren**
per	por	por
tassì *m*	táxi *m*	taxi *m*; libre *m* (Mex.)
cavolo	couve *f*	col *f*; repollo
cabina	camarote *m*	camarote *m*
mandare un cablo-gramma; cablare	passar cabograma	poner un cablegrama
cablogramma *m*	cabograma *m*	cablegrama *m*
gabbia	gaiola	jaula
Il Cairo *m*	Cairo	El Cairo *m*
dolce *m*	pastel *m*; bôlo (Br.)	torta; cake *m*
saponetta	sabonete *m*	pastilla de jabón
calendario	calendário	calendario
vitello	bezerro	ternero
polpaccio	barriga da perna	pantorrilla
fegato di vitello	fígado de vitela	hígado de ternero
chiamare	chamar	llamar
chiamare	chamar	llamar
Per favore, mi svegli alle...	Faça o favor de chamar-me a...	Favor de llamarme a la(s)...
chiamarsi	chamar-se	llamarse
biglietto da visita	cartão de visita	tarjeta de visita
callo	calo	callo
calmo; cal *m*	calmo	tranquilo
tranquillamente	com calma	con calma
Cambogia	Camboja	Camboya
cammello	camelo	camello
macchina fotografica	câmara	cámara
negozio di articoli fotografici	loja fotográfica	tienda de artículos fotográficos
potere	poder	poder
latta	lata	lata
apriscatole *m*	abridor *m* de latas	abridor *m* de latas; abrelatas *m* (Mex.)
Può...?	O senhor pode...?	¿Puede Ud...?
Può indiriz-zarmi a...?	Pode indicar-me onde está...?	¿Por dónde se va a...?
il Canadà	o Canadá	el Canadá
canadese	canadense	canadiense

English	*French*	*German*
canal	canal *m*	Kanal *m*
cancel, to	annuler	annullieren
cancer	cancer *m*	Krebs *m*
candle	chandelle *f*	Kerze *f*
candlestick	chandelier *m*	Leuchter *m*
candy	bonbons *mpl*	Süssigkeiten *fpl*
candy shop	confiserie *f*	Konfitürengeschäft *n*
cane (walking)	canne *f*	Spazierstock *m*
canned goods	boîtes *fpl* de conserves	Konserven *fpl*
canoe	canoë *m*	Kanu *n*
canteen (water)	bidon *m*	Feldflasche *f*
canvas (cloth)	toile *f*	Segeltuch *n*
cap (to wear)	casquette *f*	Mütze *f*
capital (city)	capitale *f*	Hauptstadt *f*
capital (money)	capital *m*	Kapital *n*
captain	capitaine *m*	Kapitän *m* (sea); Hauptmann *m* (army)
capture (seize), to	capturer	festnehmen
car (auto)	voiture *f*	Auto *n*
car (R.R.)	wagon *m*	Wagen *m*
carbon (chem.)	carbone *m*	Kohlenstoff *m*
carbon copy	double *m*	Durchschlag *m*
carburetor	carburateur *m*	Vergaser *m*
cardboard	carton *m*	Pappe *f*
cardinal (Cath.)	cardinal *m*	Kardinal *m*
career	carrière *f*	Laufbahn *f*
careful, to be	faire attention	vorsichtig sein
careful (cautious)	prudent	vorsichtig
careless	négligent	nachlässig
cargo	cargaison *f*	Ladung *f*
Caribbean Sea	la Mer des Caraïbes	das Karibische Meer
carload (bus.)	chargement *m*	Wagenladung *f*
carnation	oeillet *m*	Nelke *f*
carnival	carnaval *m*	Karneval *m*
carpenter	charpentier *m*	Zimmermann *m*
carpet	tapis *m*	Teppich *m*
carriage (baby-)	voiture *f* d'enfant	Kinderwagen *m*
carriage (horse-)	voiture *f*	Kutsche *f*

Italian	*Portuguese*	*Spanish*
canale *m*	canal *m*	canal *m*
annullare	cancelar	cancelar
cancro	câncer *m*; cancro	câncer *m*
candela	vela	vela
candeliere *m*	castiçal *m*	candelero
dolci *mpl*	bombons *mpl*	dulces *mpl*
negozio dei dolci	confeitaria	confitería
bastone *m*	bengala	bastón *m*
cibi *mpl* in scatola	enlatados *mpl*	conservas *fpl* alimenticias
canoa	canoa	canoa
borraccia	cantil *m*	cantimplora
tela di canapa	lona	lona
berretto	boné *m*	gorra
capitale *f*	capital *f*	capital *f*
capitale *m*	capital *m*	capital *m*
capitano	capitão	capitán *m*
catturare	capturar	prender
auto *f*: macchina	carro; automóvel *m*	coche *m*; carro
vagone *m*	vagão	coche *m*
carbonio	carbono	carbono
copia carbone	cópia a papel carbono	copia en papel *m* carbón
carburatore *m*	carburador *m*	carburador *m*
cartone *m*	papelão; cartão	cartón *m*
cardinale *m*	cardeal *m*	cardenal *m*
carriera	carreira	carrera
aver cura di	ter cuidado; estar com cuidado (Br.)	tener cuidado
cauto	cuidadoso	cuidadoso
trascurato	descuidado	descuidado
carico	carga	carga; cargamento
il mar dei Caraibi	o Mar das Antillas	el Mar Caribe
carrata	carrada	carretada
garofano	cravo	clavel *m*
carnevale *m*	carnaval *m*	carnaval *m*
falegname *m*	carpinteiro	carpintero
tappeto	tapête *m*	alfombra
carrozzina	carrinho de bebê	cochecillo para niños
carrozza	carruagem *f*; côche *m*	coche *m*

English	*French*	*German*
carrot	carotte *f*	Mohrrübe *f*
carry, to	porter	tragen
cartridge	cartouche *f*	Patrone *f*
cash (a check), to	toucher	einlösen
cashier	le caissier *m*	Kassierer *m*
cast (theat.)	distribution *f*	Rollenbesetzung *f*
castle	château *m*	Schloss *n*
castor oil	huile *f* de ricin	Rizinusöl *n*
cat	chat *m*	Katze *f*
catch, to	attraper	fangen
catch cold, to	s'enrhumer	sich erkälten
cathedral	cathédrale *f*	Dom *m*
Catholic (adj.)	catholique	katholisch
catsup	sauce *f* tomate	Ketchup *n*
cauliflower	chou-fleur *m*	Blumenkohl *m*
cause	cause *f*	Ursache *f*
cause, to	causer	verursachen
cavity (tooth)	carie *f*	Loch *n*
cease, to	cesser de	aufhören
ceiling	plafond *m*	Decke *f*
celebrate, to	célébrer	feiern
celery	céleri *m*	Sellerie *f*
cellar	cave *f*	Keller *m*
cement (n.)	ciment *m*	Zement *m*
cemetery	cimetière *m*	Friedhof *m*
center	centre *m*	Mittelpunkt *m*
centimeter (o.39 in.)	centimètre *m*	Zentimeter *m*
Central America	l'Amérique *f* Centrale	Mittelamerika *n*
central heating	chauffage *m* central	Zentralheizung *f*
century	siècle *m*	Jahrhundert *n*
Certainly!	Certainement	Gewiss
certify, to	certifier	beglaubigen
chain (n.)	chaîne *f*	Kette *f*
chair	chaise *f*	Stuhl *m*
chalk	craie *f*	Kreide *f*
chambermaid	femme *f* de chambre	Stubenmädchen *n*

Italian	*Portuguese*	*Spanish*
carota	cenoura	zanahoria
portare	levar	llevar
cartuccia	cartucho	cartucho
cambiare; incassare	descontar	hacer efectivo; cobrar; cambiar
cassiere *m*	caixa *m*	cajero
personaggi *mpl*	elenco	reparto
castello	castelo	castillo
olio *m* di ricino	óleo de rícino	aceite *m* de ricino
gatto	gato	gato
acchiappare	apanhar	coger
raffreddarsi	resfriar-se	resfriarse
cattedrale *f*	catedral *f*	catedral *f*
cattolico	católico	católico
salsa di pomodoro	môlho de tomate	salsa de tomate;—de jitomate (Mex.)
cavolfiore *m*	couve-flor *f*	coliflor *f*
causa	causa	causa
causare	causar	causar
carie *f*	cárie *f*	carie *f*
cessare	deixar de	dejar de
soffitto	teto	techo
celebrare	celebrar	celebrar
sedano	aipo	apio
cantina	porão	sótano
cemento	cimento	cemento
cimitero	cemitério	cementerio
centro	centro	centro
centimetro	centímetro	centímetro
l'America *f* Centrale	a América Central	la América Central
riscaldamento centrale; termosifone *m*	aquecimento central	calefacción *f* central
secolo	século	siglo
Certamente	Pois não; Certamente	Por supuesto
certificare	certificar	certificar
catena	cadeia	cadena
sedia	cadeira	silla
gesso	giz *m*	tiza
cameriera	criada de quarto; arrumadeira; camareira	camarera; recamarera (Mex.)

English	*French*	*German*
chamois	chamois *m*	Sämischleder *n*
champagne	champagne *m*	Sekt *m*; Champagner *m*
chance (occasion)	occasion *f*	Gelegenheit *f*; Chance *f*
change, to	changer	verändern
change clothes, to	changer de vêtements	sich umziehen
change (small-)	(petite) monnaie *f*	Kleingeld *n*
change purse	porte-monnaie *m*	Portemonnaie *n*
change the linen, to	changer les draps	Bett *n* beziehen
Change the oil!	Changez l'huile!	Wechseln Sie das Öl!
change trains, to	changer de train	umsteigen
chapel	chapelle *f*	Kapelle *f*
chapter	chapitre *m*	Kapitel *n*
charcoal	charbon *m* de bois	Holzkohle *f*
charge (to an account), to	mettre à son compte courant	anschreiben
charge account	compte *m* courant	Spesenkonto *n*
charming	charmant	reizend
chase, to	poursuivre	jagen
chat, to	causer	plaudern
cheap	bon marché	billig
cheaper	meilleur marché	billiger
check (bank)	chèque *m*	Scheck *m*
check baggage, to	faire enregistrer	aufgeben
check book	carnet *m* de chèques	Scheckbuch *n*
check (for hat, etc.)	ticket *m*	Garderobeschein *m*
check out, to	régler la note	zahlen
Check, please	L'addition, s'il vous plaît	Zahlen, bitte
checkroom	vestiaire *m*	Garderobe *f*
check (test), to	vérifier	prüfen
Check the battery!	Examinez l'eau de batterie!	Kontrollieren Sie das Wasser in der Batterie!
Check the oil!	Vérifiez le niveau d'huile!	Prüfen Sie den Ölstand!
Check the radiator!	Examinez l'eau de refroidissement!	Sehen Sie nach ob der Kühler Wasser braucht!
Check the tires!	Examinez si les pneus sont bien gonflés!	Kontrollieren Sie den Luftdruck in den Reifen!

Italian	*Portuguese*	*Spanish*
camoscio	camurça	gamuza
sciampagna	champanha	champaña
occasione *f*	ocasião *f*	ocasión *f*
cambiare	trocar; mudar	cambiar
cambiare di vestito	mudar de roupa	mudarse de ropa
spiccioli *mpl*	troco miúdo	suelto; feria (Mex.)
portamonete *m*	bolsinha; niqueleira	portamonedas *m*; monedera (Mex.)
cambiare la biancheria	trocar a roupa de cama	cambiar la ropa de cama
Cambi l'olio!	Mude o óleo!	¡Cambie el aceite!
cambiare treno	mudar de trem	cambiar de tren
cappella	capela	capilla
ϩitolo	capítulo	capítulo
carbone *m* di legna	carvão de lenha	carbón *m* de leña
mettere sul conto	pôr na conta	cargar en cuenta
conto aperto	conta corrente	cuenta abierta
incantevole	encantador	encantador
inseguire	perseguir	perseguir
chiacchierare	palestrar	charlar; platicar
a buon mercato	barato	barato
più a buon mercato	mais barato	más barato
assegno	cheque *m*	cheque *m*
spedire	despachar	facturar; checar (Mex.)
libretto d'assegni	talão de cheques	libreta de cheques
contromarca	ficha	contraseña; talón *m*
disdire la camera	sair	marcharse
Il conto, per favore	A nota, por favor	La cuenta, por favor
guardaroba *f*	vestiário	vestuario
controllare	controlar	comprobar
Esamini l'acqua della batteria!	Verifique a bateria!	¡Inspeccione el acumulador!
Verifichi il livello dell'olio!	Verifique o óleo!	¡Inspeccione el aceite!
Esamini l'acqua del radiatore!	Verifique o radiador!	¡Inspeccione el radiador!
Esamini la pressione dei pneumatici!	Verifique os pneus!	¡Inspeccione los neumáticos!

English	*French*	*German*
checking account	compte *m* (de chèques)	Scheckkonto *n*
cheek	joue *f*	Backe *f*
cheese	fromage *m*	Käse *m*
cherry	cerise *f*	Kirsche *f*
chess	échecs *mpl*	Schach *n*
chest (anat.)	poitrine *f*	Brust *f*
chest (drawers)	commode *f*	Kommode *f*
chest cold	rhume *m* de poitrine	Katarrh *m*
chew, to	mâcher	kauen
chicken (to eat)	poulet *m*	Huhn *n*
chicken pox	varicelle *f*	Windpocken *fpl*
chickpea	pois *m* chiche	Kichererbse *f*
child	enfant *m, f*	Kind *n*
Chile	le Chili	Chile *n*
Chilean (adj.)	chilien	chilenisch
chill (n.) (med.)	refroidissement *m*	Schüttelfrost *m*
chin	menton *m*	Kinn *n*
China	la Chine	China *n*
china cabinet	vitrine *f*	Porzellanschrank *m*
chinaware	porcelaine *f*	Porzellan *n*
Chinese (adj.)	chinois	chinesisch
chiropodist	pédicure *m*	Pedikürer *m*
chocolate	chocolat *m*	Schokolade *f*
choke, to	étouffer	(er) würgen
choke (on car)	étrangleur *m*	Startklappe *f*
choose (select), to	choisir	wählen
chop (n.)	côtelette *f*	Kotelett *n*
Christian (n.)	chrétien	Christ *m*
Christian name	prénom *m*	Vorname *m*
Christmas	Noël *m*	Weihnachten *fpl*
Christmas Eve	veille *f* de Noël	Heiligabend *m*
church	église *f*	Kirche *f*
cider	cidre *m*	Apfelwein *m*
cigar	cigare *m*	Zigarre *f*
cigarette	cigarette *f*	Zigarette *f*
cigarette case	porte-cigarettes *m*	Zigarettenetui *m*
cigarette holder	porte-cigarette *m*	Zigarettenspitze *f*

Italian	*Portuguese*	*Spanish*
conto in banca	conta corrente	cuenta de **cheques**
guancia	face *f*; bochecha	mejilla
formaggio	queijo	queso
ciliegia	cereja	cereza
scacchi *mpl*	xadrez *m*	ajedrez *m*
petto	peito	pecho
cassettone *m*	cômoda	cómoda
raffreddore *m* di petto	resfriado do **peito**	catarro
masticare	mascar	mascar
pollo	frango	pollo
varicella	varicela	varicela
cece *m*	grão-de-bico	garbanzo
bambino	criança	niño
il Cile *m*	o Chile	Chile
cileno	chileno	chileno
brividi *mpl*	calafrio	escalofrío
mento	queixo	barba
la Cina	a China	China
cristalliera	cristaleira	cristalera
porcellana	louça	loza
cinese	chinês	chino
pedicure *m*	pedicuro *m*	quiropodista *m*
cioccolata	chocolate *m*	chocolate *m*
soffocare	sufocar-se	ahogarse
diffusore *m*	afogamento	obturador *m*
scegliere	escolher	escoger
co(s)toletta; braciola	costeleta	chuleta; costilla (Mex.)
cristiano	cristão	cristiano
nome *m*	nome *m* de batismo	nombre *m* de **pila**
Natale *m*	Natal *m*	Navidad *f*
vigilia di Natale	véspera de Natal	Nochebuena
chiesa	igreja	iglesia
sidro	cidra	sidra
sigaro	charuto	cigarro; puro (Mex.)
sigaretta	cigarro	cigarrillo; pitillo; cigarro (Mex.)
portasigarette *m*	cigarreira	cigarrera; pitillera
bocchino	boquilha	boquilla

English	*French*	*German*
cinnamon	cannelle *f*	Zimt *m*
citizen	citoyen *m*	Bürger *m*
city	ville *f*	Stadt *f*
city hall	hôtel *m* de **ville**	Rathaus *n*
clam	palourde *f*	Muschel *f*
class (school)	classe *f*	Klasse *f*
classic (adj.)	classique	klassisch
classroom	salle *f* de **classe**	Klassenzimmer *n*
clay	argile *f*	Ton *m*
clean (adj.)	propre	rein; **sauber**
clean, to	nettoyer	reinigen
cleaner's (the)	teinturerie *f*	Reinigungsanstalt *f*
cleaning fluid	détachant *m*	(Reinigungs-) benzin *n*
clear (adj.)	clair	klar
clear soup	consommé *m*	Bouillon *f*
clerk (sales-)	vendeur *m*,-euse	Verkäufer *m*; Verkäuferin *f*
clever	habile	klug
climate	climat *m*	Klima *n*
climb, to	monter	steigen
clippers (barber's)	tondeuse *f*	Haarschneidemaschine *f*
cloak (apparel)	manteau *m*	Mantel *m*
clock	pendule *f*	Uhr *f*
close (shut), to	fermer	schliessen
closed (p.p.)	fermé	geschlossen
cloth	étoffe *f*	Stoff *m*
clothes brush	brosse *f* à **habits**	Kleiderbürste *f*
clothes closet	armoire *f*	Schrank *m*
clothespin	pince *f* à **linge**	Waschklammer *f*
clothing	vêtements *mpl*	Kleider *npl*
cloud	nuage *m*	Wolke *f*
cloudy	nuageux, -euse	bewölkt
clove (spice)	clou *m* de **girofle**	Nelke *f*
clown (n.)	clown *m*	Clown *m*
club (group)	club *m*	Verein *m*

Italian	*Portuguese*	*Spanish*
cannella	canela	canela
cittadino	cidadão	ciudadano
città	cidade *f*	ciudad *f*
municipio	prefeitura	ayuntamiento
vongola	amêijoa	almeja
classe *f*	aula	clase *f*
classico	clássico	clásico
aula	sala de aula	sala de clase
argilla	argila	arcilla
pulito	limpo	limpio
pulire	limpar	limpiar
tintoria	tinturaria	tintorería; tinte *m*
smacchiatore *m*	tira-manchas *m*	quitamanchas *m*
chiaro	claro	claro
consommé *m*	caldo	consomé *m*
commesso,-a	balconista *m, f*; vendeuse *f*	dependiente *m, f*
accorto; abile; **bravo**	hábil	ingenioso; **hábil**
clima *m*	clima *m*	clima *m*
salire	subir	subir
tosatrice *f*	máquina de cortar cabelo	maquinilla
mantello *m*	manteau *m*	abrigo
orologio	relógio	reloj *m*
chiudere	fechar	cerrar
chiuso	fechado	cerrado
tela	tecido; fazenda	tela
spazzola da **abiti**	escôva di fato; escôva de roupa (Br.)	cepillo de **ropa**
armadio	guarda-roupa	armario; ropero
molletta ferma-biancheria	pinça; prendedor *m* de roupa	pinza
abiti *mpl*	roupa	ropa
nuvola	nuvem *f*	nube *f*
nuvoloso	nublado	nublado
garofano	cravo da Índia	clavo
pagliaccio	palhaço	payaso; clown *m*
circolo	clube *m*	club *m*

English	*French*	*German*
club (stick)	massue *f*	Stock *m*
clutch (auto)	embrayage *m*	Kupplung *f*
coach (R.R.)	voiture *f;* wagon *m*	Personenwagen *m*
coal	charbon *m*	Kohle *f*
coast (sea-)	côte *f*	Küste *f*
coat (man's)	veston *m*	Rock *m*
coat (woman's)	manteau *m*	Mantel *m*
coat hanger	portemanteau *m;* cintre *m*	Kleiderbügel *m*
cockroach	cafard *m*	Kakerlak *m*
cocktail	cocktail *m*	Cocktail *m*
cocoa	cacao *m*	Kakao *m*
coconut	noix *f* de coco	Kokosnuss *f*
C.O.D.	contre remboursement	bei Lieferung
cod	morue *f*	Kabeljau *m*
cod liver oil	huile *f* de foie de morue	Lebertran *m*
coffee	café *m*	Kaffee *m*
coffee pot	cafetière *f*	Kaffeekanne *f*
coffee with cream	café-crème *m*	Kaffee mit Sahne
coffee with milk	café au lait	Kaffee mit Milch
coffin	cercueil *m*	Sarg *m*
coin	pièce *f* de monnaie	Münze *f*
cold (adj.)	froid	kalt
cold (head-)	rhume *m* de cerveau	Schnupfen *m*
cold (temp.)	froid *m*	Kälte *f*
cold cream	cold-cream *m*	Hautkrem *f*
cold cuts	viandes froides *fpl*	Aufschnitt *m*
collar	col *m*	Kragen *m*
collect (gather), to	assembler	sammeln
collect (bus.), to	encaisser	einziehen
collide (with), to	se heurter contre	zusammenstossen
collision	collision *f*	Zusammenstoss *m*
Cologne (city)	Cologne	Köln *n*
Colombia	la Colombie	Kolumbien *n*
Colombian (adj.)	colombien	kolumbienisch
colon (punct.)	deux points	Doppelpunkt *m*

Italian	*Portuguese*	*Spanish*
bastone *m*	cacête *m*	palo
frizione *f*	embreagem *f*	embrague *m*; garra (Mex.)
carrozza; vettura	carruagem *f* vagão	vagón *m*
carbone *m*	carvão de pedra	carbón de piedra
costa	costa	costa
giacca	casaco; paletó (Br.)	americana; saco
cappotto	manteau *m*	abrigo (de mujer)
attaccapanni *m*; crocetta	cabide *m*	colgador *m*
scarafaggio	barata	cucaracha
cocktail *m*	coquetel *m*	coctel *m*
cacao *m*	cacau *m*	cacao *m*
noce *f* di cocco	côco	coco
alla consegna	pago na entrega	contra reembolso
merluzzo	bacalhau *m*	bacalao
olio di fegato di merluzzo	ôleo de fígado de bacalhau	aceite de hígado de bacalao
caffè *m*	café *m*	café *m*
caffettiera	cafeteira; bule *m* de café (Br.)	cafetera
caffè con panna	café com creme	café con crema
caffè latte	café-com-leite; média	café con leche
bara	ataúde *m*	ataúd *m*
moneta	moeda	moneda
freddo	frio	frío
raffreddore *m*	constipação *f*	resfriado
freddo	frio	frío
crema per il viso	creme *f* de limpeza	colcren *m*
affettato	fatias *fpl* de carne fria	fiambres *mpl* variados
colletto	colarinho	cuello
raccogliere	reunir	reunir
riscuotere	cobrar	cobrar
scontrarsi con	chocar-se com	chocar con
collisione *f*; scontro	choque *m*	choque *m*
Colonia	Colônia	Colonia
la Colombia	a Colômbia	Colombia
colombiano	colombiano	colombiano
due punti	dois pontos	dos puntos

English	*French*	*German*
colonel	colonel *m*	Oberst *m*
color (n.)	couleur *f*	Farbe *f*
colorfast	bon teint	waschecht
color film	film *m* en couleur	Farbfilm *m*
comb	peigne *m*	Kamm *m*
comb, to	peigner	kämmen
come (p.p.)	venu (with être)	gekommen (sein)
come, to	venir	kommen
come back, to	revenir	zurückkommen
Come here, please!	Voulez-vous venir ici!	Kommen Sie bitte her!
Come in!	Entrez!	Kommen Sie herein!
come in, to	entrer	hereinkommen
comedy (theat.)	comédie *f*	Lustspiel *n*
comfortable	confortable	bequem
comma (punct.)	virgule *f*	Komma *n*
command (to)	ordonner	befehlen
commence, to	commencer	anfangen
communist (n.)	communiste *m, f*	Kommunist *m*
compact (powder)	poudrier *m*	Puderdose *f*
companion	compagnon *m*	Gefährte *m*
company (bus.)	compagnie *f*	Gesellschaft *f*
compare, to	comparer	vergleichen
compartment (R.R.)	compartiment *m*	Abteil *m*
compass (magnetic)	boussole *f*	Kompass *m*
compel, to	contraindre; forcer	zwingen
complain about, to	se plaindre de	sich beklagen über
complaint (hurt)	plainte *f*	Beschwerde *f*
complaint (protest)	réclamation *f*	Klage *f*
complete, to	achever	vollenden
completely	complètement	vollkommen
concerning	au sujet de	betreffend
concert (n.)	concert *m*	Konzert *n*
concrete (surface) (n.)	béton *m*	Beton *m*
condemn (censure), to	condamner	verurteilen
condensed milk	lait *m* condensé	Dosenmilch *f*
conducted tour	excursion *f* accompagnée	Gesellschaftsreise mit Führer

Italian	*Portuguese*	*Spanish*
colonnello	coronel *m*	coronel *m*
colore *m*	côr *f*	color *m*
(colore) stabile	(côr) firme	de color fijo
pellicola a colori	película a côres; filme *m* a côres (Br.)	película en colores
pettine *m*	pente *m*	peine *m*
pettinare	pentear	peinar
venuto (essere)	vindo	venido
venire	vir	venir
ritornare	voltar	volver; regresar
Vuol venire qui per favore!	Faça favor de vir aqui!	¡Favor de venir aquí!
Avanti!	Entre!	¡Entre!
entrare	entrar	entrar
commedia	comédia	comedia
comodo	confortável; cômodo	cómodo
virgola	vírgula	coma
comandare	mandar	mandar
cominciare	começar	empezar; comenzar
comunista *m, f*	comunista *m, f*	comunista *m, f*
portacipria	porta-pó *m*; estôjo de pó	polvera; motera (Mex.)
compagno	companheiro	compañero
compagnia	companhia	compañía
paragonare	comparar	comparar
compartimento	compartimento; cabine *f* (Br.)	compartimiento
bussola	bússola	brújula
costringere	obrigar	obligar
lamentarsi di	queixar-se de	quejarse de
lamento	queixa	queja
reclamo	reclamação *f*	reclamación *f*
completare	completar	completar
completamente	completamente	completamente
riguardo a	a respeito de; sôbre	acerca de
concerto	concerto	concierto
cemento	concreto	hormigón *m*
condannare	condenar	condenar
latte *m* condensato	leite *m* condensado	leche *f* condensada
gita turistica con guida	excursão *f* acompanhada	excursión *f* acompañada

English	*French*	*German*
conductor (mus.)	chef *m* d'orchestre	Dirigent *m*
conductor (R.R.)	contrôleur *m*	Schaffner *m*
conductor (bus)	receveur *m*	Schaffner *m*
conference (meeting)	conférence *f*	Konferenz *f*
confess (sins), to	confesser	beichten
confirm (corroborate)	corroborer	bestätigen
Confound it!	Zut!	Zum Kuckuk!
congratulate, to	féliciter	gratulieren
Congratulations!	Je vous félicite!	Ich gratuliere!
conjugate, to	conjuguer	konjugieren
conjunction (gram.)	conjonction *f*	Konjunktion *f*
connection (transp.)	correspondance *f*	Anschluss *m*
conquer, to	vaincre	besiegen
consent, to	consentir	zustimmen
consequently	par conséquent	infolgedessen
consist of, to	consister en	bestehen aus
constantly	constamment	stets
constipated	constipé	verstopft
consul	consul *m*	Konsul *m*
consulate	consulat *m*	Konsulat *n*
consult, to	consulter	zu Rate ziehen
contact lenses	lentilles *fpl* de contact	Kontaktlinsen *fpl*
contagious	contagieux, -euse	ansteckend
contain, to	contenir	enthalten
content(s)	contenu *m*	Inhalt *m*
continue, to	continuer	fortsetzen
contract (n.)	contrat *m*	Vertrag *m*
convent	couvent *m*	Kloster *n*
conversation	conversation *f*	Gespräch *n*
converse, to	converser	sich unterhalten
convince, to	convaincre	überzeugen
cook (n.)	cuisinier *m*; cuisinière *f*	Koch *m*; Köchin *f*
cook (heat food), to	(faire) cuire	kochen
cook (prepare meals)	faire la cuisine	kochen
cooky	gâteau sec *m*	Plätzchen *n*
cool (adj.)	frais; (fraîche *f*)	kühl
cool, to	refroidir	kühlen

Italian	*Portuguese*	*Spanish*
direttore *m*	regente *m* de orquestra	director *m*
controllore *m*	revisor *m*; condutor *m* (Br.)	revisor *m*
conduttore *m*	cobrador *m*	cobrador *m*
conferenza	conferência	conferencia; junta
confessare	confessar	confesar
confermare	confirmar	confirmar
Accidenti!	Com a breca!	¡Caramba!
congratulare	felicitar	felicitar
Congratulazioni!	Felicitações!	¡Felicitaciones!
coniugare	conjugar	conjugar
congiunzione *f*	conjunção *f*	conjunción *f*
coincidenza	baldeação *f*	enlace *m*
vincere	vencer	vencer
consentire	consentir	consentir
quindi	conseqüentemente	por consiguiente
consistere in	consistir de	consistir en
costantemente	constantemente	constantemente
costipato	constipado	estreñido
console *m*	cônsul *m*	cónsul *m*
consolato	consulado	consulado
consultare	consultar	consultar
lenti *mpl* a contatto	lentes *fpl* de contato	lentes *fpl* de contacto
contagioso	contagioso	contagioso
contenere	conter	contener
contenuto	conteúdo	contenido
continuare	continuar	continuar
contratto	contrato	contrato
convento	convento	convento
conversazione *f*	conversa	conversación *f*
conversare	conversar	conversar
convincere	convencer	convencer
cuoco	cozinheiro	cocinero
cuoca	cozinheira	cocinera
cuocere	cozer	cocer
cucinare	cozinhar	cocinar
pasticcino	biscoitinho	galleta; pastelito dulce
fresco	fresco	fresco
raffreddare	esfriar	enfriar

English	*French*	*German*
Copenhagen	Copenhague *f*	Kopenhagen *n*
copper (n.)	cuivre *m*	Kupfer *n*
cord (rope)	corde *f*	Strang *m*
Cordoba	Cordoue *f*	Kordova *n*
corduroy	velours *m* côtelé	Kord *m*
cork (material)	liège *m*	Kork *m*
corkscrew	tire-bouchon *m*	Korkenzieher *m*
corn (on foot)	cor *m*	Hühnerauge *n*
corn (on the cob)	épi *m* de **maïs**	Mais *m*
corn (vegetable)	maïs *m*	Mais *m*
corn plaster	coricide *m*	Hühneraugen-pflaster *n*
corned beef	corned-beef *m*	Pökelfleisch *n*
corner (inside)	coin *m*	Ecke *f*
corner (outside)	coin *m*	Ecke *f*
corporation (bus.)	société *f* (enregistrée)	A.G. (Aktienge-sellschaft *f*)
correct (adj.)	correct	richtig
correct, to	corriger	korrigieren
corridor	corridor *m*; couloir *m* (train)	Gang *m* (train); Flur *m* (bldg.)
cost (price)	prix *m*	Preis *m*
cost, to	coûter	kosten
Costa Rica	le Costa Rica	Costa Rica *n*
costly	coûteux, -euse	kostbar
cottage cheese	fromage *m* blanc	Quark *m*
cot (bed)	lit *m* de **camp**	Feldbett *n*
cotton (cloth)	coton *m*	Baumwolle *f*
cotton (absorbent)	coton *m* hydrophile	Watte *f*
couch	canapé *m*	Couch *f*
cough	toux *f*	Husten *m*
cough, to	tousser	husten
cough drops	pastilles *fpl* pour la **toux**	Hustenbonbons *mpl*
cough syrup	sirop *m* pour la **toux**	Hustensaft *m*
count, to	compter	zählen
count on (rely), to	compter **sur**	sich verlassen auf
counter (store-)	comptoir *m*	Ladentisch *m*
country (land)	pays *m*	Land *n*

Italian	*Portuguese*	*Spanish*
Copenaghen f	Copenhague	Copenhague
rame m	cobre m	cobre m
corda	corda	cuerda
Cordova	Córdova	Córdoba
velluto a coste	veludo piquê	pana
sughero	cortiça	corcho
cavatappi m	saca-rôlha m	sacacorchos m
callo	calo	callo
granturco	milho verde	elote m (Mex.); choclo (Amer.)
frumentone m	milho	maíz m
cerotto per calli	calicida m	callicida
manzo salato	bife m conservado em salmoura	cecina
canto	canto	rincón m
angolo	esquina	esquina
società anonima	sociedade f anônima	S.A. (sociedad f anônima)
corretto	correto	correcto
correggere	corrigir	corregir
corridoio	corredor m	pasillo
costo	custo	coste m
costare	custar	costar
la Costarica	a Costa Rica	Costa Rica
costoso	custoso	costoso
ricotta	requeijão	requesón m
lettino da campo	cama de lona	catre m
cotone m	algodão	algodón m
cotone m idrofilo	algodão m hidrófilo	algodón m hidrófilo
divano	divã m	diván m
tosse f	tosse f	tos f
tossire	tossir	toser
pasticche fpl per la tosse	pastilhas fpl para a tosse	pastillas fpl para la tos
sciroppo per la tosse	xarope m para tosse	jarabe m para la tos
contare	contar	contar
contare su	contar com	contar con
banco	balcão	mostrador m
paese m	país m	país m

English	*French*	*German*
country (-side)	campagne *f*	Land *n*
course (meal)	plat *m*	Gang *m*
course (of study)	cours *m*	Kursus *m*
courtyard	cour *f*	Hof *m*
cousin *f*	cousine *f*	Base *f*; Kusine *f*
cousin *m*	cousin *m*	Vetter *m*
cover (lid)	couvercle *m*	Deckel *m*
cover, to	couvrir	bedecken
cover charge	couvert *m*	Gedeckzuschlag *m*
covered (p.p.)	couvert	bedeckt
cow	vache *f*	Kuh *f*
coward	lâche *m, f*	Feigling *m*
crab	crabe *m*	Krebs *m*
cracker	biscuit *m*	Keks *m*
cradle	berceau *m*	Wiege *f*
cramp (n.)	crampe *f*	Krampf *m*
crank (handle) (n.)	manivelle *f*	Kurbel *f*
crayon (n.)	crayon *m* (de pastel)	Buntstift *m*
crazy	fou, folle	verrückt
cream	crème *f*	Sahne *f*
crew	équipage *m*	Mannschaft *f*
crooked (bent)	tortu	schief; krumm
cross (n.)	croix *f*	Kreuz *n*
cross (street, e.g.)	traverser	überqueren
cross oneself, to	se croiser	sich bekreuzigen
crossing (trip)	traversée *f*	Überfahrt *f*
crowd (n.)	foule *f*	Menge *f*
crowded (adj.)	bondé	voll; überfüllt
cruel	cruel	grausam
cruise (n.)	croisière *f*	Seereise *f*
crutch	béquille *f*	Krücke *f*
cry (weep), to	pleurer	weinen
Cuba	Cuba	Kuba *n*
Cuban (adj.)	cubain	kubanisch
cucumber	concombre *m*	Gurke *f*
cuff (sleeve)	manchette *f*	Manschette *f*

Italian	*Portuguese*	*Spanish*
campagna	campo	campo
piatto; pietanza	prato	plato
corso	curso	curso
cortile *m*	pâtio	patio
cugina	prima	prima
cugino	primo	primo
coperchio	coberta	tapa
coprire	cobrir	cubrir
coperto	couvert *m*; serviço	precio del cubierto
coperto	coberto	cubierto
vacca	vaca	vaca
codardo	cobarde *m*	cobarde *m*
granchio	caranguejo	cangrejo; jaiba (Amer.)
galletta	bolacha	galleta
culla	berço	cuna
crampo	cãibra	calambre *m*
manovella	manivela	manivela
pastello	pastel *m*	creyón *m*
pazzo	louco	loco
crema; panna	creme *m*	crema
equipaggio	tripulação *f*	tripulación *f*
storto	torcido	torcido
croce *f*	cruz *f*	cruz *f*
traversare	atravessar	atravesar
fare il segno della croce	persignar-se	santiguarse
traversata	travessia	travesía
folla	turba	muchedumbre *f*
affollato	apinhado; lotado (Br.)	atestado
crudele	cruel	cruel
crociera	cruzeiro	travesía por mar; crucero (Amer.)
gruccia	muleta	muleta
piangere	chorar	llorar
Cuba	Cuba	Cuba
cubano	cubano	cubano
cetriolo	pepino	pepino
polsino	punho de camisa	puño

English	*French*	*German*
cuff (trousers)	bord *m* (du pantalon)	Umschlag *m*
cuff link	bouton *m* de manchettes	Manschettenknopf *m*
cup	tasse *f*	Tasse *f*
cupboard	armoire *f*	Schrank *m*
cure, to	guérir	heilen
curl	boucle *f* (de cheveux)	Locke *f*
curl, to	friser	kräuseln
currant	groseille *f*	Johannisbeere *f*
currency	monnaie *f*	Währung *f*
current (elect.)	courant *m*	Strom *m*
curtain	rideau *m*	Vorhang *m*
curtain (theat.)	rideau *m*	Vorhang *m*
curved (adj.)	courbe	krumm
cushion	coussin *m*	Kissen *n*
custard	flan *m*	Eierrahm *m*
custom (habit)	l'habitude *f*	Sitte *f*
customer	client *m*	Kunde *m*
customs declaration	déclaration *f* en douane	Zollerklärung *f*
customs house	douane *f*	Zollamt *n*
customs official	douanier *m*	Zollbeamter *m*
cut	coupure *f*	Schnittwunde *f*
cut, to	couper	schneiden
cut class, to	manquer la classe	schwänzen
cute	mignon	niedlich
cypress	cyprès *m*	Zypresse *f*
daily (adv.)	tous les jours	täglich
dairy (milk bar)	laiterie *f*	Molkerei *f*
dam (dike)	digue *f*	Deich *m*
damage	dommage *m*	Schaden *m*
damage, to	endommager	beschädigen
damp (moist)	humide	feucht
dance (party)	bal *m*	Tanz *m*
dance, to	danser	tanzen
danger	danger *m*	Gefahr *f*

Italian	*Portuguese*	*Spanish*
risvolto dei calzoni	bainha (das calças)	vuelta; valenciana (Mex.)
gemello	botão de punho; abotoadura (Br.)	gemelo; mancuerna (Mex.)
tazza	chávena; xícara	taza
credenza	guarda-louça *m*	alacena
guarire	curar	curar
ricciolo	caracol *m* de cabelo	rizo
arricciare	frisar	rizar
ribes *m*	groselha	grosella
valuta; moneta	moeda corrente	moneda corriente
corrente *f*	corrente *f*	corriente *f* eléctrica
tenda; cortina	cortina	cortina
tela; sipario	pano	telón *m*
curvo	curvado	curvado
cuscino	almofada	cojín *m*
crema	(pudim *m* de) creme	flan *m*; natilla
costume *m*	costume *m*	costumbre *f*
cliente *m*	freguês *m*	parroquiano
dichiarazione *f* in dogana	declaração *f* de alfândega	declaración *f* de aduana
dogana	alfândega	aduana
doganiere *m*	funcionário da alfândega	aduanero
taglio	cortadura	cortada; corte *m*
tagliare	cortar	cortar
marinare la scuola	faltar à aula	faltar a la clase
grazioso	engraçadinho	mono; chulo; curiosito (Mex.)
cipresso	cipreste *m*	ciprés; *m* ahuehuete *m* (Mex.)
ogni giorno	diário	diariamente
latteria; cremeria	leiteria	lechería
diga	reprêsa	represa
danno	dano	daño
danneggiare	danificar	dañar
umido	úmido	húmedo
ballo	baile *m*; dança	baile *m*
ballare	bailar; dançar	bailar
pericolo	perigo	peligro

English	*French*	*German*
dangerous	dangereux, -euse	gefährlich
Danish (adj.)	danois	dänisch
Danube	le Danube	die Donau
dare, to	oser	wagen
dark (color)	sombre, foncé	dunkel
darling (n.)	chéri *m*	Liebling *m*
darn, to	repriser; stopper	stopfen
date (calendar)	date *f*	Datum *n*
date (engagement)	rendez-vous *m*	Verabredung *f*
date (fruit)	datte *f*	Dattel *f*
date of birth	date *f* de naissance	Geburtsdatum *n*
daughter	fille *f*	Tochter *f*
daughter-in-law	belle-fille *f*	Schwiegertochter
davenport	sofa *m*; divan *m*	Sofa *n*
dawn (n.)	aurore *f*	Morgendämmerung *f*
day	jour *m*	Tag *m*
day after tomorrow	après-demain	übermorgen
day before yesterday	avant-hier	vorgestern
dead	mort	tot
deaf	sourd	taub
dealer (trader)	commerçant *m*	Händler *m*
dean (Univ.)	doyen *m*	Dekan *m*
dear (beloved)	cher (*f* chère)	lieb
dear (expensive)	cher (*f* chère)	teuer
death	mort *f*	Tod *m*
debt	dette *f*	Schulden *fpl*
deceive, to	tromper	betrügen
December	décembre *m*	Dezember *m*
decide, to	se décider à	sich entschliessen
deck (of cards)	jeu *m* de cartes	Kartenspiel *n*
deck (of ship)	pont *m*	Deck *n*
deck chair	chaise *f* de pont	Liegestuhl *m*
deck steward	garçon *m* de pont	Decksteward *m*
declare (customs), to	déclarer	verzollen
decorate, to	décorer	dekorieren
deep (adj.)	profond	tief
deer	cerf *m*	Hirsch *m*
defect (flaw)	défaut *m*	Fehler *m*

Italian	*Portuguese*	*Spanish*
pericoloso	perigoso	peligroso
danese	dinamarquês	dinamarqués
il Danubio	o Danúbio	el Danubio
osare	ousar	atreverse
scuro; buio	escuro	obscuro
carissimo	benzinho	querido
rammendare	cerzir	zurcir
data	data	fecha
appuntamento	entrevista	cita
dattero	tâmara	dátil *m*
data di nascita	data do nascimento	fecha de nacimiento
figlia	filha	hija
nuora	nora	nuera
divano-letto	sofá-cama	sofá-cama
alba	aurora	alba
giorno	dia *m*	día *m*
dopodomani	depois de amanhã	pasado mañana
l'altro ieri	anteontem	anteayer
morto	morto	muerto
sordo	surdo	sordo
commerciante *m*	negociante *m*	negociante *m*
decano	decano	decano
caro	caro	querido
caro	caro	caro
morte *f*	morte *f*	muerte *f*
debito	dívida	deuda
ingannare	enganar	engañar
dicembre *m*	dezembro	diciembre *m*
decidersi	decidir	decidir (se a)
mazzo di carte	baralho	baraja
ponte *m* di coperta	coberta; convés *m*	cubierta
sedia a sdraio	cadeira de convés; preguiçosa	silla de cubierta
cameriere *m* di ponte	camaroteiro do convés	camarero de cubierta
dichiarare	declarar	declarar
decorare	decorar; enfeitar	decorar
profondo	fundo	hondo
cervo	cervo	ciervo
difetto	defeito	defecto

English	*French*	*German*
defrost, to	dégeler	entfrosten
delay	retard *m*	Verspätung *f*
delay (take long), to	retarder	säumen
delightful	précieux, -euse	entzückend
deliver, to	livrer	(über) liefern
demand (ask for), to	réclamer; exiger	verlangen
Denmark	le Danemark	Dänemark *n*
dental floss	fil *m* dentaire	Zahnfaden *m*
dentist	dentiste *m*	Zahnarzt *m*
denture	dentier *m*	Gebiss *n*
deny (contradict), to	nier	leugnen
deodorant	désodorisant *m*	Desodorierungsmittel *n*
depart, to	partir	abreisen
department store	(grand) magasin *m*	Warenhaus *n*
departure	départ *m*	Abfahrt *f*
depth	profondeur *f*	Tiefe *f*
descend, to	descendre	herabsteigen
descent	descente *f*	Abstieg *m*
describe, to	décrire	beschreiben
description	description *f*	Beschreibung *f*
desert (n.)	désert *m*	Wüste *f*
deserve, to	mériter	verdienen
design (pattern) (n.)	dessin *m*	Entwurf *m*
desire	désir *m*	Wunsch *m*
desire, to	désirer	wünschen
desk	bureau *m*	Schreibtisch *m*
dessert	dessert *m*	Nachspeise *f*
destination	destination *f*	Reiseziel *n*
destroy, to	détruire	zerstören
detour	déviation *f*	Umleitung *f*
detour, to	dévier	einen Umweg machen
develop (phot.)	développer	entwickeln
dial, to	composer (un numéro)	wählen
diamond	diamant *m*	Diamant *m*
diaper	couche *f*: lange *m*	Windel *m*
diarrhoea	diarrhée *f*	Durchfall *m*
diary	agenda *m*	Tagebuch *n*

Italian	*Portuguese*	*Spanish*
sbrinare	degelar	deshelar
ritardo	demora	demora
tardare	tardar em	tardar en
dilettevole	encantador	precioso
consegnare	entregar	entregar
richiedere	exigir	exigir
la Danimarca	a Dinamarca	Dinamarca
cotone *m* per l'igiene della bocca	sêda frouxa dental	seda dental
dentista *m, f*	dentista *m, f*	dentista *m, f*
dentiera	dentadura	dentadura
negare	negar	negar
deodorante *m*	desodorizante *m*	desodorante *m*
partire	partir	partir
grande magazzino	armazém *m*; magazine *m* (Br.)	bazar *m*; almacén *m*
partenza	saída	salida
profondità	profundidade *f*	profundidad *f*
discendere	descer	descender
discesa	descida	descenso
descrivere	descrever	describir
descrizione *f*	descrição *f*	descripción *f*
deserto	deserto	desierto
meritare	merecer	merecer
disegno	desenho	diseño
desiderio	desejo	deseo
desiderare	desejar	desear
scrivania; scrittoio	carteira; secretária	mesa; escritorio
dessert *m*	sobremesa	postre *m*
destinazione *f*	destino	destino
distruggere	destruir	destruir
deviazione *f*	desvio	desviación *f*
fare una deviazione	desviar	desviar
sviluppare	revelar	revelar
fare il numero	marcar; discar (Br.)	marcar; discar (Amer.)
diamante *m*	diamante *m*	diamante *m*
pannolino	cueiro; fralda (Br.)	pañal *m*
diarrea	diarréia	diarrea
diario	diário	diario

English	*French*	*German*
dictate (a letter)	dicter	diktieren
dictionary	dictionnaire *m*	Wörterbuch *n*
die, to	mourir	sterben
died (p.p.)	mort (être)	gestorben (sein)
difference	différence *f*	Unterschied *m*
different	différent	verschieden
difficult (hard)	difficile	schwer
difficulty	difficulté *f*	Schwierigkeit *f*
digest, to	digérer	verdauen
dine, to	dîner	(zu Mittag)essen
dimple	fossette *f*	Grübchen *n*
dining car	wagon-restaurant *m*	Speisewagen *m*
dining room	salle *f* à manger	Speisezimmer *n*
dinner (evening)	dîner *m*	Abendessen *n*
dinner (midday)	déjeuner *m*	Mittagessen *n*
direct current	courant *m* continu	Gleichstrom *m*
dirty	sale	schmutzig
disappear, to	disparaître	verschwinden
disappointed	déçu	enttäuscht
discount (n.)	remise *f*	Rabatt *m*
discover, to	découvrir	entdecken
discuss, to	discuter	diskutieren; besprechen
disease	maladie *f*	Krankheit *f*
disembark, to	débarquer	landen
dish (food)	plat *m*	Gericht *n*
disinfect, to	désinfecter	desinfizieren
dissatisfied	mécontent	unzufrieden
distance (n.)	distance *f*	Entfernung *f*
distant (far off)	lointain	entfernt
distributor (on car)	distributeur *m*	Verteiler *m*
district (locality)	district *m*	Bezirk *m*
disturb, to	déranger	stören
divide, to	diviser	teilen
divorced	divorcé	geschieden
do, to	faire	machen; tun
Do you know...? (be acquainted)	Connaissez-vous...?	Kennen Sie...?

Italian	*Portuguese*	*Spanish*
dettare	ditar	dictar
dizionario	dicionário	diccionario
morire	morrer	morir
morto (essere)	morto	muerto
differenza	diferença	diferencia
differente	diferente	diferente
difficile	difícil	difícil
difficoltà	dificuldade *f*	dificultad *f*
digerire	digerir	digerir
pranzare	jantar	comer
fossetta	covinha	hoyuelo
vagone *m* ristorante	vagão-restaurante	coche *m* comedor
sala da pranzo	sala de jantar	comedor *m*
cena	jantar *m*	cena
pranzo	jantar *m*	comida
corrente *f* continua	corrente *f* contínua	corriente *f* continua
sporco	sujo	sucio
sparire	desaparecer	desaparecer
deluso	desapontado	desengañado
sconto	desconto	descuento
scoprire	descobrir	descubrir
discutere	discutir	discutir
malattia	doença	enfermedad *f*
sbarcare	desembarcar	desembarcar
piatto	prato	plato
disinfettare	desinfetar	desinfectar
scontento	descontente	descontento
distanza	distância	distancia
lontano	distante	lejano
distributore *m*	distribuidor *m*	distribuidor *m*
distretto; rione *m*	distrito	comarca
disturbare	molestar	molestar
dividere	dividir	dividir
divorziato	divorciado	divorciado
fare	fazer	hacer
Conosce...?	O senhor conhece...?	¿Conoce Usted...?

English	*French*	*German*
Do you know...? (have knowledge)	Savez-**vous**...?	Wissen Sie...?
Do you speak...?	Parlez-**vous**...?	Sprechen Sie...?
Do you understand?	Comprenez-**vous?**	Verstehen Sie?
dock (for ships)	embarcadère *f*	Dock *n*
dock, to	arriver au **quai**	landen
doctor	docteur *m*	Arzt *m*
doctor's office	cabinet *m* du docteur	beim Arzt (at the); zum Arzt (to the)
document (n.)	document *m*	Dokument *n*
Does one have to...?	Est-ce qu'il **faut**...?	Muss man...?
dog	chien *m*	Hund *m*
doll	poupée *f*	Puppe *f*
dollar	dollar *m*	Dollar *m*
Dominican Republic	la République Dominicaine	die Dominikanische Republik
done (p.p.)	fait	getan
donkey	âne *m*	Esel *m*
Don't bother!	Ne vous dérangez **pas!**	Machen Sie sich keine Umstände!
Don't forget!	N'oubliez **pas!**	Vergessen Sie nicht!
Don't mention it!	Je vous en prie!	Nichts zu **danken!**
Don't worry!	Soyez tranquille!	Machen Sie sich keine Sorgen!
...don't you?	...n'est-ce **pas?**	...nicht **wahr?**
door	porte *f*	Tür *f*
door (vehicle)	portière *f*	Schlag *m*
doorbell	sonnette *f*	Türklingel *f*
doorman	portier *m*	Portier *m*
dormitory	dortoir *m*	Studentenheim *n*
dose (med.)	dose *f*	Dosis *f*
double (adj.)	double	doppelt
double room (1 bed)	chambre *f* à un lit pour deux personnes	Zimmer *n* mit einem Doppelbett
double room (twin beds)	chambre *f* à deux lits	Zimmer *n* mit zwei Betten
doubt	doute *m*	Zweifel *m*
doubt, to	douter	bezweifeln
doubtful	douteux, -euse	zweifelhaft
doubtless	sans **doute**	zweifellos
doughnut	beignet *m*	Pfannkuchen *m*
down (adv.)	en **bas**	hinab

Italian	*Portuguese*	*Spanish*
Sa Lei...?	O senhor sabe...?	¿Sabe Usted...?
Parla Lei...?	O senhor fala...?	¿Habla Ud...?
Capisce?	O senhor entende?	¿Entiende Ud?
molo	cais *m;* doca (Br.)	muelle *m*
attraccare	atracar	atracar
dottore *m*	médico	médico
gabinetto del medico	consultório	consultorio; consulta
documento	documento	documento
Si deve...?	É preciso...?	¿Es preciso...?
cane *m*	cão; cachorro	perro
bambola	boneca	muñeca
dollaro	dólar *m*	dólar *m;* peso (Mex.)
la Repubblica Dominicana	a República Dominicana	la República Dominicana
fatto	feito	hecho
asino	burro	burro
Non si disturbi!	Não se incomode!	¡No se moleste!
Non dimentichi!	Não se esqueça!	¡No se olvide!
Non c'è di che!	De nada!	¡No hay de qué!
Non si preoccupi!	Não se preocupe!	¡Pierda Ud. cuidado!
...non è vero?	...não é?	...¿ (no es) verdad?
porta	porta	puerta
sportello	porta; portinhola	portezuela
campanello	campainha	timbre *m*
portiere *m*	porteiro	portero
dormitorio	dormitório	dormitorio
dose *f*	dose *f*	dosis *f*
doppio	duplo	doble
camera matrimoniale	quarto para casal	cuarto con cama de matrimonio
camera a due letti	quarto com duas camas de solteiro	cuarto con camas gemelas
dubbio	dúvida	duda
dubitare	duvidar	dudar
dubbioso	duvidoso	dudoso
senza dubbio	sem dúvida	sin duda
ciambella	sonho	buñuelo; rosca (Mex.)
giù	abaixo	abajo

English	*French*	*German*
down payment	acompte *m*	Anzahlung *f*
down there	là-bas	dort unten
downstairs (below)	en bas	unten
downtown (to-)	en ville	in die Stadt
doze, to	sommeiller	schlummern
dozen	douzaine *f*	Dutzend *n*
draft (check)	traite *f*	Tratte *f*
draft (of air)	courant *m* d'air	Luftzug *m*
drapes	rideaux *mpl*	Vorhänge *mpl*
draw (sketch), to	dessiner	zeichnen
drawer (furniture)	tiroir *m*	Lade *f*
dream	rêve *m*	Traum *m*
dream, to	rêver	träumen
dress (clothe), to	habiller	anziehen
dress (frock)	robe *f*	Kleid *n*
dress (med.), to	panser	verbinden
dress shields	dessous *mpl* de bras	Armblätter *npl*
dress shirt	chemise *f* de soirée	Frackhemd *n*
dress suit (men)	habit *m*	Anzug *m*
dresser (bureau)	commode *f*	Kommode *f*
dressing (stuffing)	farce *f*	Füllung *f*
dressmaker	couturière *f*	Schneiderin *f*
drink	boisson *f*	Getränk *n*
drink, to	boire	trinken
drinking water	eau *f* potable	Trinkwasser *n*
drip, to	dégoutter	tröpfeln
drive (a vehicle), to	conduire	fahren
driver (car)	chauffeur *m*	Chauffeur *m*; Fahrer *m*
driver's license	permis *m* de conduire	Führerschein *m*
drop (n.)	goutte *f*	Tropfen *m*
drop (let fall), to	laisser tomber	fallen lassen
drown, to	se noyer	ertrinken
drugstore	pharmacie *f*	Drogerie *f*
drunk (adj.)	ivre	betrunken

Italian	*Portuguese*	*Spanish*
anticipo	**pago**; sinal *m*	entrada; enganche *m* (Mex.)
laggiù	lá em **baixo**	allí abajo
inbasso	abaixo	abajo
al **centro**	à cidade	al **centro**
dormicchiare	dormitar	dormitar
dozzina	dúzia	docena
tratta	saque *m*	giro
corrente *f* d'**aria**	corrente *f* de **ar**	corriente *f* de aire
tende *fpl*	cortinado	colgaduras *fpl*
disegnare	debuxar	dibujar
cassetto	gaveta	cajón *m*; gaveta
sogno	sonho	sueño
sognare	sonhar (com)	soñar (con)
vestire	vestir	vestir
vestito	vestido	vestido
medicare	pensar	curar
sottoascelle *fpl*	protetores *mpl* contra suor, para vestido	sobaqueras *fpl*
camicia per abito da società	camisa de goma	camisa de etiqueta
marsina	**traje** *m* a rigor	**traje** *m* de etiqueta
cassettone *m*	cômoda	cómoda
ripieno	recheio	relleno
sarta	costureira	modista
bibita; bevanda	bebida	bebida
bere	beber	beber
acqua potabile	**água** potável	agua potable
gocciolare	gotejar	gotear
condurre; guidare	dirigir; guiar	conducir; mane**jar** (Mex.)
autista; conducente *m, f*	chofer *m*	conductor *m*
patente *f* (di guida)	licença de motorista	licencia de mane**jar**
goccia	gôta	gota
lasciar ca**dere**	deixar cair	dejar caer
affogarsi	afogar-se	ahogarse
farmacia	drogaria	farmacia; botica; droguería
ubriaco, **brillo**	**bêbedo**	borracho

English	*French*	*German*
drunk (p.p.)	bu	getrunken
dry	sec, sèche	trocken
dry, to	sécher	trocknen
dry-clean, to	nettoyer à **sec**	reinigen
dry wine	vin *m* sec	trockener Wein *m*
duck (bird)	canard *m*	Ente *f*
dull (not sharp)	émoussé	stumpf
dumb (mute)	muet; muette	stumm
dumb (stupid)	bête	dumm
during	pend**ant**	während (gen.)
dust	poussière *f*	Staub *m*
dust, to	épousseter	abstäuben
dust pan	pelle *f* à ordures	Staubschaufel *f*
dusty	poussiéreux, -euse	staubig
Dutch (adj.)	holland**ais**	holländisch
duty	devoir *m*	Pflicht *f*
duty (customs)	droits *mpl* de **douane**	Zoll *m*
duty-free	exempt de **droits**	zollfrei
dye, to	teindre	färben
dysentery	dysenterie *f*	Ruhr *f*
each (every)	chaque	jeder
each one	chacun	jeder
ear (of corn)	épi *m*	Ähre *f*
ear (outer)	oreille *f*	Ohr *n*
ear (organ)	oreille *f*	Ohr *n*
earache	mal *m* d'oreille	Ohrenschmerzen *mpl*
earlier	plus tôt	früher
early (ahead of time)	de bonne **heure**	früh
earn (be paid), to	gagner	verdienen
earring	boucle *f* d'oreille	Ohrring *m*
earphone	écouteur *m*	Kopfhörer *m*
earth (land)	terre *f*	Boden *m*
earthquake	tremblement *m* de terre	Erdbeben *n*
east	est *m*	Osten *m*
Easter Sunday	dimanche *m* de Pâques	Ostersonntag *m*

Italian	*Portuguese*	*Spanish*
bevuto	bebido	bebido
secco	sêco	seco
asciugare	secar	secar
pulire a secco	limpar a sêco	limpiar en seco
vino secco	vinho sêco	vino seco
anitra	pato	pato
smussato	rombo	romo; desafilado
muto	mudo	mudo
sciocco	tolo	torpe
durante	durante	durante
polvere *m*	poeira	polvo
spolverare	limpar de pó	quitar el polvo
paletta per la spazzatura	pá de lixo	pala de recoger la basura
polveroso	poeirento	polvoriento
olandese	holandês	holandés
dovere *m*	dever *m*	deber *m*
dazio doganale; dogana	dereitos *mpl* alfandegários	derechos *mpl* de aduana
esente da dogana	livre de direitos	libre de derechos
tingere	tingir	teñir
dissenteria	disenteria	disentería
ogni	cada	cada
ognuno	cada um	cada uno
spiga	espiga	mazorca; elote *m* (Mex.)
orecchio	orelha	oreja
orecchio	ouvido	oído
mal *m* d'orecchi	dor *f* de ouvido	dolor de oído
più presto	mais cedo	más temprano
presto	cedo	temprano
guadagnare	ganhar	ganar
orecchino	brinco; pingente *m*	pendiente *m*; arete *m* (Mex.)
cuffia	fone *m* de ouvido	audífono
terra	terra	tierra
terremoto	terremoto	terremoto
est *m*	este *m;* leste *m*	este *m*
domenica di Pasqua	Domingo da Páscoa	Domingo de Pascua

English	*French*	*German*
eastern	oriental	östlich
easy	facile	leicht
eat, to	manger	essen
eaten (p.p.)	mangé	gegessen
Ecuador	l'Équateur *m*	Ekuador *n*
Ecuadorian (adj.)	équatorien	ekuadorianisch
edge (side)	bord *m*	Rand *m*
eel	anguille *f*	Aal *m*
egg	oeuf *m* (*pl* oeufs)	Ei *n*
egg-cup	coquetier *m*	Eierbecher *m*
eggplant	aubergine *f*	Eierpflanze *f*
eggshell	coquille *f* d'**oeuf**	Eierschale *f*
egg-white	blanc *m* d'**oeuf**	Eiweiss *n*
egg-yolk	jaune *m* d'**oeuf**	Dotter *m*
Egypt	l'Égypte *f*	Ägypten *n*
eight	huit	acht
eighteen	dix-huit	achtzehn
eighth	huitième	acht-
eighty	quatre-**vingts**	achtzig
either...or	soit...soit	entweder...oder
elbow	coude *m*	Ellbogen *m*
elect, to	élire	wählen
election	élection *f*	Wahl *f*
electric (adj.)	électrique	elektrisch
electric light bulb	ampoule *f* électrique	Gluhbirne *f*
electric razor	rasoir *m* électrique	Elektrorasierer *m*
electrician	électricien *m*	Elektriker *m*
electricity	électricité *f*	Elektrizität *f*
elephant	éléphant *m*	Elefant *m*
elevator	ascenseur *m*	Fahrstuhl *m*
eleven	onze	elf
elsewhere	ailleurs	anderswo
embark, to	s'embarquer	sich einschiffen
embassy	ambassade *f*	Botschaft *f*
embroider, to	broder	sticken
embroidery	broderie *f*	Stickerei *f*
emerald	émeraude *f*	Smaragd *m*
emergency	cas *m* d'urgence	Notfall *m*
emergency brake	frein *m* de secours	Handbremse *f*

Italian	*Portuguese*	*Spanish*
orientale	oriental	oriental
facile	fácil	fácil
mangiare	comer	comer
mangiato	comido	comido
l'Ecuador *m*	o Equador	el Ecuador
equatoriano	equatoriano	ecuatoriano
orlo	borda	borde *m*
anguilla	enguia	anguila
uovo (pl. uova)	ovo (pl. ovos)	huevo; blanquillo (Mex.)
portauovo	oveiro	huevera
melanzana	berinjela	berenjena
guscio d'uovo	casca de ovo	cáscara de huevo
chiaro d'uovo	clara	clara
torlo d'uovo	gema	yema
l'Egitto	o Egito	Egipto
otto	oito	ocho
diciotto	dezoito	diez y ocho
ottavo	oitavo	octavo
ottanta	oitenta	ochenta
o...o	ou...ou	o...o
gomito	cotovêlo	codo
eleggere	eleger	elegir
elezione *f*	eleição *f*	elección *f*
elettrico	elétrico	eléctrico
lampadina	lâmpada	bombilla; foco (Mex.)
rasoio elettrico	barbeador *m* elétrico	afeitadora eléctrica
elettricista *m*	eletricista *m*	electricista *m*
elettricità	eletricidade *f*	electricidad *f*
elefante *m*	elefante *m*	elefante *m*
ascensore *m*	ascensor; elevador (Br.)	ascensor *m;* elevador *m*
undici	onze	once
altrove	em outro lugar	en otra parte
imbarcarsi	embarcar-se	embarcarse
ambasciata	embaixada	embajada
ricamare	bordar	bordar
ricamo	bordado	bordado
smeraldo	esmeralda	esmeralda
emergenza	emergência	emergencia
freno a mano	freio de emergência	freno de emergencia

English	*French*	*German*
emergency exit	sortie *f* de secours	Notausgang *m*
employ (hire), to	engager	anstellen
employee	employé *m*	Angestellte *m*
employer	patron *m*	Arbeitgeber *m*
empty (adj.)	vide	leer
empty, to	vider	leeren
en route	en route	unterwegs
enamel (n.)	émail *m*	Email *n*
end (bring to an end)	terminer	beenden
end (come to an end)	finir	enden
end (conclusion)	fin *f*	Schluss *m*
endive	endive *f*	Endivie *f*
endorse (a check), to	endosser	überschreiben
endure (stand), to	supporter	ertragen
enema	lavement *m*	Klistier *n*
enemy	ennemi *m*	Feind *m*
engagement (to meet)	rendez-vous *m*	Verabredung *f*
engagement (to wed)	fiançailles *fpl*	Verlobung *f*
engine (motor)	moteur *m*	Motor *m*
engineer (prof.)	ingénieur *m*	Ingenieur *m*
England	l'Angleterre *f*	England *n*
English (adj.)	anglais	englisch
English Channel	la Manche	der Ärmelkanal
engrave, to	graver	gravieren
enjoy, to	jouir (de)	geniessen
enjoy oneself, to	s'amuser	sich unterhalten
enlarge, to	agrandir	vergrössern
enlargement	agrandissement *m*	Vergrösserung *f*
enough	assez	genug
enroll, to	se faire inscrire	sich einschreiben
enter, to	entrer (dans)	eintreten (in)
entrance	entrée *f*	Eingang *m*
entree	entrée *f*	Vorspeise *f*
envelope	enveloppe *f*	Umschlag *m*
envy, to	envier	beneiden
equal (adj.)	égal	gleich
equipment	équipement *m*	Ausrüstung *f*

Italian	*Portuguese*	*Spanish*
uscita di sicurezza	saída de emergência	salida de emergencia
impiegare	empregar	emplear
impiegato	empregado	empleado
padrone *m*	patrão	patrón *m*
vuoto	vazio	vacío
vuotare	esvaziar	vaciar
in cammino	no caminho	de camino
smalto	esmalte *m*	esmalte *m*
terminare; finire	acabar	terminar
terminarsi	acabar-se	terminarse
fine *f*	fim *m*	fin *m*
indivia	endiva	escarola
girare	endossar	endosar
sopportare	suportar	soportar
clistere *m*	enema; lavagem *f*	enema
nemico	inimigo	enemigo
appuntamento	compromisso	cita; compromiso
fidanzamento	noivado	noviazgo; compromiso
motore *m*	motor *m*	motor *m*
ingegnere *m*	engenheiro	ingeniero
l'Inghilterra	a Inglaterra	Inglaterra
inglese	inglês	inglés
la Manica	o Canal *m* da Mancha	el Canal *m* de la Mancha
incidere	gravar	grabar
godere (di)	gozar (de)	gozar (de)
divertirsi	divertir-se	divertirse
ingrandire	ampliar	ampliar
ingrandimento	ampliação *f*	ampliación *f*
abbastanza	bastante	bastante
iscriversi	matricular-se	matricularse; enrolar (Mex.)
entrare (in)	entrar (em)	entrar (en)
entrata	entrada	entrada
primo piatto	primeiro prato	entrada; principio
busta	envelope *m*	sobre *m*
invidiare	invejar	envidiar
uguale	igual	igual
equipaggiamento	equipamento	equipo

English	French	German
erase, to	effacer	ausradieren
eraser (blackboard)	éponge f; chiffon m	Wischer m
eraser (rubber)	gomme f	Radiergummi m
escalator (n.)	escalier m roulant	Rolltreppe f
escape, to	(s')échapper	entkommen; entgehen
especially	surtout	besonders
Europe	l'Europe f	Europa n
European (adj.)	européen	europäisch
European plan	chambre f sans pension	Zimmer n ohne Kost
even (adv.)	même	sogar
even though	quand même	wenn auch
evening	soir m	Abend m
evening gown	robe f du soir	Abendkleid n
ever (at any time)	jamais	je(mals)
every (each)	chaque	jeder
every day	tous les jours	jeden Tag
everybody	tout le monde	jedermann
everyone	chacun	jeder, etc.
everything	tout	alles
everywhere	partout	überall
evidently	évidemment	augenscheinlich
exactly	exactement	genau
examination	examen m	Prüfung f
examine, to	examiner	prüfen
excellent	excellent	ausgezeichnet
except (prep.)	sauf	ausser
excess baggage (weight)	excédent de poids (à payer)	Übergewicht (zu bezahlen)
excess fare	supplément m	Zuschlag m
exchange, to	changer	(aus)tauschen
excursion	excursion f	Ausflug m
excuse (pardon), to	excuser	verzeihen
Excuse me! (May I pass?)	Pardon!	Entschuldigen Sie!
exhaust pipe (auto)	tuyau m d'échappement	Auspuffrohr n
exit (n.)	sortie f	Ausgang m
expect, to	attendre	erwarten
expenses	frais mpl	Kosten fpl

Italian	*Portuguese*	*Spanish*
cancellare	borrar; apagar	borrar
cimosa	apagador *m*	borrador
gomma	borracha	goma
scala mobile	escada rolante	escalera movediza
scappare	escapar	escapar
specialmente; specie	especialmente	sobre todo
l'Europa	a Europa	Europa
europeo	europeu	europeo
camera senza pasti	quarto sem comida	cuarto sin comidas
perfino; anche	até	hasta
benchè	ainda que	aun cuando
sera	noite *f*	tarde *f*
abito da sera	vestido de baile	vestido de noche
sempre	alguma vez	alguna vez; jamás
ogni	cada	cada
ogni giorno	todos os dias	todos los días
ognuno; tutti	todo (o) mundo	todo el mundo
ciascuno	tôda a gente	cada uno
tutto	tudo	todo
dappertutto	em tôda a parte	en todas partes
evidentemente	evidentemente	por lo visto
esattamente	exatamente	exactamente
esame *m*	exame *m*	examen *m*
esaminare; verificare	examinar	examinar
eccellente	excelente	excelente
eccetto	exceto	excepto
peso eccessivo; peso in eccesso	peso excessivo	exceso de peso
supplemento	excesso de passagem	suplemento de pasaje
scambiare	cambiar	cambiar
escursione *f;* gita	excursão *f*	excursión *f*
scusare	desculpar	dispensar
Con permesso!	Com licença!	¡Con permiso!
tubo di scappamento	escape *m*	tubo de escape
uscita	saída	salida
sperare	esperar	esperar
spese *fpl*	gastos *mpl*	gastos *mpl*

English	*French*	*German*
expensive	cher; coûteux	teuer
expert (n.)	expert *m*	Fachmann *m*
explain (clarify), to	expliquer	erklären
explore, to	explorer	erforschen
export, to	exporter	exportieren
exporter	exportateur *m*	Exporteur *m*
exposure meter (phot.)	posemètre *m*	Belichtungsmesser *m*
express train	rapide *m*	Schnellzug *m*
extension cord	rallonge *f*	Verlängerungsschnur *f*
eye (n.)	oeil *m* (*pl* yeux)	Auge *n*
eyebrow	sourcil *m*	Augenbraue *f*
eyelash	cil *m*	Wimper *f*
eyelid	paupière *f*	Augenlid *n*
face	visage *m*	Gesicht *n*
facecloth	gant *m* de toilette	Waschlappen *m*
face cream	crême *f* de beauté	Hautkrem *f*
face powder	poudre *f* de riz	Puder *m*
facial (n.)	traitement *m* facial	Gesichtsmassage *f*
facial tissue	mouchoir *m* en papier	Papiertaschentuch *n*
facing (street)	donnant sur	gelegen nach
fact	fait *m*	Tatsache *f*
factory	fabrique *f*; usine *f*	Fabrik *f*
faculty (staff)	faculté *f*	Lehrkörper *m*
fade (lose color), to	se faner	verblassen
faded	fané	verblasst
fail (in exam), to	échouer à	durchfallen
fail (neglect to)	manquer de	versäumen
faint, to	s'évanouir	in Ohnmacht fallen
fair (festival)	foire *f*	Messe *f*
fair (passable)	passable	leidlich
faithful	fidèle	treu
fall (autumn)	automne *m*	Herbst *m*
fall, to	tomber	fallen
fall asleep, to	s'endormir	einschlafen
fall down, to	tomber	hinfallen
fall in love with, to	tomber amoureux de	sich verlieben in
falls (water)	chute *f*	Wasserfall *m*

Italian	*Portuguese*	*Spanish*
caro; costoso	caro; custoso	caro; costoso
esperto; perito	perito	perito
spiegare	explicar	explicar
esplorare	explorar	explorar
esportare	exportar	exportar
esportatore *m*	exportador *m*	exportador *m*
esposimetro	fotômetro	exposímetro
diretto; rapido	expresso	rápido
prolunga	fio de extensão	cordón *m* de extensión
occhio	olho (*pl* olhos)	ojo
sopracciglio	sobrancelha	ceja
ciglio	pestana	pestaña
palpebra	pálpebra	párpado
faccia	rosto; cara	cara; rostro
pezzuola da bagno	esfregão de rosto	toallita; toalla chica (Mex.)
crema per il viso	creme *m*	crema facial
cipria	pó *m* de arroz	polvos *mpl*
facciale *m*	massagem *f* facial	masaje *m* facial
fazzoletto di carta per la faccia	lenço-papel *m*	tisú *m* facial; pañuelos desechables
che dà su	dando para	dando a
fatto	fato	hecho
fabbrica	fábrica	fábrica
facoltà	faculdade *f*; professorado	facultad *f*; profesorado
sbiadire	descorar; desbotar (Br.)	descolorar
sbiadito	desbotado	descolorado
essere bocciato	sair mal	salir mal en
mancare di	deixar de	dejar de
svenire	desmaiar	desmayarse
fiera	feira	feria
passabile	regular	regular
fedele	fiel	fiel
autunno	outono	otoño
cadere	cair	caer
addormentarsi	adormecer	dormirse
cadere	cair	caerse
innamorarsi di	namorar-se de	enamorarse de
cascata	cascata	cascada

English	*French*	*German*
family	famille *f*	Familie *f*
famous	renommé; fameux	berühmt
fan (elect.)	ventilateur *m*	Ventilator *m*
fan (hand)	éventail *m*	Fächer *m*
fan (sports)	fanatique *mf*	Liebhaber *m*
fan belt (auto)	courroie *f* de ventilateur	Ventilatorriemen *m*
far (adj.)	lointain	weit
far (adv.)	loin	weit
fare (transp.)	prix *m*	Fahrpreis *m*
farm	ferme *f*	Bauernhof *m*
farmer	fermier *m*	Bauer *m*
farther	plus loin	weiter
fast (adj.)	rapide	schnell
fast (adv.)	vite	geschwind
fast, to	jeûner	fasten
fast, to be (watch)	avancer	vorgehen
fasten, to	attacher	befestigen
Fasten safety belt!	Attachez vos ceintures!	Bitte, anschnallen!
fat (obese)	gras	dick
father	père *m*	Vater *m*
father-in-law	beau-père *m*	Schwiegervater *m*
faucet (tap)	robinet *m*	Wasserhahn *m*
fault (blame)	faute *f*	Schuld *f*
favor (kindness)	grâce *f*	Gefallen *m*
fear	peur *f*	Furcht *f*
fear, to	craindre	fürchten
feather	plume *f*	Feder *f*
feature (movie)	grand film *m*	Hauptfilm *m*
February	février *m*	Februar *m*
fee	honoraires *mpl*	Gebühr *f*
feel, to	(se) sentir	fühlen
feel like (doing something), to	avoir envie de	Lust haben (etwas zu tun)
felt (material)	feutre *m*	Filz *m*
fender (auto)	garde-boue *m*; aile *f*	Kotflügel *m*
ferry (boat)	bac *m*	Fähre *f*
festival	fête *f*	Fest *n*
fever	fièvre *f*	Fieber *n*

Italian	*Portuguese*	*Spanish*
famiglia	família	familia
famoso	famoso	famoso
ventilatore *m*	ventilador *m*	ventilador *m*
ventaglio	abanico; leque *m* (Br.)	abanico
tifoso	aficionado	aficionado
cinghia del ventilatore	correia da ventoinha	correa
lontano	distante; remoto	lejano
lontano	longe; distante	lejos
prezzo del viaggio	preço de passagem	passaje *m*
fattoria; podere *m*	fazenda; sítio (Br.)	granja; rancho (Mex.)
agricoltore *m*	fazendeiro	granjero; ranchero
più lontano	mais longe	más lejos
rapido	rápido	rápido
rapidamente	depressa	de prisa; ligero (Amer.)
digiunare	jejuar	ayunar
andare avanti	estar adiantado	estar adelantado
attaccare	fixar	fijar
Allaciarsi la cintura!	Aperte o cinto!	Abroche el cinturón!
grasso	gordo	gordo
padre *m*	pai *m*	padre *m*
suocero	sogro	suegro
rubinetto	torneira; bica	grifo; llave *f*
colpa	culpa	culpa
favore *m*	favor *m*	favor *m*
paura	mêdo	miedo
temere	ter mêdo; temer	tener miedo
piuma	pena	pluma
film *m* principale	filme *m* principal	película principal
febbraio	fevereiro	febrero
onorario	honorários *mpl*	honorarios *mpl*
sentire	sentir	sentir
avere voglia di	ter vontade de	tener ganas de
feltro	fêltro	fieltro
parafango	pára-lama *m*	guardafango
nave-traghetto	barca	barco de trasbordo; chalán *m* (Amer.)
festa	festa	fiesta
febbre *f*	febre *f*	fiebre *f*

English	*French*	*German*
few (not many)	peu de	wenige
field	champ *m*	Feld *n*
fifteen	quinze	fünfzehn
fifth (adj.)	cinquième	der fünfte, etc.
fifty	cinquante	fünfzig
fig	figue *f*	Feige *f*
fight	combat *m*	Kampf *m*
fight, to	se battre	kämpfen
file (for papers)	dossier *m*	Akten *mpl*
file (tool)	lime *f*	Feile *f*
fill (make full), to	remplir	füllen
fill (teeth), to	plomber	plombieren
fill a prescription, to	faire une ordonnance	ein Rezept *n* anfertigen
fill out (a form), to	remplir	ausfüllen
Fill the tank!	Faites-le plein!	Füllen Sie bitte den Tank!
fillet (tenderloin)	filet *m*	Filet *n*
filling (teeth)	plombage *m*	Plombe *f*
film (n.)	pellicule *f*	Film *m*
filter (n.)	filtre *m*	Filter *m*
finally	finalement	endlich
find, to	trouver	finden
find out, to	vérifier	untersuchen
fine (good)	bon	fein
Fine!	Parfait!	Schön!
fine (penalty)	amende *f*	Geldstrafe *f*
Fine, thanks, and you?	Bien, merci, et vous?	Gut, danke, und Ihnen?
finger	doigt *m*	Finger *m*
finger bowl	rince-doigts *m*	Fingerschale *f*
finger wave	mise *f* en plis	Haarwelle *f*
finish (complete), to	finir; achever	vollenden
finished (ready)	prêt	fertig
Finland	la Finlande	Finnland *n*
Finnish (adj.)	finlandais	finnisch
fire (n.)	feu *m*	Feuer *n*
Fire!	Au feu!	Feuer!
fire escape	échelle *f* de sauvetage	Nottreppe *f*

Italian	*Portuguese*	*Spanish*
pochi	poucos	pocos
campo	campo	campo
quindici	quinze	quince
quinto	quinto	quinto
cinquanta	cinqüenta	cincuenta
fico	figo	higo
lotta; zuffa	briga	pelea
battersi	brigar	pelear
pratica	arquivo; fichário	archivo; fichero
lima	lima	lima
riempire	encher	llenar
impombiare; otturare	obturar	empastar
preparare una ricetta	aviar uma receita	despachar una receta
riempire	preencher	llenar
Faccia il pieno!	Encha o tanque!	¡Llene el tanque!
filetto	filé *m*	filete *m*
otturazione *f*	obturação *f*	empaste *m*
pellicola; film *m*	filme *m*; película	película
filtro	filtro	filtro
finalmente	finalmente; afinal	por fin
trovare	achar	hallar
indagare	indagar	averiguar
buono	excelente	bueno
Benissimo!	Muito bem!	¡Muy bien!
multa	multa	multa
Bene, grazie, e Lei?	Bem, obrigado, e o senhor?	Bien, gracias, y Usted?
dito (*pl* le dita *f*)	dedo	dedo
vaschetta lavadita	vaso-de-dedos *m*	lavadedos *m*
messa in piega	ondulação *f* à mão	ondulado al agua
finire	acabar; terminar	acabar; terminar
finito	pronto	listo
la Finlandia	a Finlândia	Finlandia
finlandese	finlandês	finlandés
fuoco	fogo	fuego
Al fuoco!	Incêndio!	¡Incendio!
uscita di sicurezza	escada de incêndio	escalera de salvamento

English	*French*	*German*
fire extinguisher	extincteur *m*	Feuerlöscher *m*
fireman	pompier *m*	Feuerwehrmann *m*
fireplace	cheminée *f*	Kamin *m*
firewood	bois *m* de chauffage	Brennholz *n*
first (adj.)	premier	der erste, etc.
first aid	premiers secours *mpl*	erste Hilfe *f*
first aid kit	pharmacie *f* de premier secours	Sanitätspäckchen *n*
first aid station	poste *m* de secours	Unfallhilfsposten *m*
first floor	rez-de-chaussée *m*	Erdgeschoss *n*
first of all	d'abord	zuerst
first performance	première *f*	Erstaufführung *f*
fish	poisson *m*	Fisch *m*
fish, to	pêcher	fischen
fisherman	pêcheur *m*	Fischer *m*
fishhook	hameçon *m*	Angelhaken *m*
fishline	ligne *f*	Angelschnur *f*
fishing reel	moulinet *m*	Multiplikatorrolle *f*
fishing rod	canne *f* à pêche	Angelrute *f*
fishing tackle	attirail *m* de pêche	Angelgerät *n*
fist	poing *m*	Faust *f*
fit (well, e.g.), to	aller bien	passen
five	cinq	fünf
five hundred	cinq cents	fünfhundert
fix (repair), to	réparer	reparieren
fixed price	prix fixe	feste Preis *m*
flag (n.)	drapeau *m*	Fahne *f*
flannel	flanelle *f*	Flanell *n*
flash (phot.) (n.)	flash *m*	Blitzlicht *n*
flashlight	lampe *f* de poche	Taschenlampe *f*
flashlight battery	pile *f*	Taschenlampen-batterie *f*
flat (level)	plat	flach
flat tire	pneu *m* crevé	Reifenpanne *f*
flavor (n.)	saveur *f;* goût *m*	Geschmack *m*
flea	puce *f*	Floh *m*

Italian	*Portuguese*	*Spanish*
estintore *m* (d'incendio)	extintor *m*	apagafuego; extintor *m*
pompiere *m*	bombeiro	bombero
caminetto	lareira	chimenea
legna	lenha	leña
primo	primeiro	primero
pronto soccorso	primeiros socorros *mpl*	primeros auxilios *mpl*
cassetta di pronto soccorso	estôjo de pronto socorro	botiquín *m*
posto di pronto soccorso	pôsto de primeiros socorros	puesto de primeros auxilios
primo piano	andar *m* térreo	piso bajo
prima di tutto	antes de mais nada	antes de todo
prima	estréia	estreno
pesce *m*	peixe *m*	pez *m* (alive); pescado (caught)
pescare	pescar	pescar
pescatore *m*	pescador *m*	pescador *m*
amo	anzol *m*	anzuelo
lenza	linha de pescar	sedal *m*
rocchetto	molinete *m*	carretel *m*
canna da pesca	vara de pescar	caña de pescar
arnesi *mpl* da pesca	aparelhos de pesca	avío de pesca
pugno	punho	puño
andare bene	cair bem	sentar (bien)
cinque	cinco	cinco
cinquecento	quinhentos	quinientos
riparare	consertar	reparar
prezzo fisso	preço fixo	precio fijo
bandiera	bandeira	bandera
flanella	flanela	franela
lampadina di magnesio	lâmpada de magnésio	luz *f* de magnesio
lampadina tascabile	lanterna elétrica	linterna eléctrica
pila	pilha	pila
piatto	chato	plano
pneumatico forato; gomma a terra	pneu *m* vazio; pneu furado	pinchazo; volada (Mex.)
sapore *m*	sabor *m*	sabor *m*
pulce *f*	pulga	pulga

English	*French*	*German*
fleet (n.)	flotte *f*	**Flotte** *f*
flee, to	fuir	**fliehen**
flesh	chair *f*	**Fleisch** *n*
flexible	flexible	**biegsam**
flight (air)	vol *m*	**Flug** *m*
flint	pierre *f* à briquet	**Feuerstein** *m*
flirt, to	flirter	**flirten**
flood (n.)	inondation *f*	**Über**schwemmung *f*
floor (of room)	plancher *m*	**Fussboden** *m*
floor (story)	étage *m*	**Stock** *m*
floor lamp	lampa**daire** *m*	**Stehlampe** *f*
Florence	Florence	**Florenz** *n*
florist shop	la fleuriste	**Blumenladen** *m*
flounder (fish)	carrelet *m*	**Flunder** *f*
flour	farine *f*	**Mehl** *n*
flower	fleur *f*	**Blume** *f*
fluently	couramment	**fliessend; geläufig**
fly (insect)	mouche *f*	**Fliege** *f*
fly, to	voler	**fliegen**
fly swatter	chasse-**mouches** *m*	**Fliegenklatsche** *f*
f.o.b.	franco-bord	**frei an Bord**
fog (mist)	brouillard *m*	**Nebel** *m*
fold, to	plier	**falten**
folding seat	strapon**tin** *m*	**Klappsitz** *m*
follow, to	suivre	**folgen**
following (adj.)	suivant	**folgend**
food	nourriture *f*; aliment *m*	**Speise** *f*
foot (anat.)	pied *m*	**Fuss** *m*
footwear	chaussure *f*	**Schuhwerk** *n*
for (prep.)	pour	**für**
for (conj.)	car	**denn**
for dessert	comme des**sert**	**als Nachtisch**
for example	par exemple	**zum Beispiel**
for hire	à louer	**zu vermieten**
for now	pour le mo**ment**	**zur Zeit**
for rent (signs)	à louer	**zu vermieten**
for sale	en vente	**zu verkaufen**
force, to	forcer	**zwingen**

Italian	*Portuguese*	*Spanish*
flotta	frota	flota
fuggire	fugir	huir
carne *f*	carne *f*	carne *f*
flessibile	flexível	flexible
vôlo	vôo	vuelo
pietrina	pederneira	pedernal *m*
civettare	flertar	coquetear
inondazione *f*	inundação *f*	inundación *f*
pavimento	chão; soalho	suelo
piano	andar *m*	piso
lampada a piedistallo	lâmpada de **pé**	lámpara de pie
Firenze	Florença	Florencia
fioraio	casa de flôres	florería (Amer.)
passerino	linguado	lenguado; rodaballo
farina	farinha	harina
fiore *m*	flor *f* (*pl.* flôres)	flor *f*
correntemente	correntemente	corrientemente
mosca	môsca	mosca
volare	voar	volar
scacciamosche *m*	mata-môsca *m*	matamoscas *m*
franco a bordo	franco a bordo	franco a bordo
nebbia	nevoeiro	niebla
piegare	dobrar	doblar
seggiolino pieghevole	cadeira dobradiça	silla plegadiza
seguire	seguir	seguir
seguente	seguinte	siguiente
cibo; alimento	alimento	alimento
piede *m*	pé *m*	pie *m*
calzatura	calçado	calzado
per	para; por	para; por
poichè	porque	porque
per dessert	para sobremesa	para postre
per esempio	por exemplo	por ejemplo
da noleggiare	aluga-se	a alquilar
per il momento	por agora	por ahora
affittasi	aluga-se	se alquila; se **renta** (Mex.)
in vendita	à venda	de venta
forzare	forçar	forzar

English	*French*	*German*
forced landing	atterrissage *m* forcé	Notlandung *f*
ford, to	passer à gué	durchwaten
forehead	front *m*	Stirn *f*
foreign	étranger	fremd
foreign language	langue *f* étrangère	Fremdsprache *f*
foreigner	étranger *m*	Ausländer *m*
forenoon	matinée *f*	Vormittag *m*
forest	forêt *f*	Wald *m*
forever	à jamais	für immer; ewig
forget, to	oublier	vergessen
forgive, to	pardonner	verzeihen
forgotten (p.p.)	oublié	vergessen
fork (table)	fourchette *f*	Gabel *f*
form (document)	formule *f*; fiche *f*	Formular *n*
formerly	autrefois	vorher
fort	fort *m*	Festung *f*
fortunate	heureux, -euse	glücklich
fortunately	heureusement	zum Glück
forty	quarante	vierzig
forward (mail), to	faire suivre	nachsenden
forward (adv.)	en avant	vorwärts
found (p.p.)	trouvé	gefunden
found, to	fonder	gründen
fountain	fontaine *f*	Springbrunnen *m*
fountain pen	stylo *m*	Füller *m*
fountain syringe	appareil *m* de lavements	Irrigator *m*
four	quatre	vier
fourteen	quatorze	vierzehn
fourth	quatrième	vierte *m* etc.
fox	renard *m*	Fuchs *m*
fracture (n.)	fracture *f*	Bruch *m*
frame (glasses)	monture *f*	Fassung *f*
frame (picture)	cadre *m*	Bilderrahmen *m*
France	la France	Frankreich *n*
free	libre	frei
free (gratis)	gratuit	unentgeltlich; gratis
freedom	liberté *f*	Freiheit *f*
freeze, to	geler	(ge)frieren

Italian	*Portuguese*	*Spanish*
atterraggio forzato	aterragem *f* forçada	aterrizaje *m* forzoso
guadare	vadear	vadear
fronte *f*	testa	frente *f*
straniero	estrangeiro	extranjero
lingua straniera	língua estrangeira	lengua extranjera
straniero *m*	estrangeiro	extranjero
mattina; mattinata	manhã	mañana
foresta	floresta	bosque *m*
per sempre	para sempre	para siempre
dimenticare	esquecer (-se de)	olvidar (se de)
perdonare	perdoar	perdonar
dimenticato	esquecido	olvidado
forchetta	garfo	tenedor *m*
modulo	formulário	formulario
prima	anteriormente	antes
forte *m*	forte *m*	fuerte *m*
fortunato	afortunado	afortunado
fortunatamente	felizmente	por fortuna
quaranta	quarenta	cuarenta
far seguire	fazer seguir	reexpedir
avanti	adiante	hacia adelante
trovato	achado	hallado
fondare	fundar	fundar
fontana	fonte *f*	fuente *f*
stilografica; stilo	caneta-tinteiro	plumafuente *f*
enteroclisma *m*	seringa higiênica	mangueta
quattro	quatro	cuatro
quattordici	catorze	catorce
quarto	quarto	cuarto
volpe *f*	rapôsa	zorra
frattura	fratura	fractura
montatura	armação *f*	montura
cornice *f*	porta-retratos *m*	marco
la Francia	a França	Francia
libero	livre	libre
gratis	grátis	gratis
libertà *f*	liberdade *f*	libertad *f*
gelare	gelar	congelar, helar

English	*French*	*German*
freight	marchand**ises** *fpl*	Fracht *f*
freight car	four**gon** *m*	Güterwagen *m*
French (adj.)	français	französisch
frequent	fréquent	häufig
frequently	fréquem**ment**	häufig
fresh (vs. stale)	frais (fraîche *f*)	frisch
fresh water	eau *f* douce	Süsswasser *n*
Friday	vendredi *m*	Freitag *m*
fried (adj.)	frit; sauté	gebraten
fried eggs	oeufs *mpl* sur le **plat**	Spiegeleier *npl*
fried potatoes	frites *fpl*	Bratkartoffeln *fpl*
friend	ami *m*; amie *f*	Freund *m*; **Freundin** *f*
friendly	amical	freundlich
frog	grenouille *f*	Frosch *m*
from	de	aus; von
from time to time	de temps en **temps**	von Zeit zu **Zeit**
from where	d'où	woher
front (mil.)	front *m*	Front *f*
front seat	siège *m* a**vant**	Vordersitz *m*
frozen	gelé	gefroren
fruit	fruit *m*	Obst *n*
fruit juice	jus *m* de **fruit**	Obstsaft *m*
fry, to	frire	braten
frying pan	poêle *f* à **frire**	Bratpfanne *f*
fuel (n.)	combustible *m*	Brennstoff *m*
fuel pump	pompe *f* à es**sence**	Benzinpumpe *f*
full (no space)	complet	besetzt
full (of)	plein (de)	voll (von)
funeral	funérailles *fpl*	Begräbnis *n*
funny (comical)	drôle	komisch
funny (odd)	drôle	seltsam
fur	fourrure *f*	Pelz *m*
furnished	meublé	möbliert
furniture	meubles *mpl*	Möbel *npl*
furniture store	magasin *m* de **meubles**	Möbelgeschäft *n*
fuse (elect.)	fusible *m*; plomb *m*	Sicherung *f*
future (the)	avenir *m*	Zukunft *f*

Italian	*Portuguese*	*Spanish*
merci *fpl*	frete *m*	flete *m*
carro merci	vagão de **carga**	vagón *m* de **carga**
francese	francês	francés
frequente	freqüente	frecuente
frequente**mente**	freqüente**mente**	a menudo
fresco	fresco	fresco
acqua dolce	água doce	agua dulce
venerdì *m*	sexta-feira	viernes *m*
fritto	frito	frito
uova **fritte**	ovos estrelados	huevos **fritos**
patate fritte	batatas fritas	patatas fritas
amico, amica	amigo, amiga	amigo, amiga
amichevole	amigável	amistoso
rana	rã	rana
da	de	de
di quando in quando	de quando em quando	de vez en cuando
da dove	de onde	de donde
fronte *m*	frente *m*	frente *m*
sedile *m* anteriore	assento da frente	asiento delantero
gelato	gelado	congelado; helado
frutta	fruta	fruta
succo di frutta	suco de fruta	jugo de fruta
friggere	fritar	freír
padella	frigideira	sartén *f*
combustibile *m*	combustível *m*	combustible *m*
pompa da benzina	bomba da gasolina	bomba de gasolina
completo	cheio; lotado	completo
pieno (di)	cheio (de)	lleno (de)
funerale *m*	exéquias *fpl*	funeral *m*
comico	engraçado; esquisito	divertido
bizzarro	estranho	extraño; raro
pelliccia	pele *f*	piel *f*
ammobiliato	mobilado; mobiliado (Br.)	amueblado
mobili *mpl*	móveis *mpl*	muebles *mpl*
negozio di mobili	casa de móveis	mueblería
fusibile *m*	fusível *m*	fusible *m*
futuro	futuro	porvenir *m*

English	*French*	*German*
gall bladder	vésicule *f* biliaire	Gallenblase *f*
galoshes	galoches *fpl*	Gummischuhe *mpl*
game (food)	gibier *m*	Wildbret *n*
game (match)	partie *f*	Partie *f*
gangplank	passerelle *f*	Landungssteg *m*
garage (n.)	garage *m*	Garage *f*
garbage	ordures *fpl*	Abfall *m*
garden	jardin *m*	Garten *m*
gargle, to	gargariser	gurgeln
garlic	ail *m*	Knoblauch *m*
garment	vêtement *m*	Kleidungsstück *n*
garnet	grenat *m*	Granat *m*
garter	jarretière *f*	Strumpfband *n*
gas	gaz *m*	Gas *n*
gas station	station *f* service	Tankstelle *f*
gas stove	cuisinière *f* à gaz	Gasherd *m*
gas tank (auto)	réservoir *m* (d'essence)	Benzintank *m*
gasoline	essence *f*	Benzin *n*
gate	porte *f* barrière	Tor *n* Sperre *f*
gather (meet), to	s'assembler	sich versammeln
gather (up), to	ramasser	sammeln
gauze	gaze *f*	Gaze *f*
gear (mech.)	engrenage *m*	Gang *m*
gem	gemme *f*	Edelstein *m*
gender	genre *m*	Geschlecht *n*
general (adj.)	général	allgemein
general (rank)	général *m*	General *m*
general delivery	poste restante *f*	postlagernd
generally	généralement	gewöhnlich
Geneva	Genève *f*	Genf *n*
Genoa	Gênes *f*	Genua *n*
gentleman	monsieur *m*	Herr *m*
genuine	authentique	echt
German (adj.)	allemand	deutsch
Germany	l'Allemagne *f*	Deutschland *n*
get (become), to	devenir	werden

Italian	*Portuguese*	*Spanish*
vescichetta biliare	vesícula biliar	vesícula biliar
galosce *fpl*	galochas *fpl*	chanclos *mpl*
selvaggina	caça	caza
partita	partida	partido
passerella	prancha	plancha; pasarela
autorimessa; garage *m*	garage *f*	garaje *m*
rifiuti *mpl*	desperdícios *mpl*	desperdicios *mpl*
giardino	jardim *m*	jardín *m*
gargarizzare	gargarejar	hacer gárgaras
aglio	alho	ajo
indumento	peça de roupa	prenda de vestir
granato	granate *m*	granate *m*
giarrettiera	liga	liga
gas *m*	gás *m*	gas *m*
stazione di riforni-mento	pôsto de gasolina	puesto de gasolina; gasolinera (Mex.)
cucina a **gas**	fogão a **gás**	cocina a **gas**
serbatoio benzina	tanque *m*	tanque *m*
benzina	gasolina	gasolina
cancello	portão	puerta
riunirsi	reunir-se	reunirse
raccogliere	recolher	recoger
garza	gaze *f*	gasa
ingranaggio	engrenagem *f*	engranaje *m*
gemma	gema	joya
genere *m*	gênero	género
generale	geral	general
generale *m*	general *m*	general *m*
fermo (in) posta	posta-restante *f*	entrega general; lista de correos (Mex.)
generalmente	em geral	generalmente
Ginevra *f*	Genebra	Ginebra
Genova *f*	Gênova *f*	Génova *f*
signore *m*	senhor *m*; cavalheiro	señor *m*; caballero
genuino	genuíno	genuino
tedesco	alemão	alemán
la Germania	a Alemanha	Alemania
divenire	tornar-se; fazer-se	ponerse; hacerse

English	*French*	*German*
get (fetch), to	aller chercher	holen
get (obtain), to	obtenir	bekommen
get (receive), to	recevoir	empfangen
Get a taxi, please!	Appelez un taxi, s'il vous plaît.	Bitte, rufen Sie ein Taxi!
get along without, to	se passer de	entbehren
get angry, to	se fâcher	sich ärgern
get better, to	améliorer	sich bessern
get dressed, to	s'habiller	sich anziehen
get fat, to	engraisser	zunehmen
get hurt, to	se faire mal	sich weh tun
get lost, to	s'égarer	sich verirren
get married, to	se marier (avec)	sich verheiraten (mit)
get off (descend), to	descendre	absteigen
get on, to	monter	einsteigen
get out, to	sortir	aussteigen
get ready, to	se préparer	sich vorbereiten
get seasick, to	avoir le mal de mer	seekrank werden
get sick, to	tomber malade	erkranken
get (something made)	faire faire	machen lassen
get tired, to	se fatiguer	müde werden
get up, to	se lever	aufstehen
get used to, to	s'habituer à	sich gewöhnen an
get well, to	se rétablir	gesund werden
get wet, to	se mouiller	nass werden
get worse, to	empirer	schlimmer werden
giblets	abattis *mpl*	Geflügelklein *n*
gift (present)	cadeau *m*	Geschenk *n*
gin (drink)	gin *m*	Gin *m*
ginger-ale	ginger-ale *m*	Ingwerbier *n*
ginger (spice)	gingembre *m*	Ingwer *m*
girdle (clothing)	gaine *f*	Mieder *n*
girl	jeune fille *f*	Mädchen *n*
give, to	donner	geben
give (as a gift), to	faire cadeau	schenken
Give me, please,...	Donnez-moi,...s'il vous plaît	Bitte, geben Sie mir...

Italian	*Portuguese*	*Spanish*
andare a prendere	ir buscar	ir a buscar
ottenere, procurare	obter	obtener
ricevere	receber	recibir
Per favore, mi chiami un tassi!	Faça o favor de chamar um táxi!	¡Favor de llamar un taxi!
fare a meno di	passar sem	pasarse sin
arrabbiarsi	zangar-se	enojarse
migliorare	melhorar	mejorar(se)
vestirsi	vestir-se	vestirse
ingrassarsi	engordar	engordar
farsi male	machucar-se	hacerse daño
perdersi	perder-se	perderse
sposarsi (con)	casar-se (com)	casarse (con)
scendere	descer; sair; saltar (Br.)	bajar
salire	subir; embarcar	subir
uscire	descer	salir
prepararsi	preparar-se; aprontar-se	prepararse
avere il mal di mare	enjoar	marearse
ammalarsi	adoecer	enfermar
farsi fare	mandar fazer	mandar hacer
stancarsi	cansar-se	cansarse
alzarsi	levantar-se	levantarse
abituarsi a	habituar-se a	acostumbrarse a
rimettersi	restabelecer-se	restablecerse
bagnarsi	molhar-se	mojarse
peggiorare	piorar	empeorar
frattaglie *fpl*; rigaglie *fpl*	miúdos *mpl*	menudillos *mpl*
dono; regalo	presente *m*	regalo
gin *m*	gim *m*	ginebra
ginger-ale *m*	gengibirra	cerveza de jengibre
zenzero	gengibre *m*	jengibre *m*
fascetta; cintura	cinta; espartilho	faja
ragazza	rapariga; môça (Br.)	chica; muchacha
dare	dar	dar
regalare	regalar	regalar
Per favore, mi dia...	Faça o favor de dar-me...	¡Favor de darme...!

English	*French*	*German*
Give me a light.	Donnez-moi du **feu**, s'il vous **plaît**.	Geben Sie mir bitte **Feuer**.
given (p.p.)	donné	gegeben
glad (adj.)	content	froh
glad (of), to be	se réjouir (de)	sich freuen (über)
Glad to know you!	Enchanté (de faire votre connais**sance**)!	Es freut mich sehr Sie **kenn**enzulernen!
gladly	avec plai**sir**	gerne
glance at, to	jeter un coup d'**oeil** sur	flüchtig blicken
glass (material)	verre *m*	Glas *n*
glass (container)	verre *m*	Glas *n*
glasses (eye)	lunettes *fpl*	Brille *f*
glove	gant *m*	Handschuh *m*
glove compartment	vide-**poches** *m*	Handschuhfach *n*
glue	colle *f*	Leim *m*
go (ride), to	aller	fahren
go (walk), to	aller	gehen
go abroad, to	aller à l'étranger	ins Ausland **reisen**
go ashore, to	débarquer	an **Land** gehen
go away, to	s'en aller	weggehen
Go away!	Allez-vous-**en**!	Gehen Sie **weg**!
go down, to	descendre	hinabsteigen
go fishing, to	aller à la **pêche**	**f**ischen gehen
go home, to	rentrer	nach **Hause** gehen
go in (enter), to	entrer (dans)	eintreten (in)
go out, to	sortir	ausgehen
go shopping, to	faire des **courses**	einkaufen gehen
go to bed, to	se coucher	zu Bett gehen
go to sleep, to	s'endormir	schlafen gehen
go to the movies, to	aller au cinéma	ins Kino gehen
go to the toilet, to	aller au cabinet	aufs Klosett gehen
go towards, to	se diriger **vers**	gehen (fahren) in Richtung...
goat	chèvre *f*	Ziege *f*
God	Dieu *m*	Gott *m*
godmother	marraine *f*	Patin *f*
gold	or *m*	Gold *n*

Italian	*Portuguese*	*Spanish*
Per favore, mi dia un fiammifero.	Faça o favor de dar-me um fósforo.	¡Favor de darme lumbre!
dato	dado	dado
contento	contente	contento
rallegrarsi (di)	estar contente (de)	alegrarse (de)
Piacere (di fare la Sua conoscenza!)	Muito prazer (em conhecê-lo)!	¡Tanto gusto (en conocerle)!
con piacere	com muito prazer	con mucho gusto
dare un'occhiata a	passar os olhos por	echar una mirada a
vetro	vidro	vidrio
bicchiere *m*	copo	vaso
occhiali *mpl*	óculos *mpl*	gafas *fpl;* anteojos *mpl*
guanto	luva	guante *m*
cassettino ripostiglio	porta-luvas *m*	gaveta; portaguantes *m*
colla	cola, grude *m*	cola
andare	ír	ír
andare	ir; andar	ir; andar
viaggiare all' estero	ir para o estrangeiro	ir al extranjero
sbarcare	desembarcar	desembarcarse
andarsene	ir embora	irse
Vada via!	Vá-se embora!	¡Váyase!
scendere	descer	bajar
andare a pescare	ir pescar	ir de pesca
andare a casa	ir para casa	ir a casa
entrare (in)	entrar (em)	entrar (en)
uscire	sair	salir
fare degli acquisti	ir às compras; fazer compras (Br.)	ir de compras
andare a letto; coricarsi	deitar-se, ir para a cama (Br.)	acostarse
addormentarsi	adormecer	dormirse
andare al cinema	ir ao cine	ir al cine
andare al gabinetto	ir ao banheiro	ir al excusado
dirigersi a	dirigir-se a	dirigirse a
capra	cabra	cabra
Dio	o Senhor; Deus	el Señor; Dios
madrina	madrinha	madrina
oro	ouro	oro

English	*French*	*German*
golden	d'or	golden
gone (p.p.)	allé (with être)	gegangen (with sein)
good (adj.)	bon, bonne	gut, etc.
Good afternoon!	Bonjour!	Guten Tag!
Good-by!	Au revoir!	Auf Wiedersehen!
Good day!	Bonjour!	Guten Tag!
Good evening!	Bonsoir!	Guten Abend!
Good Friday	Vendredi Saint	Karfreitag *m*
Good Heavens!	Mon Dieu!	Du lieber Gott!
good-looking	beau; joli	gut aussehend
Good luck!	Bonne chance!	Viel Glück!
Good morning!	Bonjour!	Guten Morgen!
good-natured	accommodant	gutmütig
Good night!	Bonne nuit!	Gute Nacht!
goods	marchandises *fpl*	Waren *fpl*
goose	oie *f*	Gans *f*
Gothic	gothique	gotisch
government	gouvernement *m*	Regierung *f*
governor (title)	gouverneur *m*	Gouverneur *m*
gown (dress)	robe *f*	Kleid *n*
gradually	peu à peu	allmählich
grain	grains *mpl*	Getreide *n*
gram (0.0035 oz.)	gramme *m*	Gramm *n*
Granada	Grenade *f*	Granada *n*
granddaughter	petite-fille *f*	Enkelin *f*
grandfather	grand-père *m*	Grossvater *m*
grandmother	grand-mère *f*	Grossmutter *f*
grandparents	grands-parents *mpl*	Grosseltern *pl*
grandson	petit-fils *m*	Enkel *m*
granite	granit *m*	Granit *m*
grape	raisin *m*	Traube *f*
grapefruit	pamplemousse *f*	Pampelmuse *f*
grass	herbe *f*	Gras *n*
grave (tomb)	tombe *f*	Grab *n*
gravy	sauce *f*	Sosse *f*
gray	gris	grau
grease	graisse *f*	Fett *n*
grease, to	graisser	abschmieren

Italian	*Portuguese*	*Spanish*
d'oro	dourado	dorado
andato (with essere)	ido	ido
buono, buona	bom, boa	bueno, buena
Buon giorno!	Boa tarde!	¡Buenas tardes!
Arrivederci!	Adeus!	¡Adiós!
Buon giorno!	Bom dia!	¡Buenos días!
Buona sera!	Boa noite!	¡Buenas noches!
Venerdì Santo	Sexta Feira Santa	Viernes Santo
Dio mio!	Meu Deus!	¡Dios mío!
bello	bem-parecido	guapo
Buona fortuna!	Boa sorte!	¡Buena suerte!
Buon giorno!	Bom dia!	¡Buenos días!
di buon carattere	bonachão	bonachón
Buona notte!	Boa noite!	¡Buenas noches!
merci *fpl*	mercadoria	mercancías *fpl*
oca	ganso	ganso
gotico	gótico	gótico
governo	govêrno	gobierno
governatore *m*	governador *m*	gobernador *m*
abito; vestito	vestido	vestido
poco a poco	pouco a pouco	poco a poco
grano	grão	grano
grammo	grama	gramo
Granata	Granada	Granada
nipote *f*	neta	nieta
nonno	avô	abuelo
nonna	avó *f*	abuela
nonni *mpl*	avós *mpl*	abuelos *mpl*
nipote *m*	neto	nieto
granito	granito	granito
uva	uva	uva
pompelmo	toronja	toronja
erba	grama	hierba
tomba	tumba	tumba
salsa; sugo	môlho	salsa
grigio	cinzento	gris
grasso	gordura	grasa
ingrassare	lubrificar; engraxar	lubricar; engrasar

English	*French*	*German*
Grease the car!	Graissez la voiture!	Schmieren Sie den Wagen!
greasy	graisseux,-euse	schmierig
great	grand	gross
Great Britain	la Grande Bretagne	Grossbritannien *n*
Greece	la Grèce	Griechenland *n*
Greek (adj.)	grec, grecque	griechisch
green	vert	grün
green beans	haricots verts *mpl*	grüne Bohnen *fpl*
Greenland	le Groenland	Grönland *n*
greet, to	saluer	begrüssen
grenade (mil.)	grenade *f*	Granate *f*
grilled	grillé	geröstet
grind, to	moudre	mahlen
grippe	grippe *f*	Grippe *f*
grocery	épicerie *f*	Lebensmittel-geschäft *n*
ground (earth)	terre *f*	Boden *m*
ground floor	rez-de-chaussée *m*	Erdgeschoss *n*
group (n.)	groupe *m*	Gruppe *f*
grow (get larger), to	croître	wachsen
guard (watch over), to	garder	hüten
Guatemala	le Guatemala	Guatemala *n*
guess (suppose), to	supposer	vermuten
guest	invité *m*	Gast *m*
guide (person)	guide *m*	Führer *m*
guidebook	guide *m*	(Reise)führer *m*
guitar	guitare *f*	Gitarre *f*
gulf (bay)	golfe *m*	Golf *m*
gum (anat.)	gencive *f*	Zahnfleisch *n*
gum (chewing)	chewing-gum *m*	Kaugummi *m*
gun	fusil *m*	Gewehr *n*
guy (fellow)	type *m*	Kerl *m*
gypsy	bohémien *m*, gitan *m*	Zigeuner *m*
habit (custom)	habitude *f*	Gewohnheit *f*
had (p.p.)	eu	gehabt
Hague, The	La Haye	der Haag

Italian	*Portuguese*	*Spanish*
Lubrifichi l'auto!	Lubrifique o carro!	¡Engrase el carro!
unto, grasso	engraxado	grasiento
grande	grande	grande
la Gran Bretagna	a Grã-Bretanha	la Gran Bretaña
la Grecia	a Grécia	Grecia
greco	grego	griego
verde	verde	verde
fagiolini *mpl* (verdi)	vagens *fpl*	habichuelas; ejotes *mpl* (Mex.)
la Groenlandia	a Groenlândia	Groenlandia
salutare	saudar; cumprimentar	saludar
granata	granada	granada
alla graticola	grelhado	asado a la parrilla
macinare	moer	moler
influenza	gripe *f*	gripe *f*
bottega di commestibili, drogheria	mercearia; armazém *m* (Br.)	tienda de comestibles; -de abarrotes (Mex.)
terra	terra	tierra
pianterreno	rés-do-chão; andar *m* térreo	piso bajo
gruppo	grupo	grupo
crescere	crescer	crecer
custodire	custodiar	custodiar
il Guatemala	a Guatemala	Guatemala
supporre	supor	suponer
invitato; ospite *m*	convidado; hóspede *m*	huésped *m*
guida *f*	guia *m*	guía *m*
guida *f*	guia *m*; cicerone *m*	guía *f*
chitarra	guitarra	guitarra
golfo	golfo	golfo
gengiva	gengiva	encía
gomma da masticare	goma de mascar; chiclete *m* (Br.)	goma de mascar; chicle *m* (Mex.)
fucile *m*	fuzil *m*	fusil *m*
individuo; tipo, tizio	sujeito; gajo	tipo; tío
zingaro	cigano	gitano
abitudine *f*	hábito	hábito
avuto	tido	tenido
L'Aia *f*	Haia *f*	La Haya *f*

English	*French*	*German*
hail (ice)	grêle *f*	Hagel *m*
hail, to	grêler	hageln
hair	cheveux *mpl*	Haar *n*
hairbrush	brosse *f* à cheveux	Haarbürste *f*
hair curlers	bigoudis *mpl*	Lockenwickel *f*
hair cut	coupe *f* de cheveux	Haarschnitt *m*
hairdo	coiffure *f*	Frisur *f*
hairdresser	coiffeur *m*	Friseur *m*
hair net	filet *m* à cheveux	Haarnetz *n*
hairpin	épingle *f* à cheveux	Haarnadel *f*
hair spray	fixatif *m*	Haarfixativ *n*
Haiti	Haïti *f*	Haïti *n*
half (adj.)	demi	halb
half (n.)	moitié *f*	Hälfte *f*
half an hour	une demi-**heure**	eine halbe **Stunde**
half-fare	demi-tarif *m*	Halbpreis *m*
half past (hr.)	—et demie	halb (next hour)
half soles, to put on	ressemeler	besohlen
hall	corridor *m*	(Haus) Flur *m*
halt (come to a stop)	s'arrêter	anhalten
ham	jambon *m*	Schinken *m*
ham and eggs	oeufs au jambon	Schinken und **Eier**
Hamburg	Hambourg *m*	Hamburg *n*
hammer (n.)	marteau *m*	Hammer *m*
hammock	hamac *m*	Hängematte *f*
hand	main *f*	Hand *f*
hand lotion	lotion *f* pour les **mains**	Handkrem *m*
hand baggage	bagage à main	Handgepäck *n*
hand made	fait à la **main**	angefertigt
hand towel	serviette *f* à **main**	Handtuch *n*
handbag	sac *m* à main	Handtasche *f*
handful	poignée *f*	Handvoll *f*
handkerchief	mouchoir *m*	Taschentuch *n*
handle (n.)	manche *m*	Griff *m*
handsome	beau, belle	schön
handwriting	écriture *f*	Handschrift *f*
hang (up), to	pendre	hängen

Italian	*Portuguese*	*Spanish*
grandine *f*	saraiva; granizo	granizo
grandinare	saraivar	granizar
capelli *mpl*	cabelo; pêlo	pelo; cabello
spazzola da capelli	escôva de cabelo	cepillo para la cabeza
bigodini *mpl*	frisadores *mpl*	rizadores *mpl*
taglio di capelli	corte *m* de cabelo	corte *m* de pelo
pettinatura	penteado	peinado
parrucchiere *m*	cabeleireiro	peluquero, peinador *m*
rete *f* da capelli	rede *f* de cabelo	redecilla
forcina	gancho; grampo (Br.)	horquilla
fissativo	fixador *m*	fijapelo
Haiti	Haiti	Haití
mezzo	meio	medio
metà	metade *f*	mitad *f*
una mezz'ora	uma meia hora	media hora
mezzo biglietto	meia passagem *f*	medio pasaje *m*
—e mezza	—e meia	—y media
mettere le mezze suole	pôr meias-solas	poner medias suelas
corridoio	corredor *m*	pasillo
fermarsi	parar	pararse
prosciutto	presunto	jamón *m*
uova al prosciutto	ovos fritos com presunto	jamón y huevos
Amburgo *f*	Hamburgo	Hamburgo
martello	martelo	martillo
amaca	rede *f* (de dormir)	hamaca
mano *f*	mão *f*	mano *f*
lozione *f* per le mani	loção *f* de mãos	loción *f* de manos
bagaglio a mano	bagagem *f* de mão	equipaje *m* de mano
fatto a mano	feito à mão	hecho a mano
asciugamano	toalha de rosto	toalla
borsetta	carteira; bôlsa	bolsa; petaquilla (Mex.)
manciata	punhado	puñado
fazzoletto	lenço	pañuelo
manico	cabo	mango
bello	formoso; belo	hermoso; guapo
scrittura	letra	letra
appendere	pendurar	colgar

English	French	German
hanger (clothes)	cintre *m*	Kleiderbügel *m*
hangnail	envie *f*	Niednagel *m*
happen, to	se passer	geschehen
happiness	bonheur *m*	Glück *n*
happy (glad)	heureux, heureuse	glücklich
Happy Birthday!	Bon anniversaire!	Herzlichen **Glück**-wunsch zum Geburtstag!
Happy New Year!	Bonne Année!	Ein glückliches Neujahr!
harbor	port *m*	**H**afen *m*
hard (difficult)	diffi**cile**	schwer
hard (not soft)	dur	hart
hard-boiled (egg)	dur	hartgekocht
hardly	à peine	kaum
hardware store	quincaille**rie** *f*	Eisenwarenhandlung *f*
hare	lièvre *m*	Hase *m*
Has there been...?	Y-a-t-il eu...?	Hat . . . gegeben?
hat	chapeau *m*	Hut *m*
hat box	boîte *f* à cha**peaux**	Hutschachtel *f*
hat shop	chapellerie *f* (men); modiste *f* (women)	Hutgeschäft *n*
hate, to	haïr	hassen
Havana	La Havane *f*	Havanna *n*
have, to	avoir	haben
have a cold, to	être enrhumé	erkältet sein
have a good time, to	s'amuser	sich unter**halten**
Have a nice trip!	Bon voyage!	Gute Reise!
have a passport visaed, to	faire viser un passe**port**	einen Pass revidieren lassen
Have a seat, please!	Asseyez-vous, s'il vous plaît.	Nehmen Sie **Platz**, bitte!
Have fun!	Amusez-vous!	Viel Vergnügen!
Have I time to...?	Est-ce que j'ai le temps pour...?	Habe ich **Zeit**...**zu**
have to, to	il faut...	müssen
Have you...?	Avez-vous...?	Haben Sie...?
Have you any...?	Avez-vous du (etc.)...?	Haben Sie (einige)...?

Italian	*Portuguese*	*Spanish*
attaccapanni *m*	cabide *m*	percha
pipita	raigota	padrastro
succedere; accadere	acontecer; suceder	pasar; suceder
felicità	felicidade *f*	felicidad *f*
felice	feliz	feliz
Buon compleanno!	Feliz aniversário!	¡Feliz cumpleaños!
Felice Capo d'Anno!	Feliz Ano Nôvo!	¡Feliz Año Nuevo!
porto	porto	puerto
difficile	difícil	difícil
duro	duro	duro
sodo	cozido	duro
appena	apenas; mal	apenas
negozio di ferramenta	loja de ferragens	ferretería; quincallería (Amer.)
lepre *f*	lebre *f*	liebre *f*
C'è stato...?	Tem havido...?	¿Ha habido...?
cappello	chapéu *m*	sombrero
cappelliera	chapeleira	sombrerera
cappelleria	chapelaria	sombrerería
odiare	odiar	odiar
Avana *f*	Havana *f*	La Habana *f*
avere	ter	tener
essere raffreddato	ter um resfriado	tener un resfriado
divertirsi	divertir-se	divertirse
Buon viaggio!	Boa viagem!	¡Buen viaje!
far vistare il passaporto	mandar visar o passaporte	mandar visar el pasaporte
Si accomodi, per favore!	Sente-se, por favor!	¡Tome Ud. asiento, por favor!
Si diverta!	Divirta-se!	¡Diviértase!
Ho il tempo di...?	Tenho tempo para...?	¿Tengo tiempo para...?
dovere	ter de; ter que	tener que
Ha...?	O senhor tem...?	¿Tiene Ud...?
Avete del, (etc.)...?	Tem...?	¿Tiene Ud...?

English	*French*	*German*
Have you anything to declare?	Avez-vous quelque chose à décla**rer?**	Haben Sie **etwas zu** verzollen?
hay	foin *m*	Heu *n*
he	il	er
head (anat.)	tête *f*	Kopf *m*
head (leader)	chef *m*	Direktor *m*
head (of bed)	chevet *m*	Kopfende *n*
head cold	rhume *m* de cerveau	Schnupfen *m*
head for, to	se dirig**er** vers	losfahren nach
headache	mal *m* de tête	Kopfschmerzen *mpl*
headlight	phare *m*	Scheinwerfer *m*
headwaiter	maître *m* d'hôtel	Oberkellner *m*
heal, to	guérir	heilen
health	santé *f*	Gesundheit *f*
health **certificate**	certificat *m* de santé	Gesundheits-attest *n*
healthy (well)	sain; bien portant	gesund
hear, to	entendre	hören
heard (p.p.)	entendu	gehört
hearing (sense)	ouïe *f*	Gehör *n*
hearing aid	auditif *m*	Hörapparat *m*
heart	coeur *m*	Herz *n*
heart attack	crise *f* cardiaque	Herzattacke *f*
heartburn	brûlures *fpl* d'esto**mac**	Sodbrennen *n*
heat	chaleur *f*	Hitze *f*
heat, to	chauffer	heizen
heated	chauffé	geheizt
heater	poêle *m*	Heizofen *m*
Heaven forbid!	A Dieu ne **plaise!**	Gott be**wahre!**
Heavens!	Mon **Dieu!**	Mein **Gott!**
heavy	lourd	schwer
heel (of foot)	talon *m*	Ferse *f*
heel (of shoe)	talon *m*	Absatz *m*
height	hauteur *f*	Höhe *f*
helicopter	hélicop**tère** *m*	Hubschrauber *m*
Hello!	Bonjour!	Guten **Tag!**
Hello! (phone)	Allô!	Hallo!

Italian	*Portuguese*	*Spanish*
Ha qualche cosa da dichiarare?	Tem alguma coisa a declarar?	¿Tiene Ud. algo que declarar?
fieno	feno	heno
lui	ele	él
testa	cabeça	cabeza
capo	chefe *m*	jefe *m*
capezzale *m*	cabeceira	cabecera
raffreddore *m*	constipação *f*; resfriado	resfriado
dirigersi a	encaminhar-se para; ir para	dirigirse a
mal *m* di testa	dor *f* de cabeça	dolor *m* de cabeza
faro; fanale *m*	farol *m*	faro
capo cameriere	chefe *m* de criados; chefe dos garçons (Br.)	jefe *m* del comedor
risanare; guarire	sarar; sanar	sanar
salute *f*	saúde *f*	salud *f*
certificato medico	atestado de saúde	certificado de buena salud
sano	são (*f.* sã); sadio	sano
udire; sentire	ouvir	oír
udito	ouvido	oído
udito	ouvido	oído
apparecchio acustico	aparelho de surdez	audífono
cuore *m*	coração *m*	corazón *m*
attacco cardiaco	ataque *m* cardíaco	ataque *m* cardíaco
bruciore *m* di stomaco	azia	rescoldera, acedia
calore *m*	calor *m*	calor *m*
riscaldare	aquecer; esquentar (Br.)	calentar
riscaldato	aquecido	calentado
stufa	aquecedor *m*	estufa
Dio ne liberi!	Deus me livre!	¡No lo permita Dios!
Dio mio!	Meu Deus!	¡Dios mío!
pesante	pesado	pesado
calcagno	calcanhar *m*	talón *m*
tacco	tacão *m*; salto (Br.)	tacón *m*
altezza	altura	altura
elicottero	helicóptero	helicóptero
Buon giorno! Ciao!	Olá!; alô	¿Cómo está?; ¿Qué tal?
Pronto!	Pronto!	¡Diga! ¡Bueno! (Mex.)

English	*French*	*German*
help	aide *f*	Hilfe *f*
help, to	aider	helfen (dat.)
Help!	Au secours!	Zu Hilfe!
Help yourself!	Servez-vous!	Bedienen Sie Sich!
hem (n.)	ourlet *m*	Saum *m*
hemorrhage (n.)	hémorragie *f*	Blutsturz *m*
hemorrhoids	hémorroïdes *fpl*	Hämorrhoiden *fpl*
henceforth	désormais	von nun an
her (dir. obj.)	la	sie
her (ind. obj.)	lui	ihr
her (poss. adj.)	son, sa, ses	ihr
here	ici	hier
Here is...	Voici...	Hier ist...
hereafter (after this)	dorénavant	hernach
Here's to you!	À votre santé!	Prosit!
hernia	hernie *f*	Bruch *m*
herring	hareng *m*	Hering *m*
hiccup, to	hoqueter	den Schluckauf haben
hide (conceal), to	cacher	verstecken
hide (skin)	peau *f*	Fell *n*
high	haut	hoch
highchair	chaise *f* d'enfant	Kinderstuhl *m*
high school	lycée *m*	höhere Schule *f*
highway	grande route *f*	Landstrasse *f*
hill	colline *f*	Hügel *m*
him (dir. obj.)	le	ihn
him (ind. obj.)	lui	ihm
hinge (n.)	gond *m*	Angel *f*
hip	hanche *f*	Hüfte *f*
hire (employ), to	engager	anstellen
hire (a cab), to	louer	mieten
his (poss. adj.)	son, sa, ses	sein
hit (strike), to	frapper	schlagen
hoarse	rauque	heiser
hoe (tool)	houe *f*	Hacke *f*
hold, to	tenir	halten

Italian	*Portuguese*	*Spanish*
aiuto	ajuda	ayuda
aiutare	ajudar	ayudar
Aiuto!	Socorro!	¡Socorro!
Si serva!	Sirva-se!	¡Sírvase!
orlo	bainha	bastilla
emorragia	hemorragia	hemorragia
emorroidi *fpl*	hemorróidas *fpl*	hemorroides *fpl*
d'ora in avanti	de hoje em diante	de aquí en adelante
la	a	la
le	lhe	le
il suo, etc.	o seu, etc.	su, sus
qui; qua	aqui	aquí
Ecco...	Aqui tem...	Aquí tiene...
d'ora innanzi	daqui em diante	de aquí en adelante
Alla Sua salute!	À sua saúde!	¡Salud!
ernia	hérnia	hernia
aringa	arenque *m*	arenque *m*
avere il singhiozzo	soluçar	hipar
nascondere	esconder	esconder
pelle *f*	pele *f*	piel *f*
alto	alto	alto
seggiolone *m*	cadeira de bebê	silla para bebé
scuola media superiore	escola secundária; ginásio	escuela secundaria
autostrada	auto-strada; rodovia (Br.)	carretera
collina	colina	colina
lo	o	le; lo
gli	lhe	le
cardine *m*	gonzo; dobradiça	gozne *m*; bisagra
anca	quadril *m*	cadera
impiegare	empregar	emplear
noleggiare	alugar	alquilar
suo, sua	o seu, etc.	su, sus
colpire	golpear	golpear
rauco	rouco	ronco
zappa	enxada	azada
tenere	ter	tener

English	*French*	*German*
hold (of ship)	cale *f*	Laderaum *m*
hole	trou *m*	Loch *n*
holiday	(jour de) fête *f*	Feiertag *m*
holidays	jours *mpl* fériés	Feiertage *mpl*
Holland	la Hollande	Holland *n*
hollow (adj.)	creux	hohl
holy	saint	heilig
Holy Week	Semaine *f* **Sainte**	Karwoche *f*
home	home *m*	Heim *n*
home (ward)	chez **moi** (etc.)	nach **Hause**
homesick, to be	avoir le mal du **pays**	Heimweh haben
home town	ville *f* natale	Heimatstadt *f*
Honduras	l'Honduras *m*	Honduras *n*
honest	honnête	ehrlich
honey (from bees)	miel *m*	Honig *m*
honeymoon	lune *f* de **miel**	Flitterwochen *fpl*
hood (auto)	capot *m*	Motorhaube *f*
hook (n.)	crochet	Haken *m*
hope	espoir *m*	Hoffnung *f*
hope, to	espérer	hoffen
horn (auto)	klaxon *m*	Hupe *f*
hors-d'oeuvres	hors-d'oeuvre *mpl*	Vorspeise *f*
horse	cheval *m*	Pferd *n*
horse race	course *f* de chevaux	Pferderennen *n*
horseradish	raifort *m*	Meerrettich *m*
hospital	hôpital *m*	Krankenhaus *n*
hot	chaud	heiss
hot (spicy)	piquant	scharf
hot water	eau *f* chaude	heisses Wasser *n*
hot water bottle	bouillotte *f*	Wärmflasche *f*
hotel	hôtel *m*	Hotel *n*
hour	heure *f*	Stunde *f*
house	maison *f*	Haus *n*
housewife	ménagère *f*	Hausfrau *f*
How?	Comment?	Wie?
How are you?	Comment allez-**vous**?	Wie geht es Ihnen?
How do I get to...?	Comment faut-il aller pour arriver à...?	Wie komme ich nach...?
How do you do?	Bonjour!	Guten Tag!

Italian	*Portuguese*	*Spanish*
stiva	porão *m*; estiva	bodega
buco	buraco	agujero
giorno di festa	(dia) feriado	día *m* de fiesta
ferie *fpl*	férias *fpl*	vacaciones *fpl*
l'Olanda	a Holanda	Holanda
cavo	ôco	hueco
santo	santo	santo
Settimana Santa	Semana Santa	Semana Santa
casa	lar *m*; casa	hogar *m*
a casa	para casa	a casa
essere preso da nostalgìa	ter saudades; estar com saudades (Br.)	sentir nostalgia (de)
città natale	cidade *f* natal	ciudad *f* natal
l'Honduras	o Honduras	Honduras
onesto	honesto	honrado
miele *m*	mel *m*	miel *f*
luna di miele	lua de mel	luna de miel
cofano	capô *m*	capô *m*
uncino; gancio	gancho	gancho
speranza	esperança	esperanza
sperare	esperar	esperar
clacson *m*	buzina	bocina; klaxón *m*
antipasto	acepipes *mpl*	entremeses *mpl*
cavallo	cavalo	caballo
corsa di cavalli	corrida de cavalos	carrera de caballos
rafano	rábano picante	rábano picante
ospedale *m*	hospital *m*	hospital *m*
caldo	quente	caliente
piccante	picante	picante; picoso (Mex.)
acqua calda	água quente	agua caliente
borsa dell'acqua calda	saco de água quente	bolsa de hule (para agua caliente)
albergo, hotel *m*	hotel *m*	hotel *m*
ora	hora	hora
casa	casa	casa
donna di casa; massaia	dona de casa	ama de casa
Come?	Como?	¿Cómo?
Come sta Lei?	Como vai o senhor?	¿Cómo está Ud.?
Come si può andare a...?	Por onde se vai a...?	¿Por dónde voy a...?
Come sta?	Como está?	¿Cómo está?

English	*French*	*German*
How do you like...?	Comment trouvez-vous...?	Wie gefällt Ihnen...?
How do you say...?	Comment dit-on...?	Wie sagt man...?
How do you spell...?	Comment écrit-on...?	Wie buchstabiert man...?
How do you want your...?	Comment préférez-vous...?	Wie möchten Sie Ihr...haben?
How far is it to...?	A quelle distance se trouve...?	Wie weit ist es bis...?
How goes it?	Comment ça va?	Wie geht's?
How long...?	Combien de temps...?	Wie lange...?
How long ago?	Il y a combien de temps?	Wann?
How long have you been...?	Depuis quand...? (+ present tense)	Seit wann...? (present)
How long will it take?	Combien de temps cela prendra-t-il?	Wie lange wird es dauern?
How many...?	Combien (de)...?	Wie viele...?
How much?	Combien?	Wieviel?
How much is it?	Combien est-ce?	Wieviel kostet es?
How much do I owe you?	Combien vous dois-je?	Was bin ich Ihnen schuldig?
How much do you charge?	Combien demandez-vous?	Wieviel verlangen Sie?
How much is the postage on...?	A combien doit-on affranchir...?	Wieviel beträgt das Porto...?
How old are you?	Quel âge avez-vous?	Wie alt sind Sie?
How soon?	Quand?	Wann?
however (conj.)	cependant	doch
hub cap (auto)	enjoliveur *m*	Radkappe *f*
hug, to	étreindre	umarmen
huge	énorme	riesig
hundred	cent	hundert
Hungarian (adj.)	hongrois	ungarisch
Hungary	la Hongrie	Ungarn *n*
hunger (n.)	faim *f*	Hunger *m*
hungry (famished)	affamé	hungrig
hungry, to be	avoir faim	Hunger haben
hunt, to	chasser	jagen
hunting (n.)	chasse *f*	Jagd *f*
hurricane	ouragan *m*	Orkan *m*

Italian	*Portuguese*	*Spanish*
Come le pare...?	Que lhe parece...?	¿Qué le parece...
Come si dice?	Como se diz...?	¿Cómo se dice...?
Come si scrive...?	Como se escreve...?	¿Cómo se deletrea...?
Come vuole...?	Como quer...?	¿Cómo quiere...?
Quanto é lontano di qui...?	A que distância fica...?	¿Cuánto dista de aquí a...?
Come sta?	Como vai?	¿Qué tal?
Quanto tempo...?	Quanto tempo...?	¿Cuánto tiempo...?
Quanto tempo fa?	Há quanto tempo?	¿Hace cuánto tiempo?
Da quanto tempo...? (present)	Há quanto tempo...? (present)	¿Desde cuándo...? (present)
Quanto tempo ci vorrà?	Quanto tempo leva?	¿Cuánto tiempo lleva?
Quanti...?	Quantos...?	¿Cuántos...?
Quanto?	Quanto?	¿Cuánto?
Quanto costa?	Quanto custa?	¿Cuánto vale?
Quanto le devo?	Quanto lhe devo?	¿Cuánto le debo?
Quanto chiede?	Quanto cobra?	¿Cuánto cobra?
Quanto per affrancare...?	Quanto é o porte para...?	¿Cuánto cuesta el franqueo de...?
Quanti anni ha?	Quantos anos tem?	¿Cuántos años tiene?
Quando?	Quando?	¿Cuándo a más tardar?
però; tuttavia	porém; todavia	sin embargo
testa del mozzo	calota	tapacubo
abbracciare	abraçar	abrazar
enorme	enorme	enorme
cento	cem	ciento
ungherese	húngaro	húngaro
l'Ungheria	a Hungria	Hungría
fame *f*	fome *f*	hambre *f*
affamato	faminto	hambriento
aver fame	ter fome	tener hambre
cacciare	caçar	cazar
caccia	caça	caza
uragano	furacão	huracán *m*

English	*French*	*German*
hurriedly	précipitamment	eilig
hurry, to	se dépêcher	sich beeilen
hurry, to be in a	être pressé	in Eile sein
Hurry up!	Dépêchez-vous!	Beeilen Sie sich!
hurt (be painful), to	avoir mal	schmerzen
hurt (inflict pain), to	faire mal à	weh tun
husband	mari *m*	Mann *m*
hydrant	bouche *f* d'incendie	Hydrant *m*
I	je	ich
I am an American	Je suis Américain	Ich bin Amerikaner
I am busy	Je suis occupé	Ich bin beschäftigt
I am cold	J'ai froid	Mir ist kalt
I am glad	Je suis heureux	Es freut mich
I am hot	J'ai chaud	Mir ist heiss
I am hungry	J'ai faim	Ich habe Hunger
I am in a hurry	Je suis pressé	Ich bin in Eile
I am looking for...	Je cherche...	Ich suche...
I am lost	Je me suis égaré	Ich habe mich verlaufen
I am on a diet	Je suis un régime	Ich lebe Diät
I am pleased to meet you	Je suis enchanté de faire votre connaissance	Ich freue mich Ihre Bekanntschaft zu machen
I am ready	Je suis prêt(e)	Ich bin fertig
I am seasick	J'ai le mal de mer	Ich bin seekrank
I am sick	Je suis malade	Ich bin krank
I am sleepy	J'ai sommeil	Ich bin schläfrig
I am sorry	Je (le) regrette	Es tut mir leid
I am staying at...	Je suis descendu à...	Ich wohne vorübergehend in...
I am sure	Je suis certain	Ich bin sicher

Italian	*Portuguese*	*Spanish*
in fretta	à pressa	de prisa
affrettarsi	apressar-se	apresurarse; apurarse (Amer.)
avere fretta	estar com pressa	tener prisa
Presto!	Apresse-se!	¡Apresúrese! ¡Dése prisa!
dolere	doer	doler
far male a	ferir; magoar	herir
marito	marido; espôso	marido; esposo
idrante *m*	bôca de incêndio	boca de agua
io	eu	yo
Sono americano	Sou (norte) americano	Soy (norte) americano
Sono occupato	Estou ocupado	Estoy ocupado
Ho freddo	Tenho frio; Estou com frio	Tengo frío
Sono contento	Estou contente	Me alegro
Ho caldo	Tenho calor; Estou com calor	Tengo calor
Ho fame	Tenho fome; Estou com fome	Tengo hambre
Ho fretta	Tenho pressa; Estou com pressa	Tengo prisa
Io cerco...	Eu procuro...	Yo busco...
Mi sono perduto	Estou perdido	Estoy perdido
Sono a dieta	Estou em regime	Estoy a dieta
Fortunatissimo di far la Sua conoscenza	Tenho muito prazer em conhecê-lo(-la)	Mucho gusto en conocerle(la)
Sono pronto(a)	Estou pronto(a)	Estoy listo(a)
Ho il mal di mare	Estou enjoado	Estoy mareado
Sono ammalato	Estou doente	Estoy enfermo
Ho sonno	Tenho sono; Estou com sono	Tengo sueño
Mi dispiace	Tenho pena; Sinto muito	Lo siento
Sono sceso al...	Moro em...	Me hospedo en...
Io sono sicuro	Eu estou seguro	Yo estoy seguro

English	*French*	*German*
I am thirsty	J'ai soif	Ich habe Durst
I am tired	Je suis fatigué	Ich bin müde
I am well	Je vais bien	Es geht mir gut
I beg your pardon!	Je vous demande pardon!	Verzeihung!
I can (not)	Je (ne) puis	Ich kann (nicht)
I don't feel well	Je ne vais pas bien	Mir ist nicht wohl
I don't know (acquaintance)	Je ne connais pas	Ich kenne...nicht
I don't know ('how to', fact)	Je ne sais pas	Ich weiss nicht
I don't like this	Ceci ne me plaît pas	Mir gefällt dies nicht
I don't like to...(inf.)	Je n'aime pas...	Ich mag nicht...
I don't speak...	Je ne parle pas...	Ich spreche kein...
I don't understand	Je ne comprends pas	Ich verstehe nicht
I don't want any...	Je ne veux pas de...	Ich will...nicht haben
I feel better	Je me porte mieux	Mir geht es wieder besser
I feel nauseated	J'ai des nausées	Mir ist übel
I feel sick (car or ship)	Je me sens malade	Mir ist übel
I 'get you'!	J'y suis!	Ich verstehe!
I have	J'ai	Ich habe
I have (with past part.)	J'ai	Ich habe
I have just...	Je viens de (+ inf.)	Ich habe(bin) gerade (p.p.)
I have nothing to declare (at customs)	Je n'ai rien à déclarer	Ich habe nichts zu verzollen
I have to (+ inf.)	Il me faut...	Ich muss...
I hope not!	J'espère que non	Hoffentlich nicht!
I hope so!	Je l'espère!	Hoffentlich!
I know (acquaintance)	Je connais	Ich kenne
I know (fact)	Je sais	Ich weiss
I like it (very much)	Je l'aime (beaucoup)	Es gefällt mir (sehr)
I like to...	J'aime...(+ inf.)	Ich (vb.) gern
I mean (rather)...	Je veux dire...	Ich meine...

Italian	*Portuguese*	*Spanish*
Ho sete	Tenho sêde;	Tengo sed
	Estou com sêde	
Sono stanco	Estou cansado	Estoy cansado
Sto bene	Estou bem	Estoy bien
Scusi!	Desculpe-me!	¡Perdóneme!
(Non) posso	(Não) posso	(No) puedo
Non mi sento bene	Não me sinto bem	No me siento bien
Non conosco	Não conheço	No conozco
Non so	Não sei	No sé
Questo non mi piace	Não gosto disto	No me gusta esto
Non mi piace...	Não gosto de...	No me gusta...
Non parlo...	Não falo...	No hablo...
Non capisco	Não compreendo	No entiendo
Non voglio...	Não quero...	No quiero...
Mi sento meglio	Sinto-me melhor	Me siento mejor
Mi sento nauseato	Sinto náusea	Tengo náusea
Mi sento male	Sinto-me enjoado	Me siento mareado
Ora capisco!	Compreendo!	¡Ya caigo!
Ho	Tenho	Tengo
Ho	Tenho	He
Ho appena (+ p.p.)	Acabo de (+ inf.)	Acabo de (+ inf.)
Non ho nulla da	Não tenho nada a	No tengo nada que
dichiarare	declarar	declarar
Devo...	Tenho de...	Tengo que...
Spero di no!	Tomara que não!	¡Espero que no!
	Espero que não!	
Spero di sì!	Espero; tomara que	¡Espero que sí!
	sim!	
Conosco	Conheço	Conozco
Io so	Eu sei	Yo sé
Mi piace (molto)	Gosto (muito)	Me gusta (mucho)
Mi piace... (+ inf.)	Gosto de... (+ inf.)	Me gusta... (+ inf.)
Voglio dire...	Quero dizer...	Digo..

English	*French*	*German*
I must (+ inf.)	Il me faut	Ich muss
I need	J'ai besoin de	Ich brauche
I speak	Je parle	Ich spreche
I think not	Je crois que **non**	Ich glaube **nicht**
I think so	Je crois que **oui**	Ich glaube **ja**
I understand	Je comprends	Ich verstehe
I want a haircut	Je voudrais une coupe de cheveux	Ich möchte einen Haarschnitt, bitte
I want a shave	Je voudrais me faire raser	Rasieren Sie mich, bitte
I want my shoes cleaned	Faîtes cirer mes souliers	Lassen Sie bitte meine Schuhe putzen
I want this cleaned	Je voudrais faire nettoyer ceci	Ich möchte dies reinigen lassen, bitte
I want this pressed	Je voudrais faire repasser ceci	Ich möchte dies bügeln lassen, bitte
I want this repaired	Je voudrais faire réparer ceci	Ich möchte dies reparieren lassen, bitte
I want this washed	Je voudrais faire laver ceci	Ich möchte dies waschen lassen, bitte
I was born...	Je suis né...	Ich bin...geboren
I will take (this) (said making a purchase)	Je prends (ceci)	Ich nehme (dies)
I would like...	Je voudrais...	Ich möchte...
ice	glace *f*	Eis *n*
ice box	glacière *f*	Eisschrank *m*
ice cold	glacé	eiskalt
ice cream	glace *f*	Eis *n*
ice cream ccne	cornet *m* de **glace**	Eistüte *f*
ice skate (n.)	patin *m*	Schlittschuh *m*
iced coffee	café *m* glacé	Eiskaffee *m*
iced tea	thé *m* glacé	Eistee *m*
iced water	eau *f* glacée	Eiswasser *n*
identification card	carte *f* d'identité	Ausweis *m*

Italian	*Portuguese*	*Spanish*
Devo	**Devo**; Tenho de	Tengo que; **Debo**
Ho bisogno di	Preciso de; Necessito	Necesito; Me hace **falta**
Parlo	Falo	Hablo
Credo di **no**	Acho que **não**	Creo que **no**
Penso di **sì**	Acho que sim	Creo que **sí**
Capisco	Compreendo	Entiendo
Desidero **farmi** tagliare i capelli	Desejo cortar o cabelo	Quiero cortarme el pelo
Desidero **farmi fare** la barba	Desejo fazer a **barba**	Quiero afeitarme
Fate lucidare le **mie scarpe**	Que me limpem os sapatos	Que me limpien los zapatos
Desidero che **questo** sia pulito	Queria que me **limpem** isto	Quiero que me limpien **esto**
Desidero che **questo** sia stirato	Queria que me **passem** a ferro isto	Quiero que me planchen **esto**
Desidero che **questo** sia rammendato	Queria que me consertem **isto**	Quiero que me arreglen **esto**
Desidero che **questo** sia lavato	Queria que me **lavem** isto	Quiero que me **laven** esto
Sono **nato**...	Nasci...	Nací...
Prendo (questo)	Fico com (isto)	Me quedo con **(esto)**
Vorrei...	Desejava; Gostaria de	Quisiera; Me gustaría
ghiaccio	gêlo	hielo
ghiacciaia	geladeira	nevera
ghiacciato	bem gelado	bien frío
gelato	sorvete *m*	helado; nieve *f*
cono di gelato	casquinha (Br.)	barquillo
pattino	patim *m*	patín *m* de hielo
caffè *m* ghiacciato	café *m* gelado	café *m* helado
tè *m* ghiacciato	chá *m* gelado	té *m* helado
acqua ghiacciata	água gelada	agua helada
carta d'identità	carteira de identidade	tarjeta de identidad

English	*French*	*German*
idiom	idiotisme *m*	Redewendung *f*
if	si	wenn
If you don't mind	S'il ne vous dérange pas	Wenn es Ihnen nichts ausmacht
If you please	S'il vous plaît	Bitte
ignition (auto)	allumage *m*	Zündung *f*
ill (sick)	malade	krank
illness	maladie *f*	Krankheit *f*
imagine, to	(s')imaginer	sich vorstellen
immediately	tout de suite	gleich
immigrant	immigrant *m*	Einwanderer *m*
impassable	impraticable	ungangbar
impolite	impoli	unhöflich
import, to	importer	einführen
importance	importance *f*	Wichtigkeit *f*
important	important	wichtig
importer	importateur *m*	Importeur *m*
impossible	impossible	unmöglich
impure	impur	unrein
in	dans; en	in
in a short time	tout à l'heure	bald
in advance	d'avance	im voraus
in any case	en tout cas	sowieso, jedenfalls
in case (conj.)	au cas que	falls
in case of (prep.)	en cas de	im Fall (gen.)
in fact	en effet	in der Tat
in favor of, to be	tenir pour	für sein
in front of	devant	vor
in general	en général	im allgemeinen
in order that (conj.)	pour que	damit
in order to (prep.)	pour	um...zu (inf.)
in other words	autrement dit	mit anderen Worten
in search of	à la recherche de	auf der Suche nach
in spite of	malgré	trotz (with gen.)
in style, to be	être à la dernière mode	nach der Mode sein

Italian	*Portuguese*	*Spanish*
idiotismo	idiotismo	modismo
se	se	si
Se non le dispiace	Se o senhor não faz questão	Si Ud. no tiene inconveniente
Per favore	Por favor	Por favor; Si me hace el favor
accensione *f*	ignição *f*	encendido
malato	doente	enfermo
malattia	doença	enfermedad *f*
figurarsi	imaginar	figurarse
immediatamente	imediatamente	en seguida
immigrante *m*	imigrante *m*	inmigrante *m*
impassibile	intransitável	intransitable
scortese	descortês	descortés
importare	importar	importar
importanza	importância	importancia
importante	importante	importante
importatore *m*	importador *m*	importador *m*
impossibile	impossível	imposible
impuro	impuro	impuro
in	em	en
fra poco	pouco depois	al poco rato
in anticipo	adiantado	por adelantado
in ogni caso	em todo o caso	de todos modos
in caso che	(no) caso (que)	en caso que
in caso di	em caso de	en caso de
infatti	de fato	en efecto
essere favorevole a	estar em favor de	estar por
davanti a	diante de	delante de
generalmente	geralmente	en general
affinchè	para que	para que
per	para	para
in altre parole	em outras palavras	en otros términos
alla ricerca di	em busca de	en busca de
malgrado	apesar de	a pesar de
essere di moda	estar na moda	estar de moda

English	*French*	*German*
in the afternoon	l'après-midi	am Nachmittag
in the distance	au loin	in der Ferne
in the evening	le soir	am Abend
in the fall	en automne	im Herbst
in the first place	d'abord	erstens
in the forenoon	le matin	am Vormittag
in the meantime	en attendant	inzwischen
in the middle of	au milieu de	mitten in
in the morning	le matin	am Morgen
in the open air	en plein air	unter freiem Himmel
in the spring	au printemps	im Frühling
in the summer	en été	im Sommer
in the winter	en hiver	im Winter
in vain	en vain	vergeblich
inch	pouce *m*	Zoll *m*
including	y compris	einschliesslich
income	revenu *m*	Einkommen *n*
income tax	impôt *m* sur le revenu	Einkommensteuer *f*
India	l'Inde *f*	Indien *n*
Indian (American)	indien *m*	Indianer *m*
indigestion	indigestion *f*	Verdauungsstörung *f*
Indonesia	L'Indonésie *f*	Indonesien *n*
infection	infection *f*	Ansteckung *f*
inflate, to	gonfler	aufblasen
influenza	grippe *f*	Grippe *f*
inform, to	informer	Auskunft geben
information	renseignement *m*	Auskunft *f*
ingrowing nail	ongle *m* incarné	eingewachsener Zehnagel *m*
inhabitant	habitant *m*	Bewohner *m*
inhaler	inhalateur *m*	Inhalator *m*
injection	piqûre *f*	Einspritzung *f*
injure, to	blesser	verletzen
injury	blessure *f*	Verletzung *f*
ink	encre *f*	Tinte *f*
inkwell	encrier *m*	Tintenfass *n*
inn	auberge *f*	Gasthaus *n*

Italian	*Portuguese*	*Spanish*
nel pomeriggio	à tarde	por la tarde
in lontananza	ao longe	a lo lejos
di sera	pela noite	por la noche
in autunno	no outono	en el otoño
al primo posto	em primeiro lugar	en primer lugar
la mattina	pela manhã	por la mañana
nel frattempo	entretanto	mientras tanto
nel mezzo di	no meio de	en medio de
la mattina	pela manhã	por la mañana
all'aria aperta	ao ar livre	al aire libre
in primavera	na primavera	en la primavera
d'estate	no verão	en el verano
d'inverno	no inverno	en el invierno
invano	em vão	en vano
pollice *m*	polegada	pulgada
compreso	inclusivo	incluso
rendita	renda	renta; ingresos *mpl*
tassa sulla rendita	impôsto sôbre a renda	impuesto sobre rentas
l'India	a Índia	la India
pellerossa *m*	índio	indio
indigestione *f*	indigestão *f*	indigestión *f*
Indonesia	Indonésia	Indonesia
infezione *f*	infecção *f*	infección *f*
gonfiare	inflar	inflar
influenza	gripe *f*	influenza
informare	informar	informar
informazione *f*	informação *f*	informes *mpl*
unghia incarnata	unha encravada	uñero
abitante *m*	habitante *m*	habitante *m*
inalatore *m*	inalador *m*	inhalador *m*
iniezione *f*; puntura	injeção *f*	inyección *f*
ferire	lesar; ferir	lisiar; dañar
lesione *f*	lesão *f*; dano	lesión *f*; daño
inchiostro	tinta	tinta
calamaio	tinteiro	tintero
albergo; locanda	estalagem *f*; pousada	fonda; parador *m*; posada

English	*French*	*German*
inner tube	chambre *f* à **air**	Schlauch *m*
innkeeper	aubergiste *m*	Gastwirt *m*
inquire, to	demander	sich erkundigen
insecticide	insecticide *m*	Insektenpulver *n*
inside (adv.)	dedans	drinnen
inside (inner)	intérieur	inner
inside of (prep.)	dans	innerhalb (gen.)
insist upon, to	insister	bestehen auf (dat.)
inspect, to	vérifier	prüfen
instead of	au lieu de	(an)statt (gen.)
instrument panel	planche *f* de **bord**	Schalttafel *f*
insurance	assurance *f*	Versicherung *f*
insure, to	(faire) assurer	versichern
intend to, to	avoir l'intention de	beabsichtigen
interested in, to be	s'intéresser à	sich interessieren für
interesting	intéressant	interessant
intermission (theat.)	entracte *m*	Pause *f*
interpreter	interprète *m*	Dolmetscher *m*
interrupt, to	interrompre	unterbrechen *f*
interview (n.)	entrevue *f*	Unterredung *f*
into	dans	in
introduce (bring in), to	introduire	einführen
introduce (make acquainted), to	présenter	vorstellen
invent, to	inventer	erfinden
invention	invention *f*	Erfindung *f*
inventory (bus.)	inventaire *m*	Inventar *n*
invest, to (bus.)	placer (de l'argent)	anlegen
investigate, to	examiner	untersuchen
investigation	investigation *f*	Untersuchung *f*
investment (bus.)	placement *m*	Geldanlage *f*
invitation	invitation *f*	Einladung *f*
invite, to	inviter	einladen
invoice (n.)	facture *f*	Rechnung *f*
iodine	teinture *f* **d'iode**	Jodtinktur *f*

Italian	*Portuguese*	*Spanish*
camera d'aria	câmara de ar	cámara de aire; goma (Mex.)
albergatore *m*	estalajadeiro	posadero; mesonero
domandare	indagar	preguntar
insetticida	inseticida *m*	insecticida *f*
dentro	dentro	dentro
interno	interior	interior
dentro di	dentro de	dentro de
insistere	insistir	insistir
ispezionare	examinar	registrar; revisar
invece di	em vez de	en vez de
cruscotto	painel *m* de instrumentos	tablero de instrumentos
assicurazione *f*	seguro	seguro
assicurare	segurar	asegurar
intendere	pretender; tencionar	pensar (+ inf.)
interessarsi a	interessar-se por	interesarse por
interessante	interessante	interesante
intervallo	intervalo	entreacto
interprete *m*	intérprete *m*	intérprete *m*
interrompere	interromper	interrumpir
intervista	entrevista	entrevista
in	em	en
introdurre	introduzir	introducir
presentare	apresentar	presentar
inventare	inventar	inventar
invenzione *f*	invenção *f*	invención *f*
inventario	inventário	inventario
investire	inverter	invertir
investigare	investigar	investigar
investigazione *f*	investigação *f*	investigación *f*
investimento	inversão *f*	inversión *f*
invito	convite *m*	invitación *f*
invitare	convidar	invitar
fattura	fatura	factura
l'iodio	iôdo	yodo

English	*French*	*German*
I.O.U.	billet *m* à ordre	Schuldschein *m*
Ireland	l'Irlande *f*	Irland *n*
Irish (adj.)	irlandais	irisch
iron (metal)	fer *m*	Eisen *n*
iron, to	repasser	bügeln
iron (flatiron)	fer *m* à repasser	Bügeleisen *n*
ironing board	planche *f* à repasser	Bügelbrett *n*
is	est	ist
Is it far?	Est-ce loin?	Ist es weit?
Is it necessary to...?	Faut-il...?	Muss man...
Is it time to...?	Est-il temps de...?	Ist es Zeit zu...?
Is there...?	Y a-t-il...?	Gibt es...?
Is there any mail for...?	Y a-t-il du courrier pour...?	Ist Post für...?
Is this seat free?	Est-ce que cette **place** est libre?	Ist dieser Platz **frei**?
Is this the road to...?	Est-ce que cette **route** mène a...?	Ist dies der Weg nach...?
island	île *f*	Insel *f*
...isn't it?	n'est-ce **pas**?	nicht **wahr**?
it (as subj.)	il; elle; ce	es; er; sie
it (as dir. obj.)	le; la	es; ihn; sie
It does not fit (me)	Cela ne (me) va **pas**	Es **passt** (mir) **nicht**
It doesn't matter	Ça ne fait **rien**	Das macht nichts
It does not work	Il ne marche **pas**	Es funktioniert nicht
It goes without saying	Ça va sans **dire**	Es ist selbst-verständlich
It is all the same to me	Ça m'est égal	Mir macht es **nichts** aus
It is bad weather	Il fait mauvais **temps**	Es ist **schlechtes Wetter**
It is cloudy	Le ciel est **couvert**	Es ist wolkig
It is cold (temp.)	Il fait froid	Es ist kalt
It is cool	Il fait frais	Es ist kühl
It is foggy	Il fait du brouillard	Es ist neblig
It is going to (rain)	Il va (pleuvoir)	Es wird (regnen)
It is good weather	Il fait beau	Es ist **schönes Wetter**

Italian	*Portuguese*	*Spanish*
pagherò *m*	vale *m*	pagaré *m*
l'Irlanda	a Irlanda	Irlandia
irlandese	irlandês	irlandés
ferro	ferro	hierro
stirare	passar a ferro	planchar
ferro da stiro	ferro de passar roupa; ferro de engomar	plancha
asse *f* per stirare	tábua de engomar	tabla de planchar
è; sta	é; está	es; está
È lontano?	É longe?	¿Está lejos?
Bisogna...?	É preciso...?	¿Es preciso...?
È l'ora di...?	É hora de...?	¿Es hora de...?
C'è...?	Há...?	¿Hay...?
C'è posta per...?	Ha correspondência para...?	¿Hay correo para...?
È libero questo posto?	Êste lugar está livre?	¿Está desocupado este asiento?
È questa la strada per...?	É por aqui que se vai a...?	¿Es éste el camino a...?
isola	ilha	isla
non è vero?	não é?	¿(no es) verdad?
esso; essa	êle; ela	[not expressed]
lo; la	o; a	lo; la
Non (mi) va bene	Não (me) assenta bem	No (me) sienta
Non importa	Não faz mal	No importa
Non funziona	Não funciona	No funciona
Non occorre dirlo	Não é preciso dizer	Va sin decir; Se cae de su peso
È proprio lo stesso per me	Para mim é tudo o mesmo	Me da lo mismo
Fa cattivo tempo	Faz mau tempo	Hace mal tiempo
È nuvoloso	Está nublado	Está nublado
Fa freddo	Faz frio	Hace frío
Fa fresco	Faz fresco	Hace fresco
C'è la nebbia	Faz nevoeiro	Hay neblina
fut. of verb (pioverà)	Vai(chover)	Va a(llover)
Fa bel tempo	Faz bom tempo	Hace buen tiempo

English	*French*	*German*
It is hot (temp.)	Il fait **chaud**	Es ist **heiss**
It is one o'clock	Il est une **heure**	Es ist ein **Uhr**
It is raining	Il pleut	Es regnet
It is snowing	Il neige	Es schneit
It is sunny	Il fait du **soleil**	Es ist sonnig
It is two o'clock	Il est deux **heures**	Es ist zwei **Uhr**
It is warm (temp.)	Il fait **chaud**	Es ist warm
It is windy	Il fait du **vent**	Es ist windig
It will not do (fit, suit)	Ça ne va **pas**	Das geht nicht
Italian (adj.)	italien	italienisch
Italy	l' Italie *f*	Italien *n*
itch, to	démanger	jucken
itinerary	itinéraire *m*	Reiseroute *f*
ivory (n.)	ivoire *m*	Elfenbein *n*
jack (auto)	cric *m*	Wagenheber *m*
jacket	jaquette *f*	Jacke *f*
jade (gem)	jade *m*	Nierenstein *m*
jail (n.)	prison *f*	Gefängnis *n*
jam (preserves)	confiture *f*	Marmelade *f*
janitor	concierge *m*	Hausmeister *m*; Pförtner *m*
January	janvier *m*	Januar *m*
Japan	le Japon	Japan *n*
Japanese (adj.)	japonais	japanisch
jar (vessel)	bocal *m*	Krug *m*
jaw (anat.)	mâchoire *f*	Kiefer *m*
jealous	jaloux,-ouse	eifersüchtig
jelly	gelée *f*	Gelee *n*
jet engine	moteur *m* à réaction	Düsenmotor *m*
jet plane	avion *m* à réaction	Düsenflugzeug *n*
Jew	juif *m*	Jude *m*
jewel	bijou *m*	Juwel *n*
jewel case	coffret *m*	Schmuckkasten *m*
jeweler	bijoutier *m*	Juwelier *m*
jewelry	bijouterie *f*	Schmuck *m*
jewelry store	bijouterie *f*	Juwelenhandlung *f*
Jewish (adj.)	juif, juive	jüdisch
job (employment)	emploi *m*	Arbeit *f*

Italian	*Portuguese*	*Spanish*
Fa caldo	Faz calor	Hace calor
È l'una	É uma hora	Es la una
Piove	Chove	Llueve
Nevica	Está nevando	Nieva
C'è il sole	Faz sol	Hace sol
Sono le due	São duas	Son las dos
Fa caldo	Faz calor	Hace calor
Tira vento	Faz vento	Hace viento
Non andrà bene	Não presta	No sirve
italiano	italiano	italiano
l' Italia	a Itália	Italia
prudere	prurir	picar
itinerario	itinerário	itinerario
avorio	marfim *m*	marfil *m*
cricco; cric *m*	macaco	gato
giacca	jaqueta	chaqueta; chamarra (Mex.)
giada	jade *m*	jade *m*
carcere *m*	cárcere *m*	cárcel *f*
conserva	geléia; compota	compota; conserva
portinaio	porteiro	portero; conserje *m*
gennaio	janeiro	enero
il Giappone *m*	o Japão	el Japón
giapponese	japonês	japonés
barattolo	jarro; pote *m*	jarra; bote *m*
mandibola	queixo	quijada; mandíbula
geloso	ciumento; cioso	celoso
gelatina	geléia	jalea
motore *m* a reazione	motor *m* de propulsão a jato	motor *m* de propulsión a chorro
aviogetto	avião jato	avión *m* a chorro
ebreo	judeu *m*	judío
gioiello	jóia	joya
portagioielli *m*	porta-jóias *m*	estuche *m*
gioielliere *m*	joalheiro	joyero
gioielli *mpl*	jóias *fpl*	joyas *fpl*
gioielleria	joalharia	joyería
ebraico	judaico	judío
impiego	emprêgo	empleo

English	*French*	*German*
job (task)	travail *m*	Aufgabe *f*
join (as member), to	entrer à	beitreten
join (together), to	joindre	verbinden
joint (anat.)	articulation *f*	Gelenk *n*
joke (n.)	plaisanterie *f*	Witz *m*
joke, to	plaisanter	Spass machen
journey (n.)	voyage *m*	Reise *f*
judge	juge *m*	Richter *m*
judge, to	juger	beurteilen
jug	cruche *f*	Krug *m*
juice	jus *m*	Saft *m*
July	juillet *m*	Juli *m*
jump, to	sauter	springen
June	juin *m*	Juni *m*
jungle	jungle *f*	Dschungel *f*
just (fair)	juste	gerecht
just (merely)	seulement	bloss
Just a moment, please	Un moment, s'il vous plaît	Einen Augenblick, bitte
just now	tout à l'heure	eben
keep (continue), to	continuer	fortfahren
keep (retain), to	garder	behalten
keep quiet, to	se taire	schweigen
Keep the change!	Gardez la monnaie	Es stimmt
kerosene	kérosène *m*	Kerosin *n*
kettle	bouilloire *f*	Kessel *m*
key	clef *f*	Schlüssel *m*
key ring	porte-clefs *m*	Schlüsselring *m*
kid gloves	gants *mpl* de (peau de) chevreau	Glacéhandschuhe *mpl*
kidney (anat.)	rein *m*	Niere *f*
kidney bean	haricot *m* **brun**	Schminkbohne *f*
kidneys (food)	rognons *mpl*	Nieren *fpl*
kill, to	tuer	töten
kilo(gram) (2.2 lb.)	kilo *m*	Kilogramm *n*
kilometre (⅝ mi.)	kilomètre *m*	Kilometer *n*
kind (amiable)	bon, bonne	gütig
kind (sort)	espèce *f*	Art *f*
kindergarten	école *f* maternelle	Kindergarten *m*

KINDERGARTEN 133

Italian	Portuguese	Spanish
compito; lavoro	tarefa	tarea
associarsi a	associar-se a	asociarse a
unire	juntar	juntar
giuntura	junta	coyuntura
scherzo	gracejo; pilhéria	chiste *m*
scherzare	brincar	bromear
viaggio	viagem *f*	viaje *m*
giudice *m*	juiz *m*	juez *m*
giudicare	julgar	juzgar
brocca; caraffa	jarro	jarro
succo; sugo	sumo; suco (Br.)	jugo; zumo
luglio	julho	julio
saltare	saltar	saltar
giugno	junho	junio
giungla	selva; jângal *m*	selva
giusto	justo	justo
solamente	sòmente	solamente
Un momento, per favore	Um momento, faz favor	Un momento, por favor
or ora	agora mesmo	ahora mismo
continuare	seguir	seguir
mantenere	guardar	guardar
tacere	calar-se	callarse
Tenga il resto	Fique com o troco	Quédese con la vuelta , vuelto (Mex.)
kerosene *m*	querosene *m*	kerosene *m*
caldaia; bollitore *m*	caldeira	caldera
chiave *f*	chave *f*	llave *f*
portachiavi *m*	porta-chaves *m*	llavero
guanti *mpl* di pelle di capretto	luvas *fpl* de pelica	guantes *mpl* de cabritilla
rene *m*	rim *m*	riñón *m*
fagiolino nano	feijão	judía; frijol (Amer.)
rognoni *mpl*	rins *mpl*	riñones *mpl*
uccidere	matar	matar
chilogrammo	quilograma *m*	kilogramo
chilometro	quilômetro	kilómetro
gentile	bondoso; atencioso	bondadoso
specie *f*	espécie *f*; gênero; tipo	especie *f*; clase *f*; tipo
giardino d'infanzia	jardim da infância	Jardín *m* de infancia

English	*French*	*German*
kindness (favor)	bonté *f*	Freundlichkeit *f*
kindness (goodness)	bonté *f*	Güte *f*
king	roi *m*	König *m*
kingdom	royaume *m*	Königreich *n*
kiss	baiser *m*	Kuss *m*
kiss, to	baiser; embrasser	küssen
kitchen	cuisine *f*	Küche *f*
Kleenex (or any facial tissue)	mouchoir *m* en papier	Papiertaschentuch *n*
knapsack	sac *m* à dos	Rucksack *m*
knee	genou *m*	Knie *n*
kneel, to	s'agenouiller	knien
knife	couteau *m*	Messer *n*
knit, to	tricoter	stricken
knitting (n.)	tricotage *m*	Strickarbeit *f*
knock, to	frapper	klopfen
knocker (door)	marteau *m*	Türklopfer *m*
knot	noeud *m*	Knoten *m*
know (fact, -how)	savoir	wissen
know (person, place)	connaître	kennen
known (facts)	su	gewusst
known (familiar)	connu	bekannt
Korea	la Corée	Korea *n*
Kotex (or any sanitary napkin)	serviette *f* hygiénique	Binde *f*
label (n.)	étiquette *f*	Etikett *n*
laboratory	laboratoire *m*	Laboratorium *n*
labor (-force)	travail *m*	Arbeitskraft *f*
labor union	syndicat *m*	Gewerkschaft *f*
laborer	ouvrier *m*	Arbeiter *m*
lace	dentelle *f*	Spitze *f*
lack, to	manquer de	fehlen
lacquer (n.)	laque *f*	Lack *m*
ladder	échelle *f*	Leiter *f*
ladies' room (place)	cabinet *m* de toilette	Toilette *f*
ladies' room (sign)	Dames	Damen
lady	dame *f*	Dame *f*
lake	lac *m*	See *m*
lamb (meat)	agneau *m*	Lammfleisch *n*
lamb chop	côtelette *f* d'agneau	Lammkotelett *n*
lame	boiteux, -euse	lahm

Italian	*Portuguese*	*Spanish*
gentilezza	favor *m*	favor *m*
bontà	bondade *f*	bondad *f*
re *m*	rei *m*	rey *m*
regno	reino	reino
bacio	beijo	beso
baciare	beijar	besar
cucina	cozinha	cocina
fazzolettino di **carta**	lenço-papel *m*	tisú *m* facial; pañuelos desechables
zaino	mochila	mochila; barjuleta
ginocchio	joelho	rodilla
inginocchiarsi	ajoelhar-se	arrodillarse
coltello	faca	cuchillo
lavorare a **maglia**	tricotar	hacer calceta
lavoro a **maglia**	tricô	trabajo de punto
bussare	bater	llamar
battente *m*	aldrava	aldaba; llamador *m*
nodo	nó	nudo
sapere	saber	saber
conoscere	conhecer	conocer
saputo	sabido	sabido
conosciuto	conhecido	conocido
la Corea	Coréia	Corea
pannolino	paninho; toalha higiênica	toalla higiénica; toallita
etichetta	etiquêta; rótulo	etiqueta; rótulo
laboratorio	laboratório	laboratorio
lavoro	mão *f* de obra	fuerza obrera
sindacato	sindicato operário	sindicato
lavoratore *m*	obreiro	obrero; bracero (Mex.)
merletto	renda	encaje *m*
mancare di	faltar	faltar
lacca	laca	laca
scala	escada (de **mão**)	escalera
gabinetto	toalete *f* de **senhoras**	tocador *m* de señoras
Donne; Signore	Senhoras	Damas
signora	dama	señora
lago	lago	lago
agnello	cordeiro	cordero
costoletta d'**agnello**	costeleta de **cordeiro**	chuleta de carnero
zoppo	coxo	cojo

English	*French*	*German*
lamp	lampe *f*	**Lampe** *f*
land (ground)	terre *f*	Land *n*
land (region)	contrée *f*	**Landschaft** *f*
land (from a plane), **to**	atterrir	landen
land (from a ship), **to**	débarquer	landen
landing (plane)	atterrissage *m*	**Landung** *f*
landing permit	carte *f* de débarquement	**Landungsschein** *m*
landlord	propriétaire *m, f*	**Hauswirt** *m*
landscape	paysage *m*	**Landschaft** *f*
language	langue *f*	**Sprache** *f*
lantern	lanterne *f*	**Laterne** *f*
lap (of person)	genoux *mpl*	**Schoss** *m*
lapel	revers *m* (d'habit)	**Aufschlag** *m*
lard	saindoux *m*	**Schmalz** *n*
large	grand	gross
larger	plus **grand**	**grösser**
last (final)	dernier	letzt
last (continue), **to**	durer	dauern
last (withstand use)	tenir	halten
last month	le mois dernier	letzten **Monat**
last night	hier soir	gestern Abend
last week	la semaine *f* dernière	letzte Woche
last year	l'année *f* passée	letztes **Jahr**
late	tard	spät
late (deceased)	feu	selig
late (overdue)	en retard	verspätet
late, to be	être en retard	zu spät kommen
later	plus **tard**	später
Latin (adj.)	latin	lateinisch
laugh, to	rire	lachen
laundress	blanchisseuse *f*	**Wäscherin** *f*
laundry (plant)	blanchisserie *f*	**Waschanstalt** *m*
laundry (clean)	lessive *f*	saubere **Wäsche** *f*
laundry (soiled)	linge *m* sale	schmutzige **Wäsche**
laundry list	liste *f* de blanchissage	**Wäscheliste** *f*

Italian	*Portuguese*	*Spanish*
lampada	lâmpada	lámpara
terra	terra	tierra
terra; territorio	território	territorio
atterrare	aterrar; aterrissar (Br.)	aterrizar
sbarcare	desembarcar	desembarcar
atterraggio	aterrissagem *f* aterragem (Br.)	aterrizaje *m*
permesso di sbarco	licença de desembarque	billete *m* de desembarque
proprietario	proprietário	propietario; dueño
paesaggio	paisagem *f*	paisaje *m*
lingua	língua	lengua; idioma *m*
lanterna	lanterna	linterna
grembo	regaço	regazo
rovescia	lapela	solapa
strutto	lardo	manteca
grande	grande	grande
più grande	maior	más grande
ultimo	último	último
durare	durar	durar
conservarsi	durar	durar
il mese scorso	o mês passado	el mes pasado
ieri sera	ontem à noite	anoche
la settimana scorsa	a semana passada	la semana pasada
l'anno scorso	o ano passado	el año pasado
tardi	tarde	tarde
defunto	falecido	difunto
in ritardo	atrasado	de retraso
essere in ritardo	chegar atrasado	llegar tarde
più tardi	mais tarde	más tarde
latino	latino	latino
ridere	rir	reír
lavandaia	lavandeira	lavandera
lavanderia	lavanderia	lavandería
biancheria pulita	roupa limpa	ropa limpia
biancheria sporca	roupa servida	ropa sucia
lista del bucato	rol *m* da roupa	lista de la lavandería

English	*French*	*German*
lavatory (room with toilet)	W.C. *m*; cabines *fpl*; toilette *f*	Abort *m*
law (code)	droit *m*	Recht *n*
law (statute)	loi *f*	Gesetz *n*
lawn	pelouse *f*; gazon *m*	Rasen *m*
lawn mower	tondeuse *f* à gazon	Rasenmäher *m*
lawyer	avocat *m*	Rechtsanwalt *m*
laxative (n.)	laxatif *m*	Abführmittel *n*
lay (place), to	mettre	legen
lazy	paresseux, -euse	faul
lead (metal)	plomb *m*	Blei *n*
lead (guide), to	conduire	führen
leaf	feuille *f*	Blatt *n*
leak (gas)	fuite *f*	Entweichung *f*
leak (liquid)	fuite *f*	Leck *m*
leak (gas), to	fuir	entweichen
leak (liquid), to	fuir	lecken
lean (bend), to	se pencher	sich hinneigen
lean (meat)	maigre	mager
learn, to	apprendre	lernen
learn (find out), to	apprendre	erfahren
leather	cuir *m*	Leder *n*
leave (depart), to	partir	abreisen
leave (let stay), to	laisser	lassen
leave a message, to	laisser un mot pour	eine Mitteilung *f* hinterlassen
lecture (n.)	conférence *f*	Vorlesung *f*
leek	poireau *m*	Lauch *m*
left (adj.)	gauche	link-
left handed	gaucher	linkshändig
leg	jambe *f*	Bein *n*
legation	légation *f*	Gesandtschaft *f*
lemon	citron *m*	Zitrone *f*
lemonade	citronnade *m*	Limonade *f*
lend, to	prêter	leihen
length	longueur *f*	Länge *f*
lengthen, to	allonger	verlängern
lens (of glasses)	verre *m*	Linse *f*
lens (phot.)	objectif *m*	Objektiv *n*

Italian	*Portuguese*	*Spanish*
gabinetto	lavatório; retrete *f*	excusado; retrete *m*
legge *f*	lei *f*	ley *f*
legge *f*	estatuto	estatuto
prato (rasato)	gramado; relva	césped *m*
falciatrice *f* per prati	segadeira (de grama)	cortacésped *m*
avvocato	advogado	abogado
lassativo	purgante *m*; laxante *m*	laxante *m*; purgante *m*
porre	pôr	poner
pigro	preguiçoso	perezoso; flojo (Amer.)
piombo	chumbo	plomo
condurre	conduzir	conducir
foglia	fôlha	hoja
fuga	fuga	fuga
perdita; falla	fuga	fuga
sfuggire	verter	escaparse
perdere	verter	salirse
inclinarsi	inclinar-se	inclinarse
magro	magro	magro
imparare	aprender	aprender
apprendere	inteirar-se de	enterarse de
cuoio	couro	cuero
partire	partir	partir
lasciare	deixar	dejar
lasciare un messaggio	deixar um recado	dejar un recado
conferenza	conferência	conferencia
porro	porro	puerro
sinistro	esquerdo	izquierdo
mancino	canhoto	zurdo
gamba	perna	pierna
legazione *f*	legação *f*	legación *f*
limone *m*	limão	limón *m*; lima (Mex.)
limonata	limonada	limonada
prestare	emprestar	prestar
lunghezza	comprimento	largo
allungare	alongar	alargar
lente *f*	lente *f*	lente *f*
obiettivo	objetiva	objetivo

English	*French*	*German*
Lent	Carême *m*	Fastenzeit *f*
lentil	lentille *f*	Linse *f*
leprosy	lèpre *f*	Aussatz *m*
less (adj.)	moindre	weniger
less (adv.)	moins	weniger
lesson	leçon *f*	Aufgabe *f*
lest (conj.)	de peur que	damit...nicht
let (allow), to	laisser	lassen
Let's go!	Allons!	Gehen wir!
letter (alphabet)	lettre *f*	Buchstabe *m*
letter (message)	lettre *f*	Brief *m*
letter box	boîte *f* aux **lettres**	Briefkasten *m*
letter of credit	lettre *f* de crédit	Kreditbrief *m*
letter opener	ouvre-**lettres** *m*	Brieföffner *m*
lettuce	laitue *f*	(Kopf)salat *m*
level (flat)	plat	platt
lever	levier *m*	Hebel *m*
library	bibliothèque *f*	Bibliothek *f*
license (a permit)	permis *m*	Bescheinigung *f*
license plate (auto)	plaque *f* d'immatriculation	Nummernschild *n*
lid (cover)	couvercle *m*	Deckel *m*
lie (be located), to	se trouver	liegen
lie (deceive), to	mentir	lügen
lie (falsehood)	mensonge *m*	Lüge *f*
lie down, to	se coucher	sich hinlegen
lieutenant	lieutenant *m*	Leutnant *m*
life	vie *f*	Leben *n*
lifeboat	canot *m* de sauvetage	Rettungsboot *n*
life buoy	bouée *f* de sauvetage	Rettungsboje *f*
lifeguard (beach)	garde-plage *m*	Bademeister *m*
life preserver	ceinture *f* de sauvetage	Schwimmweste *f*
lift (raise), to	lever	aufheben
light (n.)	lumière *f*	Licht *n*
light (not dark)	clair	hell
light (in weight)	léger (*f* légère)	leicht
light, to	allumer	anzünden
lighter (smoking)	briquet *m*	Feuerzeug *n*

Italian	*Portuguese*	*Spanish*
quaresima	quaresma	cuaresma
lenticchia	lentilha	lenteja
lebbra	lepra	lepra
meno	menos	menos
meno	menos	menos
lezione *f*	lição *f*	lección *f*
per tema che	para que **não**	para que **no**
lasciare	deixar	dejar
Andiamo!	Vamos!	¡Vamos!
lettera	letra	letra
lettera	carta	carta
buca delle lettere	caixa do correio	buzón *m*
lettera di credito	carta de crédito	carta de crédito
tagliacarte *m*	abre-cartas *m*	abridor *m* de cartas
lattuga	alface *f*	lechuga
piatto	plano	plano
leva	alavanca	palanca
biblioteca	biblioteca	biblioteca
patente *f*	licença	licencia
targa	chapa	placa de matrícula
coperchio	tampa	tapa
trovarsi	estar colocado	estar sobre
mentire	mentir	mentir
bugia	mentira	mentira
coricarsi	deitar-se	acostarse
tenente *m*	tenente *m*	teniente *m*
vita	vida	vida
scialuppa di salvatag-gio	barco salva-vidas	bote *m* de salvavidas
salvagente *m*	bóia de salvamento	boya salvavidas
bagnino	salvavidas *m*	salvavidas *m*
cintura di salvatag-gio	salva-vidas *m*	salvavida(s) *m*
sollevare	levantar	levantar
luce *f*	luz *f*	luz *f*
chiaro	claro	claro
leggero	leve	ligero
accendere	acender	encender
accendisigari *m*	isqueiro	encendedor *m*

English	*French*	*German*
lighter fluid	essence *f* à briquet	Benzin *n*
lighthouse	phare *m*	Leuchtturm *m*
lightning (flash)	foudre *f*	Blitz *m*
like (adv.)	comme	wie
like (similar)	semblable	ähnlich
like (be fond of), to	aimer	gern haben
likewise	de même	ebenfalls
lily	lis *m*	Lilie *f*
lima bean	fève *f*	Saubohne *f*
lime (fruit)	limette *f*	Limone *f*
limp, to	boiter	hinken
line (mark)	ligne *f*	Linie *f*
linen (fabric)	toile *f* de **lin**	Leinen *n*
lingerie	lingerie *f*	Damenunterwäsche *f*
lining	doublure *f*	Futter *n*
lion	lion *m*	Löwe *m*
lip	lèvre *f*	Lippe *f*
lipstick	rouge *m* à **lèvres**	Lippenstift *m*
liquid (n.)	liquide *m*	Flüssigkeit *f*
liquor	spiritueux *mpl*	Spirituosen *fpl*
Lisbon	Lisbonne *f*	Lissabon *n*
list (n.)	liste *f*	Liste *f*
listen to, to	écouter	zuhören
liter (1.05 qts.)	litre *m*	Liter *m*
little (not much)	peu de	wenig
little (small)	petit	klein
live (be alive), to	vivre	leben
live (dwell), to	demeurer	wohnen
liver	foie *m*	Leber *f*
living room	salon *m*	Wohnzimmer *n*
load (fill), to	charger	laden
loaf of bread	pain *m*	Brot *n*; Laib *m*
loan	emprunt *m*	Anleihe *f*
loan, to	prêter	leihen
lobby (foyer)	foyer *m*	Foyer *n*
lobster	homard *m*	Hummer *m*

Italian	*Portuguese*	*Spanish*
benzina per accendi-tore	gasolina para isqueiro	combustible *m* para encendedor
faro	farol *m*	faro
lampo	relâmpago	relámpago
come	como	como
simile	semelhante	semejante
piacere	gostar de	gustar
parimenti	igualmente	igualmente
giglio	lírio	lirio
fava	fava	haba
limetta	lima	lima; limón *m* (Mex.)
zoppicare	coxear	cojear
linea	linha	línea
lino	linho	lino
biancheria personale	lingerie *f*	ropa blanca
fodera	forro	forro
leone *m*	leão	león *m*
labbro (le labbra *fpl*)	lábio; beiço	labio
rossetto (per le labbra)	bâton *m*; batom *m*	lápiz *m* para los labios
liquido	líquido	líquido
liquore *m*	bebida alcoólica	licor *m*
Lisbona	Lisboa	Lisboa
lista	lista	lista
ascoltare	escutar	escuchar
litro	litro	litro
poco	pouco	poco
piccolo	pequeno	pequeño
vivere	viver	vivir
abitare	morar	morar
fegato	fígado	hígado
salotto	sala de visitas; sala de estar	sala
caricare	carregar	cargar
pane *m*	pão	pan *m*; bollo (Mex.)
prestito	empréstimo	préstamo
(im)prestare	emprestar	prestar
atrio; vestibolo	vestíbulo; foyer *m*	foyer *m*; vestíbulo
aragosta	lagosta	langosta

English	*French*	*German*
lock (fastening)	serrure *f*	Schloss *n*
lock (waterway)	écluse *f*	Schleuse *f*
lock, to	fermer à clef	schliessen
locket	médaillon *m*	Medaillon *n*
locksmith	serrurier *m*	Schlosser *m*
London	Londres *m*	London *n*
long	long, longue	lang
long for, to	avoir grande envie de	sich sehnen (nach)
Look!	Regardez!	Schauen Sie!
look (aspect)	aspect *m*	Aussehen *n*
look (glance)	regard *m*	Blick *m*
look at, to	regarder	anschauen
look for, to	chercher	suchen
look forward to, to	s'attendre à	sich freuen auf
look like (resemble)	ressembler à	sich ähneln
Look out!	Attention!	Passen Sie auf!
loose (not tight)	ample	weit
loosen, to	desserrer	auflockern
lose, to	perdre	verlieren
lose one's way, to	s'égarer	sich verirren
lose sight of, to	perdre de vue	aus den Augen verlieren
loss	perte *f*	Verlust *m*
lost (p.p.)	perdu	verloren
lottery ticket	billet *m* de loterie	Los *n*
loud (noisy)	bruyant	laut
loud (resounding)	fort	laut
loud (showy)	voyant	auffällig
loud-speaker	haut-parleur *m*	Lautsprecher *m*
lounge (n.)	salon *m*	Diele *f*
louse	pou *m*	Laus *f*
love	amour *m*	Liebe *f*
love, to	aimer, adorer	lieben
lovely	charmant	reizend
low	bas, basse	niedrig
lower (let down), to	baisser	senken
lower berth	couchette *f* inférieure	Unterbett *n*

Italian	*Portuguese*	*Spanish*
serratura	fechadura	cerradura; chapa (Mex.)
chiusa	esclusa	esclusa
chiudere a chiave	fechar à chave	cerrar con llave
medaglione *m*	medalhão	guardapelo
magnano; fabbro	serralheiro	cerrajero
Londra *f*	Londres	Londres
lungo	comprido	largo
desiderare	ter saudades de	anhelar
Guardi!	Olhe!	¡Mire!
aspetto	aspecto	aspecto
sguardo	olhada	mirada
guardare	olhar (para)	mirar
cercare	buscar; procurar	buscar
non vedere l'ora di	anticipar	anticipar con placer
somigliare	parecer-se com	parecerse a
Attenzione!	Cautela! Cuidado!	¡Cuidado!
sciolto	frouxo; folgado (Br.)	flojo; suelto
allentare	afrouxar	aflojar
perdere	perder	perder
smarrirsi	extraviar-se	extraviarse
perdere di **vista**	perder de **vista**	perder de **vista**
perdita	perda	pérdida
perduto	perdido	perdido
biglietto **della** lotteria	décimo (⅒th)	décimo (⅒th); cachito (Mex.)
rumoroso	ruidoso	ruidoso
forte	forte	fuerte
vistoso	vistoso; berrante	vistoso
altoparlante *m*	alto-falante *m*	altoparlante *m*
sala	salão de espera	salón *m*
pidocchio	piolho	piojo
amore *m*	amor *m*	amor *m*
amare	amar	amar
bello	bonito; belo	precioso
basso	baixo	bajo
abbassare	abaixar	bajar
cuccetta inferiore	cama de **baixo**; leito inferior (Br.)	cama baja

English	*French*	*German*
luck	chance *f*	Glück *n*
lucky	heureux, heureuse	glücklich
luggage	bagages *mpl*	Gepäck *n*
luggage shop	magasin *m* d'articles de voyage	Lederwarengeschäft *n*
lukewarm	tiède	lauwarm
lunch	déjeuner *m*	Mittagessen *n*
lunch, to	déjeuner	zu Mittag essen
lung	poumon *m*	Lunge *f*
Lyon	Lyon *f*	Lyon *n*
macaroni	macaroni *m*	Makkaroni *fpl*
machine	machine *f*	Maschine *f*
machine gun	mitrailleuse *f*	Maschinengewehr *n*
mackerel	maquereau *m*	Makrele *f*
made (p.p.)	fait	gemacht
made to order	fait sur mesure	nach Mass
magazine	revue *f*	Zeitschrift *f*
magnificent	magnifique	herrlich
mahogany	acajou *m*	Mahagoniholz *n*
maid (servant)	bonne *f*	Dienstmädchen *n*
maiden name	nom *m* de jeune fille	Mädchenname *m*
mail (n.)	poste *f*	Post *f*
mail (something), to	mettre à la poste	aufgeben
mailbox	boîte *f* aux lettres	Briefkasten *m*
main dish	pièce *f* de résistance	Hauptgericht *n*
main floor	rez-de-chaussée *m*	Erdgeschoss *m*
main (home) office	siège *m* social	Zentralverwaltung *f*
main street	rue *f* principale	Hauptstrasse *f*
major (rank)	commandant *m*	Major *m*
make, to	faire	machen
make an appointment, to	prendre un rendez-vous (avec)	eine Verabredung machen
make connections, to	faire la correspondance	Anschluss haben
make fun of, to	se moquer de	auslachen
make up a bed, to	faire un lit	beziehen
make use of, to	se servir de	benutzen
malaria	malaria *f*	Malaria *f*

Italian	*Portuguese*	*Spanish*
fortuna	sorte *f*	suerte *f*
fortunato	afortunado	afortunado
bagaglio	bagagem *f*	equipaje *m*
valigeria	loja de malas	talabartería
tiepido	môrno	tibio
colazione *f*	almôço; lanche *m* (Br.)	almuerzo
fare la colazione	almoçar; lanchar (Br.)	almorzar
polmone *m*	pulmão	pulmón *m*
Lione *f*	Lião *m*	Lyon *m*
maccheroni *mpl*	macarrão	macarrones *mpl*
macchina	máquina	máquina
mitragliatrice *f*	metralhadora	ametralladora
scombro *m*	cavala	caballa; escombro
fatto	feito	hecho
fatto su misura	feito sob medida	hecho a (la) medida
rivista	revista	revista
magnifico	magnífico	magnífico
mogano	mogno; acaju *m*	caoba
cameriera	criada; camareira	criada; doncella; recamarera (Amer.)
nome *m* di signorina	nome *m* de solteira	apellido de soltera
posta	correio	correo
impostare, imbucare	postar; pôr no correio	echar al correo
buca delle lettere	caixa de correio	buzón *m*
piatto principale	prato principal	plato principal
piano principale	andar *m* térreo	piso principal
sede *f* principale	casa matriz; sede *f*	casa matriz
strada principale	rua principal	calle *f* principal
maggiore *m*	major *m*	comandante *m*
fare	fazer	hacer
fissare un appuntamento	marcar uma hora para	hacer una cita
prendere la coincidenza a	fazer baldeação	hacer enlace
burlarsi di	fazer troça de	burlarse de
rifare il letto	fazer a cama	hacer la cama
servirsi di	servir-se de	servirse de
malaria	malária	malaria

English	*French*	*German*
male (adj.)	mâle	männlich
man	homme *m*	Mann *m*
manager	gérant *m*	Geschäftsführer *m*
manicurist	manucure *f*	Maniküre *f*
Man overboard!	Homme à la **mer**!	Mann über **Bord**!
many	beaucoup de	viele
map (n.)	carte *f*	Landkarte *f*
marble	marbre *m*	Marmor *m*
March	mars *m*	März *m*
market (n.)	marché *m*	Markt *m*
market place	place *f* du **marché**	Marktplatz *m*
marmalade	marmelade *f*	Marmelade *f*
marriage	mariage *m*	Ehe *f*
married	marié	verheiratet
married couple	ménage *m*	Ehepaar *n*
marry, to	se marier (avec)	sich verheiraten (mit)
Marseilles	Marseille *f*	Marseille *n*
marvelous	merveilleux, -euse	wunderbar
mashed potatoes	purée *f* de pommes de terre	Kartoffelbrei *m*
mason (order)	franc-maçon *m*	Freimaurer *m*
mass (church)	messe *f*	Messe *f*
massage	massage *m*	Massage *f*
mast	mât *m*	Mast *m*
masterpiece	chef-d'oeuvre *m*	Meisterwerk *n*
match (light)	allumette *f*	Streichholz *n*
match (go well **with**)	aller bien en**semble**	zu**sammenpassen**
material (cloth)	étoffe *f*	Stoff *m*
maternity dress	robe *f* de grossesse	Umstandskleid *n*
mattress	matelas *m*	Matratze *f*
May	mai *m*	Mai *m*
May I...?	Est-il permis de...?	Darf ich...?
May I introduce...?	Permettez-moi de vous présenter...?	Darf ich...vorstellen?
May I speak to...?	Puis-je parler à...?	Kann ich mit... sprechen?
maybe	peut-être	vielleicht

Italian	*Portuguese*	*Spanish*
maschio	másculo	macho
uomo (pl. uomini)	homem *m*	hombre *m*
gerente *m*	gerente *m*	gerente *m*
manicure *m*	manicura	manicura
Uomo in mare!	Homen ao mar!	¡Hombre al agua!
molti	muitos	muchos
carta	mapa *m*	mapa *m*
marmo	mármore *m*	mármol *m*
marzo	março	marzo
mercato	mercado	mercado
mercato	mercado; feira	plaza de mercado
marmellata	marmelada	mermelada
matrimonio	matrimônio	matrimonio
sposato	casado	casado
sposi *mpl*	casal *m*	matrimonio
sposare	casar-se (com)	casarse (con)
Marsiglia *f*	Marselha *f*	Marsella
meraviglioso	maravilhoso	maravilloso
puré *m* di patate	purê *m* de batatas	puré *m* de patatas
frammassone *m*	mação	masón *m*
messa	missa	misa
massaggio	massagem *f*	masaje *m*
albero	mastro	mástil *m*
capolavoro	obra-prima	obra maestra
fiammifero; cerino	fósforo	fósforo; cerilla (of wax); cerillo (Mex.)
accompagnarsi bene a	combinar com	hacer juego con
stoffa	tela	tela
vestito per la gravidanza	vestido para gestantes	vestido de maternidad
materasso	colchão	colchón *m*
maggio	maio	mayo
È permesso...?	Dá-me licença de...?	¿Se puede...?
Permette che le presenti...?	Dá-me licença para apresentar...?	Permítame presentarle...?
Posso parlare con...?	Posso falar com...?	¿Me permite hablar con...?
forse	talvez; quiçá	tal vez; quizá

English	*French*	*German*
mayonnaise	mayonnaise *f*	Mayonaise *f*
mayor	maire *m*	Bürgermeister *m*
me	me; moi	mich (acc.), mir (dat.)
meal	repas *m*	Mahlzeit *f*
mean (have in mind)	vouloir dire	meinen
mean (malicious)	vilain	boshaft
mean (signify), to	signifier	bedeuten
meaning (sense)	signification *f*	Meinung *f*
meanwhile	en attendant	inzwischen
measles	rougeole *f*	Masern *fpl*
measure, to	mesurer	messen
meat	viande *f*	Fleisch *n*
meat balls	boulettes *fpl*	Fleischklösse *mpl*
meat market	boucherie *f*	Fleischerei *f*
mechanic	mécanicien *m*	Mechaniker *m*
medicine	médicament *m*	Arznei *f*
medicine cabinet	pharmacie *f* de famille	Arzneischränkchen
medicine dropper	compte-gouttes *m*	Tropfenzähler *m*
Mediterranean Sea	mer *f* Méditerranée	Mittelmeer *n*
medium (weight)	moyen	mittelschwer
medium (-done)	à point	nicht sehr durchgebraten
meet (as planned), to	retrouver	treffen
meet (encounter), to	rencontrer	begegnen (dat.)
meeting	réunion *f*	Versammlung *f*
melon (cantaloupe)	melon *m*	Melone *f*
melt, to	fondre	schmelzen
member	membre *m*	Mitglied *n*
memorize, to	apprendre par coeur	auswendig lernen
mend, to	raccommoder	flicken
men's room (the place)	W.C.; cabinets *mpl*	Herrentoilette *f*
men's room (the sign)	Messieurs	Herren
mention, to	mentionner	erwähnen
menu	carte *f*	Speisekarte *f*
merchant	commerçant *m*	Kaufmann *m*
meringue	meringue *f*	Meringe *f*
Merry Christmas!	Joyeux Noël!	Fröhliche Weihnachten!

Italian	*Portuguese*	*Spanish*
maionese *f*	maionese *f*	mayonesa
sindaco	prefeito	alcalde *m*
mi; me	me; mim	me; mí
pasto	refeição *f*	comida
voler dire	querer dizer	querer decir
cattivo	mesquinho	mezquino
significare	significar	significar
significato	significação *f*	sentido
nel frattempo	no entanto	entretanto
rosolia; morbillo	sarampo	sarampión *m*
misurare	medir	medir
carne *f*	carne *f*	carne *f*
polpette *fpl*	almôndegas *fpl*	albóndigas *fpl*
macelleria	açougue *m*	carnicería
meccanico	mecânico	mecánico
medicina	medicamento	medicina
cassettina-farmacia	armário de remédios	botiquín *m*
contagocce *m*	conta-gotas *m*	cuentagotas *m*; gotero *m* (Mex.)
mare *m* Mediterraneo	mar *m* Mediterrâneo	mar *m* Mediterráneo
medio	médio	mediano
a mezza cottura	médio	mediano; no muy cocido
incontrarsi	encontrar	encontrar
incontrare	encontrar	encontrar
riunione *f*	reunião *f*	reunión *f*
melone *m*	melão	melón *m*
fondere	derreter	derretir
membro	membro; sócio	miembro; socio
imparare a memoria	decorar	aprender de memoria
rammendare	consertar	remendar
gabinetto (uomini)	toalete *f* de homens	retrete *m*
Uomini	Homens	Caballeros
menzionare	mencionar	mencionar
menù *m*; lista	menu *m*; cardápio	menú *m*; lista
commerciante *m*	negociante *m*	comerciante *m*
meringa	merengue *m*; suspiro	merengue *m*
Buon Natale!	Feliz Natal!	¡Feliz Navidad!

English	*French*	*German*
mess kit	gamelle *f*	Kochgeschirr *n*
message	message *m*	Mitteilung *f*
messenger	messager *m*	Bote *m*
metal (n.)	métal *m*	Metall *n*
meter (39.37 in.)	mètre *m*	Meter *n*
meter (taxi-)	compteur *m*	Taxameter *n*
Mexican (adj.)	mexicain	mexikanisch
Mexico	le Mexique	Mexiko *n*
middle (n.)	milieu *m*	Mitte *f*
midnight	minuit *m*	Mitternacht *f*
Milan	Milan	Mailand *n*
mile (1.6 km.)	mille *m*	Meile *f*
mileage (distance)	kilométrage *m*	Entfernung *f*
milk	lait *m*	Milch *f*
million	million *m*	Million *f*
mine (pit)	mine *f*	Bergwerk *n*
mine (poss. pron.)	le mien, etc.	meiner, -e, -(e)s
mineral water	eau *f* minérale	Mineralwasser *n*
minister (cabinet)	ministre *m*	Minister *m*
minister (church)	pasteur *m*	Pfarrer *m*
minus (less)	moins	weniger
minute	minute *f*	Minute *f*
mirror	miroir *m*	Spiegel *m*
misfortune	malheur *m*	Unglück *n*
miss (young lady)	mademoiselle *f*	Fräulein *n*
miss (feel the loss of)	regretter	vermissen
miss the train, to	manquer le **train**	den Zug verpassen
mistake (error)	erreur *f*	Fehler *m*
mistaken, to be	se tromper	sich irren
misunderstand, to	mal comprendre	missverstehen
mitten	moufle *f*	Fausthandschuh *m*
mix, to	mélanger	mischen
mixer (electric)	mixeur *m* électrique	Mixer *m*
model (copy) (n.)	modèle *m*	Modell *n*
modern	moderne	modern
modest	modeste	bescheiden

Italian	*Portuguese*	*Spanish*
gavetta	marmita	utensilios *mpl* de rancho
messaggio	recado; mensagem *f*	recado; mensaje *m*
messaggero, fattorino	mensageiro	mensajero
metallo	metal *m*	metal *m*
metro	metro	metro
tassametro	taxímetro	taxímetro
messicano	mexicano	mexicano
il Messico	o México	México
mezzo	meio	medio
mezzanotte *f*	meia-noite *f*	medianoche *f*
Milano	Milão	Milán
miglio	milha	milla
chilometraggio	quilometragem *f* milhagem *f* (Br.)	kilometraje *m*
latte *m*	leite *m*	leche *f*
milione *m*	milhão	millón *m*
miniera; mina	mina	mina
mio, etc.	o meu, etc.	el mío, etc.
acqua minerale	água mineral	agua mineral
ministro	ministro	ministro
pastore *m*	pastor *m*	pastor *m*
meno	menos	menos
minuto	minuto	minuto
specchio	espelho	espejo
disgrazia; sventura	desgraça	desgracia
signorina	senhorinha	señorita
sentire l'assenza di	ter saudades de	echar de menos
perdere il treno	perder o trem	perder el tren
sbaglio	erro	error *m*
sbagliarsi	equivocar-se	equivocarse
intendere male	entender mal	entender mal
mezzo-guanto	mitene *m*	mitón *m*
mescolare	mesclar; misturar	mezclar
frullino elettrico	batedeira	mezcladora; batidor *m* eléctrico
modello	modelo	modelo
moderno	moderno	moderno
modesto	modesto	modesto

English	*French*	*German*
moist (damp)	humide	feucht
molasses	mélasse *f*	Zuckersirup *m*
moldy	moisi	schimmelig
moment	moment *m*	Augenblick *m*
monastery	monastère *m*	Kloster *n*
Monday	lundi *m*	Montag *m*
monetary unit (each country)	franc *m*	Mark *f*
money	argent *m*	Geld *n*
money changer	changeur *m*	Geldwechsler *m*
money order	mandat-poste *m*	Geldanweisung *f*
monk	moine *m*	Mönch *m*
monkey	singe *m*	Affe *m*
month	mois *m*	Monat *m*
monument	monument *m*	Denkmal *n*
moon	lune *f*	Mond *m*
mop (n.)	balai *m* à laver	Mop *m*; Scheuerlappen *m*
more	plus (de)	mehr
more (some-)	davantage	mehr
more or less	plus ou moins	mehr oder weniger
moreover	de plus	ausserdem
morning	matin *m*	Morgen *m*
Morocco	le Maroc	Marokko *n*
mortgage (n.)	hypothèque *f*	Hypothek *f*
mortgage, to	hypothéquer	verpfänden
Moscow	Moscou *m*	Moskau *n*
mosquito	moustique *m*	Moskito *m*
mosquito net	moustiquaire *f*	Moskitonetz *n*
most (adv.)	(le) plus	am meisten
most (almost all)	presque tout	meist
most of (adj.)	la plupart de	die meisten-
mother	mère *f*	Mutter *f*
mother-in-law	belle-mère *f*	Schwiegermutter *f*
motor	moteur *m*	Motor *m*
motorcycle	motocyclette *f*	Motorrad *n*
mountain	montagne *f*	Berg *m*
mouse	souris *f*	Maus *f*

Italian	*Portuguese*	*Spanish*
umido	úmido	húmedo
melassa	melaço; melado	melaza
ammuffito	mofado	mohoso
momento	momento	momento
monastero	mosteiro	monasterio
lunedì *m*	segunda-feira	lunes *m*
lira	escudo (Portugal) cruzeiro (Br.)	peseta (Spain) peso (Mex.)
denaro; soldi *mpl*	dinheiro	dinero; plata (Amer.)
cambiavalute *m*	cambista *m*	cambista *m*
vaglia *m*	vale *m* postal	giro postal
monaco	monje *m*	monje *m*
scimmia	macaco	mono
mese *m*	mês *m* (*pl* meses)	mes *m*
monumento	monumento	monumento
luna	lua	luna
spazzolone *m*	esfregão de assoalho	aljofifa; estropajo; trapeador *m* (Amer.)
più (di)	mais	más
più	mais	más
più o meno	mais ou menos	más o menos
inoltre	além disso	además
mattina	manhã	mañana
il Marocco	Marrocos	Marruecos
ipoteca	hipoteca	hipoteca
ipotecare	hipotecar	hipotecar
Mosca *f*	Moscou *m*	Moscú *m*
zanzara	mosquito	mosquito; zancudo (Amer.)
zanzariera	mosquiteiro	mosquitero
(il) più	mais	más
quasi	quase tudo	casi todo
la maggior parte di	a maior parte de	la mayor parte de
madre *f*	mãe *f*	madre *f*
suocera	sogra	suegra
motore *m*	motor *m*	motor *m*
motocicletta	motocicleta	motocicleta
montagna	montanha	montaña
topo	ratinho; camundongo (Br.)	ratón *m*

English	*French*	*German*
mouth	bouche *f*	Mund *m*
mouthwash	eau *f* dentifrice	Mundwasser *n*
move (residence)	déménager	umziehen
move (one's position)	se déplacer; bouger	sich bewegen
move (something)	déplacer	bewegen
movie camera	caméra *f*	Filmkamera *f*
movies	cinéma *m*	Kino *n*
Mr.	monsieur *m*	Herr *m*
Mrs.	Madame *f*	Frau *f*
much	beaucoup (de)	viel
mucilage	mucilage *m*	Klebstoff *m*
mud	boue *f*	Schlamm *m*
muffler (auto)	silencieux *m*	Schalldämpfer *m*
muffler (to wear)	cache-nez *m*	Halstuch *n*
mule	mulet *m*	Maultier *n*
mumps	oreillons *mpl*	Ziegenpeter *m*
Munich	Munich *m*	München *n*
muscle	muscle *m*	Muskel *m*
museum	musée *m*	Museum *n*
mushroom	champignon *m*	Champignon *m*
music	musique *f*	Musik *f*
musical comedy	opérette *f*	Operette *f*
musician	musicien *m*	Musiker *m*
must (be obliged)	devoir	müssen
Must I...?	Dois-je...?	Muss ich...?
mustache	moustache *f*	Schnurrbart *m*
mustard	moutarde *f*	Senf *m*
mutton	mouton *m*	Hammelfleisch *n*
mutton chop	côtelette *f* de mouton	Hammelkotelett *n*
my	mon, ma, mes	mein, etc.
My...hurts	...me fait mal	...tut mir weh
My name is...	Je m'appelle...	Ich heisse...
nail (finger)	ongle *m*	Nagel *m*
nail (metal)	clou *m*	Nagel *m*
nail brush	brosse *f* à ongles	Nagelbürste *f*
nail clipper	coupe-ongles *m*	Nagelschere *f*
nail file	lime *f* à ongles	Nagelfeile *f*

Italian	*Portuguese*	*Spanish*
bocca	bôca	boca
colluttorio	colutório	enjuagadientes *m*
sgomberare	mudar-se	mudarse
muoversi	mover-se	moverse
muovere	mover	mover
cinepresa	máquina de cine	máquina de cine
cinema *m*	cinema *m*; cine *m*	cine *m*
signore *m*	senhor *m*	señor *m*
signora	senhora	señora
molto	muito	mucho
mucillaggine *f*	mucilagem *f*	mucílago
fango	lama; lôdo	lodo
silenziatore *m*	silenciador *m*	silenciador *m*
sciarpa	cachecol *m*	bufanda
mulo	mula	mula
orecchioni *mpl*	papeira, caxumba (Br.)	paperas *fpl*
Monaco *m* diBaviera	Munique	Munich *m*
muscolo	músculo	músculo
museo	museu *m*	museo
fungo	cogumelo; fungo	seta
musica	música	música
operetta	comédia musical	zarzuela
musicista *m*	músico	músico
dovere	dever	deber
Devo...?	Devo...?	¿Debo...?
baffi *mpl*	bigode *m*	bigote *m*
mostarda; senapa *f*	mostarda	mostaza
montone *m*	carne *f* de carneiro	carnero
costoletta di montone	costeleta de carneiro	chuleta de carnero
(il) mio, etc.	(o) meu *m*; (a) minha *f*	mi, mis
...mi fa male	Dói-me...	Me duele ...
Mi chiamo...	Chamo-me...	Me llamo...
unghia	unha	uña
chiodo	prego; cravo	clavo
spazzolino da unghie	escôva de unhas	cepillo para las uñas
forbicine *fpl* da unghie	alicate *m* de unhas	cortauñas *m*
lima da unghie	lima de unhas	lima para las uñas

English	*French*	*German*
nail polish	vernis *m* à ongles	Nagellack *m*
nail polish remover	dissolvant *m*	Nagellackentferner *m*
naked	nu	nackt
name	nom *m*	Name *m*
name, to	nommer	nennen
namely	à savoir	nämlich
nap (a snooze)	somme *m*	Schläfchen *n*
napkin	serviette *f*	Serviette *f*
napkin ring	rond *m* de serviette	Serviettenring *m*
Naples	Naples *m*	Neapel *n*
narrow	étroit	schmal
nation	nation *f*	Nation *f*
national (adj.)	national	national
nationality	nationalité *f*	Nationalität *f*
native (adj.)	natif	(ein) heimisch
native (n.)	natif *m*	Eingeborene *m*
natural	naturel	natürlich
navy	marine *f*	Marine *f*
near (adv.)	près	nah
near (prep.)	près de	neben
nearly	presque	beinahe; fast
neat (tidy)	propre	sauber
necessary	nécessaire	nötig
neck	cou *m*	Hals *m*
necklace	collier *m*	Halsband *n*
necktie	cravate *f*	Krawatte *f*
need	besoin *m*	Not *f*
need, to	avoir besoin de	brauchen
needle	aiguille *f*	Nadel *f*
needless	inutile	unnötig
negative (phot.)	négatif *m*	Negatif *n*
negligee	peignoir *m*	Neglige *n*
negotiate, to	négocier	verhandeln über
Negro	nègre *m*	Neger *m*
neighbor	voisin *m*	Nachbar *m*
neighborhood	voisinage *m*	Nachbarschaft *f*
Neither do I	Ni moi non plus	Ich auch nicht

Italian	*Portuguese*	*Spanish*
smalto per le unghie	esmalte *m* de unhas	esmalte *m* para uñas
acetone *m*	acetona;	quitaesmalte *m*;
	removedor *m*	acetona
nudo	nu (*f* nua)	desnudo
nome *m*	nome *m*	nombre *m*
nominare	nomear	nombrar
cioè	a saber; isto é	a saber
sonnellino	soneca; sesta	siesta
tovagliolo	guardanapo	servilleta
portatovagliolo *m*	argola de guardanapo	servilletero
Napoli *f*	Nápoles	Nápoles
stretto	estreito	estrecho
nazione *f*	nação *f*	nación *f*
nazionale	nacional	nacional
nazionalità	nacionalidade *f*	nacionalidad *f*
indigeno; nativo	nativo	nativo
indigeno	natural *m*	natural *m*
naturale	natural	natural
marina	marinha	marina
vicino	perto	cerca
vicino a	perto de	cerca de
quasi	quase	casi
nitido	nítido	ordenado
necessario	necessário	necesario; preciso
collo	pescoço	cuello
collana	colar *m*	collar *m*
cravatta	gravata	corbata
bisogno	necessidade *f*	necesidad *f*
avere bisogno di	precisar de	necesitar
ago *m*	agulha	aguja
inutile	inútil; desnecessário	innecesario
negativa	negativo	negativo
negligé *m*; vestaglia	peignoir *m*	bata
trattare	negociar	negociar
negro	preto	negro
vicino	vizinho	vecino
vicinato	vizinhança	vecindad *f*
Neppure io	Eu também não	Ni yo tampoco

English	*French*	*German*
neither...nor	ne...ni...ni	weder...noch
nephew	neveu *m*	Neffe *m*
nerve (anat.)	nerf *m*	Nerv *m*
nervous	nerveux, -euse	nervös
nest (n.)	nid *m*	Nest *n*
net (n.)	filet *m*	Netz *n*
Netherlands (the)	les Pays-**Bas**	die Niederlande
never	ne...jamais	nie (mals)
Never mind	N'importe	Lass gut sein
nevertheless	néanmoins	trotzdem
new	nouveau- ,elle	neu
news	nouvelles *fpl*	Nachricht *f*
newspaper	journal *m*	Zeitung *f*
newsreel	actualités *fpl*	Wochenschau *f*
newsstand	kiosque *m* à journaux	Zeitungskiosk *m*
New Year's Eve	veille *f* du Nouvel **An**	Silvesterabend *m*
New York	New-York *m*	Neuyork *n*
next (following)	suivant	nächst
next (then)	ensuite	dann
next day (the)	lendemain *m*	am nächsten **Tag**
next door	à côté	nebenan
next month	le mois prochain	nächsten Monat
next to (along side)	á côté de	nebenan
next week	la semaine prochaine	nächste Woche
next year	l'année prochaine	nächstes **Jahr**
Nicaragua	le Nicaragua	Nikaragua *n*
nice	agréable	nett
Nice	Nice *f*	Nizza *n*
nickel (metal)	nickel *m*	Nickel *n*
nickname	surnom *m*	Spitzname *m*
niece	nièce *f*	Nichte *f*
night	nuit *f*	Nacht *f*
night before last	avant-hier **soir**	vorgestern abend
night club	boîte *f* de **nuit**	Nachtklub *m*; Nachtlokal *n*
nightgown	chemise *f* de **nuit**	Nachthemd *n*

Italian	*Portuguese*	*Spanish*
non . . . nè . . . nè	nem...nem	ni...ni
nipote *m*	sobrinho	sobrino
nervo	nervo	nervio
nervoso	nervoso	nervioso
nido	ninho	nido
rete *f*	rêde *f*	red *f*
i Paesi Bassi	os Países Baixos	los Países Bajos
mai	nunca	nunca
Non importa	Não faz mal;	No importa;
	Não importa	No le hace
tuttavia	contudo; todavia	sin embargo
nuovo	nôvo (*f* nova)	nuevo
notizia	notícia	noticias *fpl*
giornale *m*	jornal *m*	periódico
cinegiornale *m*	noticiário	actualidades *fpl*
chiosco di giornali;	quiosque *m*; ban-	puesto de
edicola	ca de jornais	periódicos
vigilia di	véspera de	víspera de
Capodanno	Ano Bom	Año Nuevo
Nuova York *f*	Nova Iorque *f*	Nueva York *f*
prossimo; seguente	seguinte; próximo	próximo; siguiente
quindi	logo	luego
il giorno seguente	o dia seguinte	al día siguiente
accanto	ao lado; vizinho de	al lado
mese prossimo	o mês que vem	el mes que viene
vicino a	junto de	junto a
la settimana	a semana que vem	la semana que viene
prossima		
l'anno prossimo	o ano que vem	el año que viene
Nicaragua	a Nicarágua	Nicaragua
simpatico	bom; bonito;	simpático
	agradável	
Nizza	Niza	Niza
nichelio	níquel *m*	níquel *m*
soprannome *m*	apelido	apodo
nipote *f*	sobrinha	sobrina
notte *f*	noite *f*	noche *f*
l'altra sera	ante-ontem à noite	anteanoche
ritrovo *m*	boite *f*	cabaret *m*
notturno		café *m* cantante
camicia da notte	camisola;	camisa de dormir;
	camisa de dormir	camisón *m* (Amer.)

English	*French*	*German*
night light	veilleuse *f*	**Nacht**licht *n*
nightmare	cauche**mar** *m*	**Alp**druck *m*
nine	neuf	neun
nine hundred	neuf **cents**	neunhundert
nineteen	dix-neuf	neunzehn
ninety	quatre-vingt-**dix**	neunzig
ninth	neuvième	der **neunte**, etc.
nipple (for bottle)	tétine *f*	**Saug**hütchen *n*
no	non	nein
no (not any)	aucun, au**cune**	kein, etc.
No **admittance!**	Défense d'en**trer!**	Eintritt verboten!
no longer	ne...**plus**	nicht mehr
no one (nobody)	ne...**personne**	niemand
No parking!	Défense de stationn**er!**	**Parken** verboten!
No smoking!	Défense de fu**mer!**	Rauchen verboten!
No, thank you	Non, merci	Danke, nein
No trespassing!	Accès inter**dit!**	**Durchgang** verboten!
noise	bruit *m*	**Lärm** *m*
noisy	bruyant	laut; geräuschvoll
nonstop	sans es**cale** (ar**rêt**)	ohne **Halt**
none (pron.)	aucun	keine, etc.
noodles	nouilles *fpl*	**N**udeln *fpl*
noon	midi *m*	**Mittag** *m*
north (n.)	nord *m*	**Norden** *m*
northern	du **nord**	nördlich
North Sea	la Mer du **Nord**	die **Nordsee**
Norway	la Norvège	Norwegen *n*
Norwegian (adj.)	norvé**gien**	norwegisch
nose	nez *m*	**Nase** *f*
nosebleed	saignement *m* de **nez**	**Nasenbluten** *n*
nostril	narine *f*	**Nasenloch** *n*
not	ne...**pas**	nicht
not at all	pas du **tout**	gar nicht
not even	pas **même**	nicht einmal
not much	pas beaucoup	nicht viel
not only...but also	non seulement... mais aussi	nicht nur...sondern auch

Italian	*Portuguese*	*Spanish*
lampadina da notte	lamparina	lamparilla
incubo	pesadelo	pesadilla
nove	nove	nueve
novecento	novecentos	novecientos
diciannove	dezenove	diez y nueve
novanta	noventa	noventa
nono	nono	noveno
capezzolo	bico de mamadeira	tetilla
no	não	no
nessun, etc.	nenhum, etc.	ningún, etc.
Vietato l'ingresso!	Entrada proibida!	¡Se prohibe la entrada!
non...(vb.) più	já não	ya no
nessuno	ninguém	nadie
Parcheggio vietato!	Proibido estacionar!	¡Prohibido estacionarse!
Vietato fumare!	Proibido fumar!	¡Prohibido fumar!
No, grazie	Obrigado	Gracias
Vietato il passaggio!	Proibido passar!	¡Prohibida la entrada!
rumore *m*	barulho; ruído	ruido
rumoroso	barulhento; ruidoso	ruidoso
senza scalo; diretto	direto; sem escalas	sin escala
nessuno	nenhum	ninguno
taglierini *mpl*	talharins *mpl*	tallarines *mpl*
mezzogiorno	meio-dia *m*	mediodía *m*
nord *m*	norte *m*	norte *m*
settentrionale	do norte	del norte
il Mare del Nord	o Mar do Norte	el Mar del Norte
la Norvegia	a Noruega	Noruega
norvegese	norueguês	noruego
naso	nariz *m*	nariz *f*
emorragia nasale	hemorragia nasal	hemorragia nasal
narice *f*	narina	ventana de la nariz
non	não	no
niente affatto	nada	nada
nemmeno	nem mesmo	ni aun
non molto	não muito	no mucho
non solo...ma anche	não só...mas também	no sólo...sino también

English	*French*	*German*
not so fast!	pas si vite!	nicht so schnell!
Not that I know of	Pas que je sache	Nicht, dass ich es weiss
not yet	pas encore	noch nicht
notary (public)	notaire *m*	Notar *m*
notebook (pocket)	carnet *m*	Notizbuch *n*
notebook (school)	cahier *m*	Heft *n*
nothing	ne...rien	nichts
nothing else	rien de plus	nichts weiteres
notice (see), to	remarquer	bemerken
notice (n.)	avis *m*	Ankündigung *f*
notify, to	aviser	benachrichtigen
notions store	mercerie *f*	Kramladen *m*
nougat	nougat *m*	Marzipan *m*
noun	substantif *m*	Substantiv *n*
novel (n.)	roman *m*	Roman *m*
novelist	romancier *m*	Romanschriftsteller *m*
November	novembre *m*	November *m*
now	maintenant	jetzt; nun
now and then	de temps en temps	von Zeit zu Zeit
nowadays	de nos jours	heutzutage
nowhere	nulle part	nirgends
number (numeral)	numéro *m*	Nummer *f*
number (quantity)	nombre *m*	Zahl *f*
numerous	nombreux, -euse	zahlreich
nun	religieuse *f*	Nonne *f*
nurse (n.)	infirmière *f*	Krankenschwester *f*
nursemaid	bonne *f* (d'enfants)	Kindermädchen *n*
nursing bottle	biberon *m*	Saugflasche *f*
nut (food)	noix *f*	Nuss *f*
nut (for bolt)	écrou *m*	Schraubenmutter *f*
nutcracker	casse-noisettes *m*	Nussknacker *m*
nutmeg	muscade *f*	Muskat *m*
nylon	nylon *m*	Nylon *n*
oak	chêne *m*	Eiche *f*
oar	rame *f*	Ruder *n*
oatmeal	farine *f* d'avoine	Hafergrütze *f*
oats (grain)	avoine *f*	Hafer *m*
obey, to	obéir	gehorchen

Italian	*Portuguese*	*Spanish*
non così in fretta	não tão depressa!	¡no tan de prisa!
Ch'io sappia, no	Que eu saiba, não	No que yo sepa
non ancora	ainda não	todavía no
notaio	notário; tabelião	notario
taccuino	caderneta; agenda	libreta; agenda
quaderno	caderno	cuaderno
niente	nada	nada
nient' altro	mais nada	nada más
notare	notar; observar	notar
avviso	notícia; aviso	aviso
notificare	avisar; notificar	avisar
merceria	armarinho	mercería
torrone *m*	nugá *m*	turrón *m*
sostantivo	substantivo	substantivo
romanzo	romance *m*; novela	novela
romanziere *m*	novelista *m, f*	novelista *m, f*
novembre	novembro	noviembre
adesso; ora	agora	ahora
di quando in quando	de quando em quando	de vez en cuando
oggidì; oggigiorno	hoje em dia	hoy día
in nessun luogo	em parte alguma	en ninguna parte
numero	número	número
quantità	número	número
numeroso	numeroso	numeroso
monaca; suora	freira; monja	monja
infermiera	enfermeira	enfermera
governante *f*	ama	niñera
poppatoio	mamadeira	biberón *m*
noce *f*	noz *f*	nuez *f*
dado	porca	tuerca
schiaccianoci *m*	quebra-nozes *m*	cascanueces *m*
noce *f* moscata	noz-moscada	nuez *f* moscada
nailon *m*	nailon *m*	nilón *m*
quercia	carvalho	roble *m*
remo	remo	remo
farinata d'avena	farinha de aveia	harina de avena
avena	aveia	avena
ubbidire	obedecer	obedecer

English	*French*	*German*
obliged to, to be	devoir	müssen
obtain, to	obtenir	erhalten
obvious	évident	offenbar
occasionally	de temps en **temps**	ab und zu
occupation (calling)	métier *m*	Beruf *m*
occupied (sign)	occupé	besetzt
occur (happen), to	avoir **lieu**	vorkommen
ocean	océan *m*	Ozean *m*
October	octobre *m*	Oktober *m*
oculist	oculiste *m*	Augenarzt *m*
odd (not even)	impair	ungerade
odd (queer)	étrange	sonderbar
odor	odeur *f*	Geruch *m*
of	de	von
Of course!	Naturelle**ment!**	Natürlich!
offer	offre *f*	Angebot *n*
offer, to	offrir	anbieten
office (bus.)	bureau *m*	Büro *n*
office (position)	office *m*	Amt *n*
office hours	heures *fpl* de **bureau**	Sprechstunden *fpl*
officer	officier *m*	Offizier *m*
official (adj.)	officiel	amtlich
official (n.)	fonction**naire** *m*	Beamte *m*
often	souvent	oft
oil	huile *f*	Öl *n*
oil, to	huiler	ölen
oil filter	filtre *m* à huile	Ölfilter *m*
ointment	onguent *m*	Salbe *f*
old	vieux, vieille	alt
older	plus **vieux**	älter
olive	olive *f*	Olive *f*
olive oil	huile *f* d'**olive**	Olivenöl *n*
omelet	omelette *f*	Omelette *f*
on	sur	auf
on account of	à cause de	wegen (with gen.)
on board	à bord	an Bord
on deck	sur le **pont**	an Deck

Italian	*Portuguese*	*Spanish*
dovere	ter que; ter de; dever	tener que
ottenere; procurare	obter, conseguir	obtener; conseguir
ovvio	óbvio	obvio
di quando in quando	de quando em quando	de vez en cuando
occupazione *f*	ocupação *f*	ocupación *f*
occupato	ocupado	ocupado
occorrere	ocorrer	ocurrir
oceano	oceano	océano
ottobre	outubro	octubre
oculista *m*	oculista *m*	oculista
dispari	ímpar	impar
raro	estranho; exquisito	extraño
odore *m*	cheiro; odor *m*	olor *m*
di	de	de
Certo!	Pois não!	¡Claro!; ¡Cómo no!
offerta	oferta	oferta
offrire	oferecer	ofrecer
ufficio	escritório	oficina; despachol
ufficio	ofício	oficio
ore *fpl* d'ufficio	horas *fpl* de trabalho	horas *fpl* de oficina
ufficiale *m*	oficial *m*	oficial *m*
ufficiale	oficial	oficial
funzionario	oficial *m*; funcionário	funcionario
spesso	freqüentemente; muitas vêzes	a menudo
olio	óleo	aceite *m*
lubrificare	lubrificar	engrasar; aceitar
filtro dell'olio	filtro de azeite	filtro de aceite
unguento	ungüento	ungüento
vecchio; anziano	velho; antigo	viejo; antiguo
più vecchio	mais velho	mayor
oliva	azeitona	aceituna
olio (d'oliva)	azeite *m* de oliva	aceite *m* de oliva
frittata	omeleta	tortilla
su	sôbre; em	en; sobre
a causa di	por causa de	a causa de
a bordo	a bordo	a bordo
sopra coperta	no convés	sobre cubierta

English	*French*	*German*
on foot	à pied	zu Fuss
on horseback	à cheval	zu Pferde
on purpose	exprès	mit Absicht
on sale	à vendre	zu verkaufen
on the contrary	au contraire	im Gegenteil
on the other hand	d'autre part	dagegen
on the whole	à tout prendre	im grossen und **ganzen**
on time	à l'heure	pünktlich
on top of	au dessus de	auf
On what floor?	À quel étage?	In welchem **Stock?**
once (one time)	une fois	einmal
once more	encore une **fois**	noch einmal
one	un, une	ein, etc.
one must...	il faut	man muss
one-way street	sens unique	Einbahnstrasse
one-way ticket	billet *m* d'aller	einfache **Fahrkarte** *f*
onion	oignon *m*	Zwiebel *f*
only (merely)	seulement	nur
only (sole)	seul	einzig
onyx	onyx *m*	Onyx *m*
open (not closed)	ouvert	offen
open, to	ouvrir	öffnen; **aufmachen**
Open the door!	Ouvrez la **porte!**	Machen Sie die **Tür** auf!
opening (aperture)	ouverture *f*	Öffnung *f*
opera	opéra *m*	Oper *f*
opera glasses	jumelles *fpl*	Opernglas *n*
operate (handle), to	faire mar**cher**	betreiben
operate (med.)	opérer	operieren
operation (med.)	opération *f*	Operation *f*
operator (phone)	telephoniste *f*; mademoiselle! *f*	Telefonistin *f*; Fräulein! *n*
opinion	opinion *f*	Ansicht *f*; Meinung *f*
opposite	en face	gegenüber
opposite (n.)	opposé *m*	Gegenteil *n*
optician	opticien *m*	Optiker *m*
optional	facultatif	wahlfrei
or	ou	oder
orange	orange *f*	Apfelsine *f*
orange (color)	orangé	orange
orange juice	jus *m* d'orange	Orangensaft *m*

Italian	*Portuguese*	*Spanish*
a piedi	a pé	a pie
a cavallo	a cavalo	a caballo
apposta {	de propósito	de propósito
in vendita	à venda	de venta
al contrario	ao contrário	al contrario
d'alta parte	por outro lado	por otra parte
nell'insieme	em geral	en general
a tempo	a tempo; na hora	a tiempo
in cima di	acima de	encima de
A che piano?	Em que andar?	¿En qué piso?
una volta	uma vez	una vez
ancora una volta	mais uma vez	una vez más
uno, una	um, uma	uno, una
si deve	precisa	hay que
senso unico	direção única	vía única; trânsito (Mex.)
biglietto semplice	bilhete *m* simples	billete *m* sencillo
cipolla	cebola	cebolla
soltanto	sòmente; só	sólo; solamente
unico, solo	único	único
onice *m*	ónix *m*	ónice *m*
aperto	aberto	abierto
aprire	abrir	abrir
Apra la porta!	Abra a porta!	¡Abra la puerta!
apertura	abertura	abertura
opera	ópera	ópera
binocolo	binóculo de teatro	gemelos *mpl* de teatro
far funzionare	fazer funcionar	manejar
operare	operar	operar
operazione *f*	operação *f*	operación *f*
telefonista	telefonista	telefonista; ¡central! *f* (Mex.)
opinione *f*	opinião *f*	opinión *f*
di fronte	em frente	enfrente
opposto	contrário	contrario
ottico	ó(p)tico	óptico
facoltativo; a scelta	facultativo	facultativo
o	ou	o
arancia	laranja	naranja
arancione	alaranjado	naranjado
succo d'arancia	suco de laranja	jugo de naranja

English	*French*	*German*
orangeade	orangeade *f*	Orangeade *f*
orchard	verger *m*	Obstgarten *m*
orchestra	orchestre *m*	Orchester *n*
orchestra seat	fauteuil *m* d'**orchestre**	Parkettplatz *m*
orchid	orchidée *f*	Orchidee *f*
order (command)	ordre *m*	Befehl *m*
order (command), to	ordonner	befehlen
order (for goods)	commande *f*	Bestellung *f*
order (purchase), to	comman**d**er	bestellen
ordinary wine	vin *m* ordi**naire**	Tafelwein *m*
organ (anat.)	organe *m*	Organ *n*
organ (mus.)	orgue *m*	Orgel *f*
organize, to	organiser	einrichten
original (adj.)	original	ursprünglich
ornament (n.)	ornement *m*	Zierde *f*
orphan (n.)	orphelin *m*; orpheline *f*	Waise *m, f*; Waisenkind *n*
osteopath	ostéopathe *m*	Osteopath *m*
other (adj.)	autre	ander-
otherwise	autrement	anders
ought (vb.)	devoir	sollen
ounce	once *f*	Unze *f*
our	notre, nos	unser, etc.
out (forth)	dehors	heraus
out (not in)	(au) dehors	aus
out of date	passé de **mode**	unmodern
out of order	dérangé	ausser Betrieb
out of print	épuisé	vergriffen
out of style	démodé	aus der Mode
outboard motor	hors-bord *m*	Aussenbordmotor *m*
outdoors (adv.)	au dehors	draussen
outlet (elect.)	prise *f* de **courant**	Steckdose *f*
outside (adj.)	extérieur	äussere
outside (adv.)	en dehors	draussen
outside of	en dehors de	ausserhalb (gen.)
oven	four *m*	Ofen *m*
over (above)	sur	über
over (finished)	fini	vollendet

Italian	*Portuguese*	*Spanish*
aranciata	laranjada	naranjada
frutteto	pomar *m*	huerto
orchestra	orquestra	orquesta
poltroncina	cadeira de platéia	butaca de platea
orchidea	orquídea	orquídea
ordine *m*	ordem *f*	orden *f*
ordinare	ordenar	ordenar
ordinazione *f*	pedido	pedido
ordinare	pedir	pedir
vino da tavola	vinho da casa	vino de mesa
organo	órgão	órgano
organo	órgão	órgano
organizzare	organizar	organizar
originale	original	original
ornamento	ornamento	ornamento
orfano, a	órfão, órfã	huérfano, a
osteopatico	osteopata *m*	osteópata *m*
altro	outro	otro
altrimenti	de outro modo	de otro modo
dovere	dever	deber
oncia	onça	onza
nostro, etc.	nosso, etc.	nuestro, etc.
fuori	fora	fuera
fuori	fora	afuera
fuori moda	fora de moda	pasado de moda
fuori servizio; non funziona	fora de serviço não funciona	descompuesto; no funciona
esaurito	esgotado	agotado
fuori moda	fora de moda	pasado de moda
motore *m* fuoribordo	motor *m* de pôpa	motor *m* fuera de borda
all'aperto	ao ar livre	al aire libre
presa	tomada de corrente	enchufe *m*; toma
esterno	exterior	exterior
fuori	fora	afuera
fuori di	fora de	fuera de
forno	forno	horno
sopra	sôbre	sobre
finito	acabado; terminado	terminado

English	*French*	*German*
overcoat	pardessus *m*	Überzieher *m*
overnight (adv.)	pour la nuit	übernacht
oversea(s) (adj.)	d'outre-mer	überseeisch
overturn, to	renverser	umstürzen
overweight (luggage)	excédent de bagages	Übergewicht *n*
owe, to	devoir	schuldig sein (dat.)
owl	hibou *m*	Eule *f*
own (adj.)	propre	eigen
own, to	posséder	besitzen
owner	propriétaire *m*	Besitzer *m*
ox	boeuf *m*	Ochs *m*
oxygen	oxygène *m*	Sauerstoff *m*
oyster	huître *f*	Auster *f*
Pacific (Ocean)	Pacifique *m*	Stiller Ozean *m*
pack (baggage), to	faire les valises	packen
pack (of cigarettes)	paquet *m* de cigarettes	Päckchen *n* Zigaretten
pack (wrap), to	emballer	verpacken
package	colis *m*	Paket *n*
padlock	cadenas *m*	Hängeschloss *n*
page (leaf)	page *f*	Seite *f*
page (someone), to	faire appeler	suchen lassen
paid (p.p.)	payé	bezahlt
pail	seau *m*	Eimer *m*
pain	douleur *f*	Schmerz *m*
pain, to	avoir mal à	schmerzen
paint	peinture *f*	Farbe *f*
paint (something), to	peindre	anstreichen; malen
painter	peintre *m*	Maler *m*
painting	peinture *f*	Gemälde *n*
pair (a)	une paire	ein Paar
pajamas	pyjama *m*	Schlafanzug *m*
palace	palais *m*	Palast *m*
pale	pâle	blass
palm (of hand)	paume *f*	Handfläche *f*
palm (tree)	palmier *m*	Palme *f*
Palm Sunday	dimanche *m* des Rameaux	Palmsonntag *m*

Italian	*Portuguese*	*Spanish*
soprabito	sobretudo	sobretodo
per una notte	por uma noite	una sola noche
d'oltremare	de ultramar	de ultramar
capovolgere	virar	volcar
eccedenza di peso	excesso de peso	exceso de peso
dovere	dever	deber
gufo	coruja	búho
proprio	próprio	propio
possedere	possuir	poseer
proprietario	dono	dueño
bue *m* (pl. buoi)	boi *m*	buey *m*
ossigeno	oxigênio	oxígeno
ostrica	ostra	ostra; ostión *m* (Mex.)
Pacifico	Pacífico	Pacífico
fare i bagagli	fazer as malas	hacer la maleta
pacchetto di sigarette	maço de cigarros	cajetilla; paquete *m*
impaccare	embrulhar; empacotar	envolver; empacar
pacco	pacote *m*	paquete *m*
lucchetto	cadeado	candado
pagina	página	página
far chiamare	chamar	llamar
pagato	pago	pagado
secchio	balde *m*	balde *m*
dolore *m*; pena	dor *f*	dolor *m*
dolere	doer	doler
colore *m*	pintura	pintura
dipingere	pintar	pintar
pittore *m*	pintor *m*	pintor *m*
pittura	pintura	pintura
un paio	um par	un par
pigiama *m*	pijama *m*	pijama *m*
palazzo	palácio	palacio
pallido	pálido	pálido
palmo	palma da mão	palma
palma	palmeira	palma
Domenica delle Palme	Domingo de Ramos	Domingo de Ramos

English	*French*	*German*
Panama	le Panama	Panama *n*
pancake	crêpe *f*	Eierkuchen *m*
pane (of glass)	vitre *f*	Fensterscheibe *f*
pansy	pensée *f*	Stiefmütterchen *n*
panties	culotte *f*	Unterhose *f*
pantry	garde-manger *m*	Speisekammer *f*
pants (trousers)	pantalon *m*	Hose *f*
papaya	papaye *f*	Papaja *m*
paper	papier *m*	Papier *n*
paper clip	attache *f*	Heftklammer *f*
paper handkerchiefs	mouchoirs *mpl* en papier	Papiertaschentücher *npl*
parachute (n.)	parachute *m*	Fallschirm *m*
parade	défilé *m*	Parade *f*
paragraph	paragraphe *m*	Absatz *m*
Paraguay	le Paraguay	Paraguay *n*
Paraguayan (adj.)	paraguayen	paraguayisch
parasol	parasol *m*	Sonnenschirm *m*
parcel	paquet *m*; colis *m*	Paket *n*
parcel post	colis *m* postal	Paketpost *f*
pardon (forgive), to	pardonner	verzeihen
Pardon? (What did you say?)	Comment?	Wie, bitte?
Pardon me!	Excusez-moi!	Entschuldigen Sie!
parents	parents *mpl*	Eltern *pl*
Paris	Paris *m*	Paris *n*
park	parc *m*	Park *m*
park, to	stationner; garer	parken
parking lot	parking *m*	Parkplatz *m*
parlor	salon *m*	Wohnzimmer *n*
parrot	perroquet *m*	Papagei *m*
parsley	persil *m*	Petersilie *f*
parsnip	panais *m*	Pastinak *m*
part (share) (n.)	part *f*	Teil *m*
partner (bus.)	associé *m*	Teilhaber *m*
partridge	perdrix *f*	Rebhuhn *n*
party (celebration)	fête *f*	Fest *n*

Italian	*Portuguese*	*Spanish*
il **Panama**	o Panamá	Panamá
frittella	panqueca	panqueque *m*
(lastra di) **vetro**	vidro	vidrio
viola del pensiero	**amor**-perfeito	pensamiento
mutandine *fpl*	calcinhas *fpl*	pantaletas *fpl*; calzones *mpl*
dispensa	despensa	despensa
pantaloni *mpl*	cal**ç**as *fpl*	pantalones *mpl*
papaya	mamão	papaya
carta	papel *m*	papel *m*
fermaglio *m*	clipe *m* (para **papéis**)	sujetapapeles *m*
fazzolettini *mpl* di carta	lenços *mpl* de papel	tisú *m* facial; pañuelos *mpl* de papel
paracadute *m*	pára-quedas *m*	paracaídas *m*
parata	desfile *m*	desfile *m*
paragrafo	parágrafo	párrafo
il Paraguai	o Paraguai	el Paraguay
paraguaiano	paraguaio	paraguayo
ombrellino *m*	pára-sol *m*; sombrinha	parasol *m*
pacco	embrulho; pacote *m*	paquete *m*
pacco postale	encomenda postal	paquete *m* postal
perdonare	perdoar	perdonar
Come?	Como disse?	¿Mande?; ¿Cómo?
Scusi!	Desculpe-me!; perdoe-me!	¡Perdóneme!
genitori *mpl*	pais *mpl*	padres *mpl*
Parigi *f*	Paris	París
parco *m*	parque *m*	parque *m*
parcheggiare; parcare	estacionar	aparcar; estacionar
parcheggio	estacionamento	estacionamiento
salotto	salão	sala
pappagallo	papagaio	loro; papagayo
prezzemolo	salsa	perejil *m*
pastinaca	pastinaca	pastinaca
parte *f*	parte *f*	parte *f*
socio	sócio	socio
pernice *f*	perdiz *f*	perdiz *f*
festa	festa	fiesta

English	*French*	*German*
party (evening)	soirée *f*	Abendgesellschaft *f*
pass (an exam), to	réussir à un examen	bestehen
pass (go by), to	passer	vorbeigehen
passenger	passager *m*	Passagier *m*
passenger train	train *m* de voyageurs	Personenzug *m*
passport	passeport *m*	Pass *m*
past (gone by) (adj.)	passé	vergangen
past, the (n.)	passé *m*	Vergangenheit *f*
pastor (church)	pasteur *m*	Pfarrer *m*
pastry	pâtisserie *f*	Gebäck *n*
pastry shop	pâtisserie *f*	Konditorei *f*
patent (right) (n.)	brevet *m*	Patent *n*
patent leather	cuir *m* verni	Glanzleder *n*
path	sentier *m*	Pfad *m*
patient (forbearing)	patient	geduldig
patient (invalid)	malade *m, f*	Kranke *m, f*; Patient *m*
patience	patience *f*	Geduld *f*
pawn, to	mettre en gage	verpfänden
pawnshop	mont-de-piété *m*	Leihhaus *n*
pay a visit, to	faire une visite	einen Besuch machen
pay attention, to	faire attention	aufpassen
pay cash, to	payer comptant	bar bezahlen
pay duty (on), to	payer les droits de douane	verzollen
pay for, to	payer	bezahlen
payment	paiement *m*	Zahlung *f*
pea	petit pois *m*	Erbse *f*
peace	paix *f*	Frieden *m*
peaceful (calm)	paisible	ruhig
peach	pêche *f*	Pfirsich *m*
peak (of mountain)	cime *f*	Spitze *f*
peanut	cacahuète *f*	Erdnuss *f*
pear	poire *f*	Birne *f*
pearl	perle *f*	Perle *f*
peasant	paysan *m*	Bauer *m*
peculiar (strange)	singulier	sonderbar
pedestrian	piéton *m*	Fussgänger *m*

Italian	*Portuguese*	*Spanish*
serata	tertúlia	tertulia
superare un esame	passar (no exame)	salir bien en un examen
passare	passar	pasar
passeggero	passageiro	pasajero
treno passeggeri	trem *m* de passageiros	tren *m* de pasajeros
passaporto	passaporte *m*	pasaporte *m*
passato	passado	pasado
passato	passado	pasado
pastore *m*	pastor *m*	pastor *m*
paste *fpl*; pasticceria	pastéis *mpl*	pasteles *mpl*
pasticceria	pastelaria	pastelería
brevetto	patente *f*	patente *f*
copale *f*	verniz *m*	charol *m*
sentiero	senda	sendero
paziente	paciente	paciente
paziente *m, f*	doente *m, f*	paciente *m, f*
pazienza	paciência	paciencia
impegnare	empenhar	empeñar
monte *m* di pietà	casa de penhores	casa de empeños
fare una visita	fazer uma visita	hacer una visita
fare attenzione	prestar atenção	prestar atención
pagare in contanti	pagar à vista	pagar al contado
pagare dogana	pagar os direitos de alfândega	pagar los derechos de aduana
pagare	pagar	pagar
pagamento	pagamento	pago
pisello	ervilha	guisante *m*; chícharo (Mex.)
pace *f*	paz *f*	paz *f*
tranquillo	tranqüilo	tranquilo
pesca (pl. pesche)	pêssego	melocotón *m*; durazno
picco	cume *m*	cumbre *f*
arachide *f*	amendoim *m*	maní *m*; cacahuete *m*
pera	pêra (*pl* peras)	pera
perla	pérola	perla
contadino	camponês *m*	campesino
strano	singular	singular
pedone *m*	transeunte *m*; pedestre *m, f*	transeúnte *m*; peatón *m*

English	*French*	*German*
pedometer	podomètre *m*	Schrittmesser *m*
peel, to	peler	schälen
Peking	Pékin *f*	Peking *n*
pen	plume *f*	Feder *f*
pencil	crayon *m*	Bleistift *m*
pencil sharpener	taille-crayon *m*	Bleistiftspitzer *m*
penicillin	pénicilline *f*	Penicillin *n*
people (persons)	gens *mpl*	Leute pl
people (populace)	peuple *m*	Volk *n*
pepper (seasoning)	poivre *m*	Pfeffer *m*
pepper (vegetable)	poivron *m*	Pfeffer *m*
pepper shaker	poivrière *f*	Pfefferstreuer *m*
per cent	pour cent	Prozent *n*
per day	par jour	pro Tag
per hour	par heure	pro Stunde
per month	par mois	pro Monat
per week	par semaine	pro Woche
performance (theat.)	représentation *f*	Vorstellung *f*
perfume	parfum *m*	Parfüm *n*
perhaps	peut-être	vielleicht
period (punct.)	point *m*	Punkt *m*
permanent (wave)	permanente *f*	Dauerwelle *f*
permission	permission *f*	Erlaubnis *f*
permit, to	permettre	zulassen; erlauben
person	personne *f*	Person *f*
personal	personnel	persönlich
personal effects	effets *mpl* personnels	persönliche Sachen *fpl*
perspire, to	transpirer	schwitzen
persuade, to	persuader	überreden
Peru	le Pérou	Peru *n*
Peruvian (adj.)	péruvien	peruanisch
petticoat	jupon *m*	Unterrock *m*
pharmacy	pharmacie *f*	Apotheke *f*
pheasant	faisan *m*	Fasan *m*
Philippines	les Philippines *fpl*	die Philippinen
photograph	photographie *f*	Photographie *f*; Foto *n*
photograph, to	photographier	photographieren

Italian	*Portuguese*	*Spanish*
pedometro	pedômetro; conta-passos *m*	podómetro
mondare	descascar; pelar	pelar; mondar
Pechino	Pequim *m*	Pekín
penna	pena; caneta	pluma
matita	lápis *m*	lápiz *m*
temperamatite *m*	apontador *m* de lápis	sacapuntas *m*
penicillina	penicilina	penicilina
gente *f*	gente *f*	gente *f*
popolo	povo	pueblo
pepe *m*	pimenta	pimienta
peperone *m*	pimentão	pimiento
pepaiola	pimenteira	pimentero
per cento	por cento	por ciento
al giorno	por dia	al día
all' ora	por hora	por hora
al mese	por mês	por mes
alla settimana	por semana	por semana
rappresentazione *f*	representação *f*	representación *f*
profumo	perfume *m*	perfume *m*
forse	talvez; quiçá	tal vez; quizá(s)
punto	ponto	punto
permanente *f*	permanente *f*	permanente *f*
permesso	licença	permiso
permettere	permitir	permitir
persona	pessoa	persona
personale	pessoal	personal
effetti *mpl* personali	objetos *mpl* de uso pessoal	efectos *mpl* personales
sudare	suar	sudar
persuadere	persuadir	persuadir
il Perù	o Peru	el Perú
peruviano	peruano	peruano
sottoveste *f*	anágua; saia	enaguas *fpl*
farmacia	farmácia	farmacia
fagiano	faisão	faisán *m*
le Filippine	as Filipinas	las Filipinas
fotografia	fotografia	fotografía
fotografare	fotografar	retratar; fotografiar

English	*French*	*German*
photographer	photographe *m*	Photograph *m*
physician	médecin *m*	Arzt *m*
piano	piano *m*	Klavier *n*
pick out (choose), to	choisir	auswählen
pick up, to	recueillir	aufheben
pick up the mail, to	faire la levée	die Post holen
pickles	cornichons *mpl*	Essiggurken *fpl*
pickpocket	pickpocket *m*	Taschendieb *m*
picnic	pique-nique *m*	Picknick *n*
picture	image *f*; tableau *m*	Bild *n*
pie	tarte *f*	(Obst) Torte *f*
pie à la mode	"pie" *m* avec glace	Torte *f* mit Eis
piece	morceau *m*	Stück *n*
pier	quai *m*	Kai *m*
pig	cochon *m*	Schwein *n*
pigeon	pigeon *m*	Taube *f*
pigskin	peau *f* de porc	Schweinsleder *n*
pile (heap) (n.)	tas *m*	Haufen *m*
pill	pilule *f*; comprimé *m*	Pille *f*
pillow	oreiller *m*	Kissen *n*
pillow case	taie *f* d'oreiller	Kissenbezug *m*
pilot (n.)	pilote *m*	Pilot *m*
pimple	bouton *m*	Pickel *m*
pin	épingle *f*	Stecknadel *f*
pinch (be tight), to	serrer	drücken
pine (tree)	pin *m*	Kiefer *f*
pineapple	ananas *m*	Ananas *f*
pink	rose	blassrot; rosa
pipe (smoking)	pipe *f*	Pfeife *f*
pipe (tube)	tuyau *m*	Röhre *f*
pipe cleaner	cure-pipes *m*	Pfeifenreiniger *m*
pistol	pistolet *m*	Pistole *f*
piston	piston *m*	Kolben *m*
piston ring	segment *m* de piston	Kolbenring *m*
pitcher (container)	cruche *f*	Krug *m*
place (lay), to	poser	legen
place (site)	endroit *m*	Platz *m*

Italian	*Portuguese*	*Spanish*
fotografo	fotógrafo	fotógrafo
medico	médico	médico
piano	piano	piano
scegliere	escolher	escoger
raccogliere	apanhar	recoger
fare la levata delle lettere	recolher o correio	recoger el correo
sottaceti *mpl*	picles *mpl*	encurtidos *mpl*
borsaiuolo	ratoneiro	ratero
picnic *m*	piquenique *m*	jira; picnic *m*
quadro	quadro	cuadro
torta ; pasticcio	torta	pastel *m*
crostata con gelato	torta à moda	pastel con helado
pezzo	peça; pedaço	pedazo
molo	cais *m*; molhe *m*	muelle *m*
porco	porco	puerco; cerdo
piccione *m*	pombo	pichón *m*
pelle *f* di cinghiale	couro de porco	cuero de cerdo
mucchio; catasta	montão; pilha	montón *m*
pillola	pílula; cápsula	píldora
guanciale *m*	almofada; travesseiro (Br.)	almohada
federa	fronha	funda de almohada
pilota *m*	pilôto	piloto
foruncolo	espinha	grano
spillo	alfinête *m*	alfiler *m*
pressare	apertar	apretar
pino	pinheiro	pino
ananasso	ananás *m*; abacaxi *m* (Br.)	piña; ananá(s)
rosa	côr-de-rosa	rosado
pipa	cachimbo	pipa
tubo	tubo	tubo
nettapipe *m*	limpa-cachimbo *m*	limpiapipas *m*
pistola	pistola	pistola
pistone *m*; stantuffo	pistão	pistón *m*; émbolo
segmento (del pistone)	anel de segmento	anillo de émbolo
brocca	jarro; cântaro	jarro; cántaro
collocare	colocar	colocar
luogo	lugar *m*	lugar *m*

English	*French*	*German*
plain (clear)	clair	deutlich
plain (level land)	plaine *f*	Ebene *f*
plain (simple)	simple	einfach
plan	plan *m*	Plan *m*
plan, to	projeter	planen
plane (air-)	avion *m*	Flugzeug *n*
planet	planète *f*	Planet *m*
plank (wood)	planche *f*	Brett *n*
plant (factory)	usine *f*	Betriebsanlage *f*; Fabrik *f*
plant (growing)	plante *f*	Pflanze *f*
plant, to	planter	pflanzen
plaster (walls) (n.)	plâtre *m*	Gips *m*
plastic (n.)	plastique *m*	Kunststoff *m*
plate (dish)	assiette *f*	Teller *m*
platform (R.R.)	quai *m*	Bahnsteig *m*
platform ticket	ticket *m* de **quai**	Bahnsteigkarte *f*
platinum	platine *f*	Platin *n*
play (theat.) (n.)	pièce *f* de **théâtre**	(Theater)stück *n*
play (a game), to	jouer à	spielen
play (instrument), to	jouer de	spielen
play cards, to	jouer aux **cartes**	Karten spielen
playing cards	cartes *fpl* à **jouer**	Spielkarten *fpl*
pleasant	agréable	angenehm
please, to	plaire	gefallen (dat.)
Please!	S'il vous plaît!	Bitte!
Please direct me to...	Voulez-vous bien m'indiquer où se trouve...	Bitte, zeigen Sie mir, wo...
Pleased to meet you!	Enchanté de faire votre connaissance!	Es freut mich sehr, Sie kennenzulernen!
pleasure	plaisir *m*	Vergnügen *n*
pliers	pinces *fpl*	Zange *f*
plow	charrue *f*	Pflug *m*
plow, to	labourer	pflügen
plug (elect.)	prise *f*	Stecker *m*
plug (spark)	bougie *f*	Zündkerze *f*
plug (stopper)	tampon *m*	Stöpsel *m*

Italian	*Portuguese*	*Spanish*
chiaro	claro	claro
pianura	planura	llanura
semplice	simples	sencillo
piano	plano	plan *m*
progettare	planejar; projetar	proyectar; planear
aereo	aeroplano; avião	avión *m*; aeroplano
pianeta *m*	planêta *m*	planeta *m*
tavola	prancha	tabla
fabbrica	fábrica	fábrica
pianta	planta	planta
piantare	plantar	plantar; sembrar
intonaco	gêsso	yeso
plastica	plástico	plástico
piatto	prato	plato
marciapiede *m*	plataforma	andén *m*
biglietto d'entrata	bilhete *m* de gare	billete *m* de andén
platino	platina	platino
spettacolo	peça de teatro	drama *m*; pieza
giocare	jogar; brincar	jugar
suonare	tocar	tocar
giocare a carte	jogar cartas	jugar a los naipes
carte da giuoco	cartas de jogar	naipes *mpl*; cartas *fpl*
piacevole	agradável; simpático (persons)	agradable; simpático (persons)
piacere	agradar	agradar
Per piacere!	Por favor!	¡Por favor!
Per favore, potrebbe dirigirmi a...	Faça favor de indicar o caminho para...	Favor de decirme dónde está...
Piacere di fare la Sua conoscenza!	Muito prazer em conhecê-lo!	¡Tanto gusto en conocerle!
piacere *m*	prazer *m*	gusto; placer *m*
pinze *fpl*	alicate *m*	alicates *mpl*
aratro	arado	arado
arare	arar	arar
spina, presa	tomada	enchufe *m*; clavija
candela	vela (de ignição)	bujía
tappo	tampão	tapón *m*

English	*French*	*German*
plum	prune *f*	Pflaume *f*
plumber	plombier *m*	Klempner *m*
plus	plus	plus
p.m.	de l'après-midi; du soir	nachmittags
pneumonia	pneumonie *f*	Lungenentzündung *f*
poach (eggs), to	pocher	pochieren
poached (eggs)	poché	verlorene (Eier)
pocket (n.)	poche *f*	Tasche *f*
pocket (adj.)	de poche	taschen-
pocketbook	portefeuille *m*	Handtasche *f*
pocketknife	canif *m*	Taschenmesser *n*
poem	poème *m*	Gedicht *n*
poet	poète *m*	Dichter *m*
poetry	poésie *f*	Dichtung *f*
point (place)	point *m*	Punkt *m*
point (sharp end)	pointe *f*	Spitze *f*
point to, to	montrer	deuten auf
point of, to be on the	être sur le point de	im Begriff sein
poison (n.)	poison *m*	Gift *n*
poisonous	venimeux; vénéneux	giftig
Poland	la Pologne	Polen *n*
police	police *f*	Polizei *f*
police station	commissariat *m* de police	Polizeiwache *f*
policeman	agent *m* de police	Schutzmann *m*, Polizist *m*
policy (insurance)	police *f*	Police *f*
polio	paralysie *f* infantile	Kinderlähmung *f*
Polish (adj.)	polonais	polnisch
polish, to	polir	putzen
polite	poli	höflich
politeness	politesse *f*	Höflichkeit *f*
pomade	pommade *f*	Pomade *f*
pomegranate	grenade *f*	Granatapfel *m*
poor	pauvre	arm
popcorn	maïs *m* éclaté	Röstmais *m*

Italian	*Portuguese*	*Spanish*
prugna; susina	ameixa	ciruela
idraulico	encanador *m*; bombeiro (Br.)	plomero; fontanero
più	mais	más
del pomeriggio	da tarde; da noite	de la tarde; de la noche
polmonite *f*	pneumonia	pulmonía
cuocere le uova in camicia; affogare	escalfar	escalfar
affogato	escalfado; cozido	escalfado; poché (Mex.)
tasca	algibeira; bôlso (Br.)	bolsillo; bolsa (Amer.)
tascabile	de bôlso	de bolsillo
portafoglio	bôlsa	cartera
temperino	canivete *m*	cortaplumas *m*
poema *m*	poema *m*	poema *m*
poeta *m*	poeta *m*	poeta *m*
poesia	poesia	poesía
punto	ponto	punto; lugar *m*
punta	ponta	punta
indicare	indicar	señalar
essere sul punto di	estar a ponto de	estar a punto de
veleno	veneno	veneno
velenoso	venenoso	venenoso
la Polonia	a Polônia	Polonia
polizia	polícia	policía
questura, posto di polizia	esquadra, pôsto de polícia (Br.)	comisaría
agente *m* di polizia; guardia *f*	polícia *m*; guarda *m*	policía *m*; agente *m* de policía
polizza	apólice *f* de seguro	póliza
paralisi *f* infantile	polio (mielite) *f*	polio (mielitis) *f*
polacco	polonês	polaco
pulire, lucidare	polir	pulir
cortese	cortês	cortés
cortesia	cortesia	cortesía
pomata	pomada	pomada
melagrana	romã	granada
povero	pobre	pobre
granturco arrostito	pipoca	palomitas *fpl* (de maíz)

English	*French*	*German*
pope	pape *m*	Papst *m*
popular	populaire	beliebt
population	population *f*	Bevölkerung *f*
porcelain	porcelaine *f*	Porzellan *n*
porch	véranda *f*	Veranda *f*
pork	porc *m*	Schweinefleisch *n*
pork chop	côtelette *f* de **porc**	Schweinskotelett *n*
port (harbor)	port *m*	Hafen *m*
port (left side)	bâbord *m*	Backbord *m*
port of call	escale *f*	Anlaufhafen *m*
port wine	porto *m*	Portwein *m*
portable (adj.)	portatif	tragbar
porter (baggage)	porteur *m*	Gepäckträger *m*
porthole	hublot *m*	Luke *f*
portion	portion *f*	Portion *f*
portrait	portrait *m*	Bildnis *n*
Portugal	le Portugal	Portugal *n*
Portuguese (adj.)	portugais	portugiesisch
possess, to	posséder	besitzen
possible	possible	möglich
post (position)	poste *m*	Posten *m*
post card (picture)	carte *f* postale illustrée	Ansichtskarte *f*
post card (plain)	carte *f* postale	Postkarte *f*
post office	bureau *m* de poste	Postamt *n*
post office box	boîte *f* postale	Postfach *n*
postage	port *m*	Porto *n*
postage stamp	timbre-**poste** *m*	Briefmarke *f*
postman	facteur *m*	Briefträger *m*
postpaid	affranchi	franko
postpone, to	remettre	verschieben
pot (chamber-)	vase *m* de **nuit**	Nachttopf *m*
pot (container)	pot *m*	Topf *m*
potato	pomme *f* de **terre**	Kartoffel *f*
pottery	poterie *f*	Töpferwaren *fpl*
poultice (n.)	cataplasme *m*	Breiumschlag *m*

Italian	Portuguese	Spanish
papa m	papa m	papa m
popolare	popular	popular
popolazione f	população f	población f
porcellana	porcelana	porcelana
veranda	pórtico; varanda	pórtico; terraza (Mex.)
carne f di maiale	carne f de porco	carne f de puerco
costoletta di maiale	costeleta de porco	chuleta de puerco
porto	porto	puerto
babordo	bombordo	babor m
scalo	porto de escala	puerto de escala
porto	vinho do Porto	oporto
portatile	portátil	portátil
facchino	bagageiro; carregador (Br.)	mozo; maletero; cargador (Mex.)
oblò	portinhola; vigia	portilla
porzione f	porção f	porción f
ritratto	retrato	retrato
il Portogallo	Portugal	Portugal
portoghese	português	portugués
possedere	possuir	poseer
possibile	possível	posible
posto	pôsto	puesto
cartolina illustrata	postal m ilustrado	tarjeta postal ilustrada; vista
cartolina postale	cartão postal	tarjeta postal
ufficio postale	correio	casa de correos; correo
casella postale	caixa postal	apartado; casilla (Amer.)
affrancatura	porte m	porte m; franqueo
francobollo	selo	sello de correo; estampilla (Amer.); timbre m (Mex.)
postino	carteiro	cartero
franco di porto	porte pago	porte pagado
posporre	adiar	posponer
orinale m	urinol m	orinal m; bacinilla
pentola	pote m	pote m
patata	batata	patata; papa (Amer.)
terracotta	olaria	alfarería; loza
cataplasma m	cataplasma	cataplasma

English	*French*	*German*
pound (.45 kilo)	livre *f*	Pfund *n*
pour, to	verser	giessen
pour (rain), to	pleuvoir à **verse**	in Strömen regnen
poverty	pauvreté *f*	Armut *f*
powder (dust)	poudre *f*	Staub *m*
powder (face)	poudre *f*	(Gesichts) puder *m*
powder puff	houppette *f*	Puderquaste *f*
powdered sugar	sucre *m* en **poudre**	Puderzucker *m*
power (authority)	pouvoir *m*	Macht *f*
power of attorney	procuration *f*	Vollmacht *f*
powerful	puissant	mächtig
practice, to	pratiquer	üben
Prague	Prague *m*	Prag *n*
praise	louange *f*	Lob *n*
praise, to	louer	loben
pray, to	prier	beten
prayer	prière *f*	Gebet *n*
preach, to	prêcher	predigen
prefer, to	préférer;	vorziehen; lieber haben
	aimer **mieux**	
preferably	de préférence	am liebsten
pregnant	enceint (e)	schwanger
preparation	préparation *f*	Vorbereitung *f*
prepare, to	préparer	vorbereiten
preposition (gram.)	préposition *f*	Präposition *f*
prescribe (med.)	ordonner	verschreiben
prescription (med.)	ordonnance *f*	Rezept *n*
present (current)	actuel	gegenwärtig
present (gift)	cadeau *m*	Geschenk *n*
present, the	présent *m*	Gegenwart *f*
president	président *m*	Präsident *m*
president (univ.)	recteur *m*	Rektor *m*
press (iron), to	repasser	bügeln
pressure cooker	autocuiseur *m*	Dampfkochtopf *m*
pretend, to	feindre	vorgeben
pretty	joli	hübsch
pretty (fairly)	assez	ziemlich

Italian	*Portuguese*	*Spanish*
libbra	libra	libra
versare; mescere	verter	verter; echar
piovere a catinelle	chover a cântaros	llover a cántaros
povertà *f*	pobreza	pobreza
polvere *f*	pó *m*; pólvora	polvo
cipria	pó de arroz	polvos *mpl* (para la cara)
piumino da (cipria)	pompom *m*	borla; mota (Mex.)
zucchero in polvere	açúcar em pó	azúcar fino
potere *m*	poder *m*	poder *m*
procura	procuração *f*	poder *m*
potente	poderoso	poderoso
praticare	praticar	practicar
Praga *f*	Praga *f*	Praga *f*
lode *f*	louvor *m*	alabanza
lodare	louvar	alabar
pregare	rezar	rezar
preghiera	oração *f*	oración *f*
predicare	predicar	predicar
preferire	preferir	preferir
di preferenza	de preferência	de preferencia
gravida; incinta	prenhe; grávida	preñada
preparazione *f*	preparação *f*	preparación *f*
preparare	preparar	preparar
preposizione *f*	preposição *f*	preposición *f*
prescrivere	receitar	recetar
ricetta	receita	receta
attuale	atual	actual
regalo; presente *m*	presente *m*	regalo
presente *m*	presente *m*	presente *m*
presidente *m*	presidente *m*	presidente *m*
rettore *m*	reitor *m*	rector *m*
stirare	passar a ferro	planchar
pentola a pressione	panela de pressão	olla a presión; olla express (Mex.)
fingere	fingir	fingir
bello	bonito; lindo	bonito; lindo; chulo (Mex.)
abbastanza	bastante	bastante

English	*French*	*German*
prevent, to	empêcher	verhüten
previous (adj.)	antérieur	vorhergehend
price (n.)	prix *m*	Preis *m*
priest	prêtre *m*; curé *m*	Priester *m*
prince	prince *m*	Prinz *m*
princess	princesse *f*	Prinzessin *f*
print (phot.) (n.)	épreuve *f*	Abzug *m*
print, to	imprimer	drucken
print (phot.), to	tirer	abziehen
printed matter	imprimés *mpl*	Drucksache *f*
printer	imprimeur *m*	Drucker *m*
prison	prison *f*	Gefängnis *n*
prisoner	prisonnier *m*	Gefangene *m, f*
private (personal)	privé	privat
private bath	salle *f* de bains privée	Privatbad *n*
prize (n.)	prix *m*	Preis *m*
probably	probablement	wahrscheinlich
problem	problème *m*	Problem *n*
procure, to	obtenir	verschaffen
produce, to	produire	hervorbringen
product	produit *m*	Erzeugnis *n*
profession	profession *f*	Beruf *m*
professor	professeur *m*	Professor *m*
program	programme *m*	Programm *n*
prohibit, to	prohiber	verbieten
promise	promesse *f*	Versprechen *n*
promise, to	promettre	versprechen
pronoun (gram.)	pronom *m*	Pronomen *n*
pronounce, to	prononcer	aussprechen
pronunciation	prononciation *f*	Aussprache *f*
propeller	hélice *f*	Schraube *f*
protect, to	protéger	schützen
protection	protection *f*	Schutz *m*
protest	protestation *f*	Einspruch *m*
protest, to	protester	protestieren
Protestant (n.)	protestant(e) *m, f*	Protestant *m*
proud	orgueilleux, -euse	stolz
proverb	proverbe *m*	Sprichwort *n*

Italian	*Portuguese*	*Spanish*
prevenire	prevenir; impedir	impedir
precedente	prévio	previo; anterior
prezzo	preço	precio
prete *m*	padre *m*; sacerdote *m*	cura *m*; sacerdote *m*
principe *m*	príncipe *m*	príncipe *m*
principessa	princesa	princesa
copia	positivo; cópia	copia
stampare	imprimir	imprimir
stampare	copiar	tirar; imprimir
stampati *mpl*	impressos *mpl*	impresos *mpl*
tipografo	impressor *m*	impresor *m*
prigione *f*	prisão *f*	cárcel *f*
prigioniero	prisioneiro	prisionero
privato	privado	privado
bagno privato	banheiro anexo	cuarto de baño particular
premio	prêmio	premio
probabilmente	provàvelmente	probablemente
problema *m*	problema *m*	problema *m*
procurare	obter	obtener
produrre	produzir	producir
prodotto	produto	producto
professione *f*	profissão *f*	profesión *f*
professore *m*	professor *m*; lente *m*	profesor *m*
programma *m*	programa *m*	programa *m*
proibire	proibir	prohibir
promessa	promessa	promesa
promettere	prometer	prometer
pronome *m*	pronome *m*	pronombre *m*
pronunziare	pronunciar	pronunciar
pronunzia	pronúncia	pronunciación *f*
elica	hélice *f*	hélice *f*
proteggere	proteger	proteger
protezione *f*	proteção *f*	protección *f*
protesta	protesto	protesta
protestare	protestar	protestar
protestante *m*	protestante *m*	protestante *m*
orgoglioso	orgulhoso	orgulloso
proverbio	provérbio	refrán *m*

English	*French*	*German*
provide, to	fournir	besorgen
provided that	pourvu que	wenn nur
province	province *f*	Provinz *f*
prune (n.)	pruneau *m*	Backpflaume *f*
psychiatrist	psychiatre *m*	Psychiater *m*
public (adj.)	public	öffentlich
publish, to	publier	herausgeben
pudding	pouding *m*	Pudding *m*
Puerto Rico	le Porto-Rico	Portorico *n*
pull, to	tirer	ziehen
pulley	poulie *f*	Rolle *f*
pulse	pouls *m*	Puls *m*
pump (fuel, car)	pompe *f*	Pumpe *f*
pumpkin	potiron *m*	Kürbis *m*
punch (drink)	punch *m*	Punsch *m*
puncture (n.)	crevaison *f*	Reifenpanne *f*
punish, to	punir	strafen
pupil (eye)	pupille *f*	Pupille *f*
pupil (student)	élève *m, f*	Schüler *m*
purchase	achat *m*	Einkauf *m*
purchase, to	acheter	kaufen
pure	pur	rein
purple (adj.)	violet	purpurn
purpose (aim) (n.)	but *m*	Absicht *f*
purse (woman's)	sac *m* à main	Handtasche *f*
purser (ship)	commissaire *m*	Zahlmeister *m*
push, to	pousser	stossen
put (p.p.)	mis	gelegt
put (place), to	mettre	legen
put on (clothes), to	mettre	anziehen
put out (fire), to	étouffer	löschen
put out the light, to	éteindre	abdrehen
put up at, to	descendre	absteigen
putty	mastic *m*	Glaserkitt *m*
Pyrenees, The	les Pyrénées	die Pyrenäen
quail (bird)	caille *f*	Wachtel *f*
quality (grade)	qualité *f*	Qualität *f*
quantity	quantité *f*	Menge *f*

Italian	*Portuguese*	*Spanish*
provvedere	prover	proveer
purchè	contanto que	con tal que
provincia	província	provincia
prugna secca	ameixa sêca	ciruela pasa
psichiatra *m*	psiquiatra	psiquiatra *m, f*
pubblico	público	público
pubblicare	publicar	publicar
budino	pudim *m*	pudín *m*
il Portorico	Porto-Rico	Puerto Rico
tirare	puxar	tirar
puleggia	polia; polé *f*	polea
polso	pulso	pulso
pompa	bomba	bomba
zucca	abóbora	calabaza; ayote *m* (Mex.)
ponce *m*	ponche *m*	ponche *m*
foratura; bucatura	furo no pneu	pinchazo
punire	castigar	castigar
pupilla	menina do olho	pupila
alunno; allievo	aluno	alumno
compra; acquisto	compra	compra
comprare	comprar	comprar
puro	puro	puro
porpora	roxo	morado
scopo	propósito	propósito
borsa	bôlsa (para dinheiro)	bolsa; bolso
commissario	comissário	contador *m*
spingere	empurrar	empujar
messo	pôsto	puesto
mettere	pôr	poner
mettersi	vestir	ponerse
estinguere	apagar	apagar
spegnere	apagar	apagar
scendere	hospedar-se	hospedarse
mastice *m*	massa de vidraceiro	masilla
i Pirenei	os Pireneus	los Pirineos
quaglia	codorniz *f*	codorniz *f*
qualità	qualidade *f*	calidad *f*
quantità	quantidade *f*	cantidad *f*

English	*French*	*German*
quarrel	querelle *f*	Streit *m*
quarrel, to	se quereller	streiten
quarter (part)	quart *m*	Viertel *n*
quarter of...	...moins un **quart**	ein Viertel vor...
quarter past...	...et **quart**	ein Viertel nach...
queen	reine *f*	Königin *f*
question	question *f*	Frage *f*
question (query), to	interroger	befragen
quick	rapide	schnell
quickly	vite	schnell
quiet (no motion)	tranquille	ruhig
quiet (no noise)	silencieux, -euse	still
quilt (cover)	courtepointe *f*	Steppdecke *f*
quince	coing *m*	Quitte *f*
quinine	quinine *f*	Chinin *n*
quit (stop), to	cesser de	aufhören
quite (somewhat)	un **peu**	etwas
quote, to	citer	zitieren
rabbi	rabbin *m*	Rabbiner *m*
rabbit	lapin *m*	Kaninchen *n*
race (contest)	course *f*	Wettlauf *m*
race (human)	race *f*	Rasse *f*
rack (baggage)	filet *m*	Gepäcknetz *n*
race track (horses)	hippodrome *m*	Hippodrom *n*
racket (noise)	vacarme *m*	Lärm *m*
racket (tennis)	raquette *f* (de tennis)	Tennisschläger *m*
radiator (car)	radiateur *m*	Kühler *m*
radiator (room)	radiateur *m*	Heizkörper *m*
radio (set)	poste *m* de radio	Radio *n*
radish	radis *m*	Radieschen *n*
rag (cloth)	chiffon *m*	Putzlappen *m*
railroad	chemin *m* de fer	Eisenbahn *f*
railroad station	gare *f*	Bahnhof *m*
railway guide	indicateur *m* des chemins de fer	Kursbuch *n*

Italian	*Portuguese*	*Spanish*
alterco	rixa	riña
litigare	rixar	reñir
quarto	. . . quarta parte *f*	cuarta parte *f*
. . . meno un quarto	um quarto para. . .	. . . menos cuarto
. . . e un quarto	. . . e um quarto	. . . y cuarto
regina	rainha	reina
domanda	pergunta	pregunta
interrogare	interrogar	interrogar
rapido	rápido	rápido

rapidamente	depressa;
	  ràpidamente
		de prisa;
		  rápidamente

quieto	quieto	quieto
silenzioso	silencioso	silencioso
coltrone *m*	colcha	colcha
(mela)cotogna	marmelo	membrillo
chinino	quinino	quinina
smettere di	deixar de	dejar de
un poco	um pouco	algo
citare	citar	citar
rabbino	rabino	rabí *m*
coniglio	coelho	conejo
corsa	curso	carrera
razza	raça	raza
reticella	rêde *f;* porta-mala (Br.)	red *f;* rejilla
ippodromo	hipódromo	hipódromo
fracasso	barulho	alboroto
racchetta da tennis	raqueta	raqueta
radiatore *m*	radiador *m*	radiador *m*
radiatore *m*	esquentador *m*	radiador *m*
radio *f*	rádio	radio
ravanello; radice *f*	rabanete *m*	rábano
straccio	trapo	trapo
ferrovia	caminho de ferro; estrada de ferro (Br.)	ferrocarril *m*
stazione *f*	estação *f*	estación *f* de ferrocarril

guida ferroviaria	guia dos caminhos
	  de ferro
		guía de ferro-
		  carriles

English	*French*	*German*
rain	pluie *f*	Regen *m*
rain, to	pleuvoir	regnen
raincoat	imperméable *m*	Regenmantel *m*
raise (lift up), to	lever	heben
raisin	raisin *m* sec	Rosine *f*
rake (tool)	râteau *m*	Harke *f*
rancid	rance	ranzig
range (mountain)	chaîne *f*	Bergkette *f*
rapid (adj.)	rapide	schnell
rare (not common)	rare	selten
rare (meat)	saignant	nicht durchgebraten
rash (med.)	éruption *f*	Hautausschlag *m*
raspberry	framboise *f*	Himbeere *f*
rat	rat *m*	Ratte *f*
rate (exchang-)	cours *m* (du change)	Kurs *m*
rate (price)	tarif *m*	Gebühr *f*
rather (on the other hand)	plutôt	vielmehr
rather (quite)	assez	ziemlich
rather (I would-)	j'aimerais mieux	ich möchte lieber
raw	cru	roh
rayon	rayonne *f*	Kunstseide *f*
razor	rasoir *m*	Rasiermesser *n*
razor (safety)	rasoir *m* de sûreté	Rasierapparat *m*
razor blade	lame *f* de rasoir	Rasierklinge *f*
reach (arrive at), to	arriver (à)	erreichen
reach (extend to), to	s'étendre à	reichen
read (p.p.)	lu	gelesen
read, to	lire	lesen
reader (person)	lecteur *m*	Leser *m*
ready	prêt	bereit; fertig
ready made	confectionné	Konfektion *f*
real (actual)	réel	wirklich
real estate	biens-fonds *mpl*	Grundeigentum *n*
realize (recognize)	se rendre compte de	einsehen
really (actually)	vraiment	wirklich
really (truly)	vraiment	wirklich
rear (adj.)	d'arrière	hinter...

Italian	*Portuguese*	*Spanish*
pioggia	chuva	lluvia
piovere	chover	llover
impermeabile *m*	impermeável *m*	impermeable *m*
sollevare	levantar	levantar
uva passa	passa	pasa
rastrello	ancinho	rastrillo
rancido	rançoso; râncido	rancio
catena	cordilheira	cordillera
rapido	rápido	rápido
raro	raro	raro
al sangue	mal-passado; sangrento	poco asado; medio crudo
eruzione *f*	erupção *f*	erupción *f*
lampone *m*	framboesa	frambuesa
topo	rato	rata
cambio	câmbio	tipo de cambio
tariffa	taxa	tarifa
piuttosto	antes	más bien
abbastanza	bastante	bastante
preferirei	preferiria	preferiría
crudo	cru	crudo
raion *m*	rayon *m*	rayón *m*
rasoio	navalha de barba	navaja de afeitar; rasurador (Mex.)
rasoio di sicurezza	gilete *f*	máquina de afeitar
lametta (da rasoio)	lâmina de gilete	hojita de afeitar
arrivare (a)	chegar (à)	llegar (a)
estendersi fino a	estender-se	extenderse
letto	lido	leído
leggere	ler	leer
lettore *m*	leitor *m*	lector *m*
pronto	pronto	listo
confezionato	feito	hecho
vero	real	real
beni *mpl* immobili	bens *mpl* imóveis	bienes *mpl* raíces
rendersi conto di	dar-se conta de	darse cuenta de
in realtà	na realidade	realmente
veramente	realmente	de veras
di dietro	traseiro	posterior

English	*French*	*German*
rear view mirror	rétroviseur *m*	Rückspiegel *m*
reason (cause)	raison *f*	Grund *m*
reasonable (price)	raisonnable	preiswert
rebate (n.)	remise *f*	Rabatt *m*
receipt	reçu *m*	Quittung *f*
receipt, to	acquitter	quittieren
receive, to	recevoir	bekommen
received (p.p.)	reçu *m*	bekommen
recent	récent	neu
recently	récemment	neulich; kürzlich
recipe	recette *f*	Rezept *n*
recite, to	réciter	vortragen
recognize, to	reconnaître	erkennen
recommend, to	recommander	empfehlen
recommendation	recommendation *f*	Empfehlung *f*
record (phonog.)	disque *m*	Schallplatte *f*
record player	tourne-disque *m*	Grammophon *n*; Plattenspieler *m*
recover (get back)	récupérer	zurückbekommen
recover (get well)	se rétablir	sich erholen
red	rouge	rot
redcap (porter)	porteur *m*	Gepäckträger *m*
Red Cross	Croix *f* Rouge	Rotes Kreuz *n*
red-haired	roux, rousse	rothaarig
red wine	vin *m* rouge	Rotwein *m*
refreshment stand	buvette *f*	Büfett *n*
refreshments	rafraîchissements *mpl*	Erfrischungen *fpl*
refrigerator	réfrigérateur *m*; frigo *m*	Eisschrank *m*; Kühlschrank *m*
refund	remboursement *m*	Rückzahlung *f*
refund, to	rembourser	zurückzahlen
refuse, to	refuser	verweigern
regarding (about)	au sujet de	in Bezug auf
region	région *f*	Gegend *f*
register (a letter), to	recommander	einschreiben
register (at a hotel)	s'inscrire	einschreiben
regret, to	regretter	bedauern
regular (ordinary)	régulier	gewöhnlich
reject, to	rejeter	ablehnen

Italian	*Portuguese*	*Spanish*
specchio retrovisivo	espelho retrovisor	retrovisor *m*
ragione *f*	razão *f*	razón *f*
modico	módico; razoável	módico
rimborso	desconto	rebaja
ricevuta	recibo	recibo
dare una ricevuta	passar recibo	poner el recibí
ricevere	receber	recibir
ricevuto	recebido	recibido
recente	recente	reciente
recentemente	recentemente	recientemente
ricetta	receita	receta
recitare	recitar	recitar
riconoscere	reconhecer	reconocer
raccomandare	recomendar	recomendar
raccomandazione *f*	recomendação *f*	recomendación *f*
disco	disco	disco
giradischi *m*	fonógrafo; toca-discos *m*	fonógrafo; tocadiscos *m*
riavere; ricuperare	recuperar	recobrar
guarire	restabelecer-se	reponerse
rosso	vermelho	rojo; colorado
facchino	bagageiro; môço; carregador (Br.)	mozo; cargador (Mex.)
Croce *f* Rossa	Cruz *f* Vermelha	Cruz *f* Roja
dai capelli rossi	ruivo	pelirrojo
vino rosso	vinho tinto	vino tinto
buffet *m*	bufete *m*	cantina
rinfreschi *mpl*	refrescos *mpl*	refrescos *mpl*
frigorifero	refrigerador *m*; geladeira (Br.)	frigorífico; nevera (Mex.)
rimborso	reembôlso	reembolso
rimborsare	reembolsar	reembolsar
rifiutare	recusar	rehusar
riguardo a	a respeito de	acerca de
regione *f*	região *f*	región *f*
raccomandare	regist(r)ar	certificar
iscriversi sul registro	registrar-se	firmar el registro
dispiacersi	sentir	sentir
ordinario	regular	regular
rigettare	rejeitar	rechazar

English	*French*	*German*
relate (tell), to	raconter	erzählen
relative (kinsman)	parent *m*	Verwandte *m, f*
release (let go of), to	lâcher	freilassen
reliable	sûr	zuverlässig
religion	religion *f*	Religion *f*
rely on, to	se fier à	sich verlassen auf (acc.)
remain (be left), to	rester	übrigbleiben
remain (stay behind)	rester	bleiben
remark, to	faire une observation	bemerken
remarkable	remarquable	bemerkenswert
remedy (n.)	remède *m*	Heilmittel *n*
remember, to	se souvenir de	sich erinnern an (acc.)
remind, to	rappeler	erinnern
remove, to	enlever	beseitigen
rent	loyer *m*	Miete *f*
rent, to	louer	mieten
repair, to	réparer	reparieren
repairs	réparations *fpl*	Reparatur *f*
repeat, to	répéter	wiederholen
Repeat, please!	Répétez, s'il vous plaît.	Bitte, wiederholen Sie!
reply	réponse *f*	Antwort *f*
reply, to	répondre	antworten
reporter	reporter *m*	Berichterstatter *m*
republic	république *f*	Republik *f*
request	demande *f*	Bitte *f*
request, to	demander	bitten; ersuchen
require, to	exiger	fordern; verlangen
rescue, to	sauver	retten
research	recherche(s) *f(pl)*	Forschung *f*
resemble, to	ressembler à	gleichen; ähneln
reservation (advance order)	réservation *f*	Vorbestellung *f*
reserve (order in advance), to	réserver	reservieren
reserved seat	place *f* réservée	der belegte (reservierte) Platz
reside, to	demeurer	wohnen
residence	domicile *m*	Wohnort *m*

Italian	*Portuguese*	*Spanish*
raccontare	relatar	contar; relatar
parente *m*	parente *m*	pariente *m*
rilasciare	soltar	soltar
sicuro	digno de confiança	digno de confianza
religione *f*	religião *f*	religión *f*
confidare	confiar em	confiar en
rimanere	restar	quedar
rimanere; restare	ficar	quedarse
osservare	fazer uma observação	observar
straordinario	notável	notable
rimedio	remédio	remedio
ricordarsi di	lembrar-se de	acordarse de
ricordare	lembrar	recordar
rimuovere	afastar	quitar
pigione *f*; affitto	renda; aluguel *m*	alquiler *m*; renta (Mex.)
affittare	arrendar; alugar	alquilar; rentar (Mex.)
riparare	consertar	reparar; componer
riparazioni *fpl*	conserto	reparaciones *fpl*
ripetere	repetir	repetir
Per favore, ripeta!	Faça favor de repetir!	¡Repita, por favor!
risposta	resposta	respuesta
rispondere	responder	responder
reporter *m*	repórter *m*	repórter *m*; reportero
repubblica	república	república
richiesta	pedido	petición *f*
richiedere	solicitar; pedir	pedir
esigere	exigir	exigir
salvare	salvar	salvar
indagine *f*; ricerca	investigação *f*	investigación *f*
assomigliare a	assemelhar-se a	asemejarse a
prenotazione *f*	reservação *f*	reservación *f*
riservare; prenotare	reservar	reservar
posto riservato	assento reservado	asiento reservado
dimorare	morar	morar; residir
domicilio	domicílio; residência	domicilio

English	*French*	*German*
resident (n.)	habitant *m*	Einwohner *m*
resign, to	démissionner	zurücktreten
resist, to	résister à	widerstehen
resort (spa)	station *f* thermale	Kurort *m*
resort (summer)	station *f* d'été	Sommerfrische *f*
respect, to	respecter	achten
respond, to	répondre	antworten
rest (remainder)	reste *m*	Rest *m*
rest (repose)	repos *m*	Ruhe *f*
rest, to	se reposer	sich ausruhen
rest room	cabinet *m* d'aisance, toilette *f*	Toilette *f*; Klosett *n*; Abort *m*
restaurant	restaurant *m*	Restaurant *n*
result (n.)	résultat *m*	Ergebnis *n*
retail	détail *m*	Einzelhandel *m*
return	retour *m*	Rückkehr *f*
return (go back), to	retourner	zurückkehren
return (give back), to	rendre	zurückgeben
return ticket	billet *m* de retour	Rückfahrkarte *f*
return trip	voyage *m* de retour	Rückfahrt *f*
review (go over), to	revoir	wiederholen
revive, to	ressusciter	wiederbeleben
reward, to	récompenser	belohnen
Rhine (river)	le Rhin	der Rhein
Rhone (river)	le Rhône	die Rhone
rhubarb	rhubarbe *f*	Rhabarber *m*
rib	côte *f*	Rippe *f*
ribbon	ruban *m*	Band *n*
rice	riz *m*	Reis *m*
rich (adj.)	riche	reich
ride (n.)	promenade *f*	Fahrt *f*
ride (in car), to	aller en voiture	fahren
right (vs. left)	droit	recht
right (correct)	correct	richtig
right, to be	avoir raison	recht haben
right away	tout de suite	sofort; gerade jetzt
right of way, to have the	avoir la priorité	Vorfahrt haben

Italian	*Portuguese*	*Spanish*
residente *m*	residente *m*	residente *m*
dimettersi	demitir-se de	dimitir
resistere a	resistir	resistir
stazione *f* climatica	estação *f* de águas	balneario
stazione *f* estiva	estação de veraneio	estación *f* de veraneo
rispettare	respeitar	respetar
rispondere	responder	responder
resto	resto	resto
riposo	repouso	descanso
riposarsi	repousar; descansar	descansar
gabinetto	toalete *m*	lavabo; retrete *m*
ristorante *m*; trattoria	restaurante *m*	restaurante *m*; restorán *m*
risultato	resultado	resultado
vendita al minuto	varejo	venta al por menor
ritorno	volta	regreso; vuelta
ritornare	voltar; regressar	regresar; volver
rendere	devolver	devolver
biglietto di ritorno	bilhete *m* de volta	billete *m* de vuelta
viaggio di ritorno	viagem *f* de volta	viaje *m* de vuelta
rivedere	rever	repasar
risuscitare	ressuscitar	resucitar
ricompensare	recompensar	recompensar
il Reno	o Reno	el Rin
il Rodano	o Ródano	el Ródano
rabarbaro	ruibarbo	ruibarbo
costola	costela	costilla
nastro	fita	cinta
riso	arroz *m*	arroz *m*
ricco	rico	rico
passeggiata	passeio	paseo
andare in automobile	passear	pasear en auto
destro	direito	derecho
corretto	correto	correcto
aver ragione	ter razão	tener razón
proprio ora; subito	agora mesmo	ahora mismo; ahorita
aver la precedenza	ter o direito de precedência	tener el derecho de tránsito

English	*French*	*German*
rim (wheel)	jante *f*	Felge *f*
ring (jewelry)	bague *f*; anneau *m*	Ring *m*
ring, to	sonner	klingeln
ringworm	teigne *f*	Flechte *f*
rinse, to	rincer	ausspülen
rip, to	déchirer	abreissen
ripe (vs. green)	mûr	reif
river	rivière *f*; fleuve *m*	Fluss *m*
road	route *f*	Strasse *f*
road map	carte *f* routière	Autokarte *f*
roast, to	rôtir	braten
roast beef	rosbif *m*	Rinderbraten *m*
roast pork	rôti *m* de porc	Schweinebraten *m*
roast veal	rôti *m* de veau	Kalbsbraten *m*
roast(ed) (adj.)	rôti	gebraten
rob, to	voler	berauben
robber	voleur *m*	Räuber *m*
robe (gown)	robe *f* de chambre	Robe *f*; Schlafrock *m*
rock (cliff)	roc *m*	Felsen *m*
rocket	fusée *f*	Rakete *f*
rocking chair	chaise *f* à bascule	Schaukelstuhl *m*
roll (bread)	petit pain *m*	Brötchen *n*
roll (of film)	rouleau *m*; bobine *f*	Rollfilm *m*
Rome	Rome *f*	Rom *n*
roof	toit *m*	Dach *n*
room (hotel)	chambre *f*	Zimmer *n*
room (house)	pièce *f*	Zimmer *n*
room (space)	place *f*	Raum *m*
roommate	camarade *m, f* de chambre	Zimmerkollege
room steward (ship)	steward *m*	Steward *m*
root (n.)	racine *f*	Wurzel *f*
rope	corde *f*	Seil *n*; Strick *m*
rosary	rosaire *m*	Rosenkranz *m*
rose (flower)	rose *f*	Rose *f*
rot, to	pourrir	faulen

Italian	*Portuguese*	*Spanish*
cerchione *m*	aro	aro
anello	anel *m*	anillo; sortija
suonare	soar	sonar
tigna	tinha	tiña
risciacquare	enxaguar	enjuagar
strappare	rasgar	rasgar
maturo	maduro	maduro
fiume *m*	rio	río
strada	caminho; estrada	camino; carretera
carta stradale	mapa *m* turístico; mapa de estradas	mapa *m* de carretera; mapa itinerario
arrostire	assar	asar
arrosto di manzo; rosbif *m*	rosbife *m*; carne *f* assada	rosbif *m*; carne *f* asada
arrosto di maiale	carne *f* de porco assado	carne de puerco asada
arrosto di vitello	carne de vitela assada	carne de ternera asada
arrostito	assado	asado
rubare; derubare	roubar	robar
ladro	ladrão	ladrón *m*
veste *f* da camera	roupão	bata
roccia	rocha	roca
razzo	foguete *m*	cohete *m*
sedia a dondolo	cadeira de balanço	mecedora
panino	pãozinha	panecillo; bolillo (Mex.)
rotolo di pellicola	rôlo	rollo
Roma	Roma	Roma
tetto	teto	techo
camera	quarto	cuarto
stanza	quarto; peça	pieza
spazio *m*	espaço	espacio
compagno (a) di camera	companheiro (a) de quarto	compañero (a) de cuarto
cameriere *m* (di bordo)	camaroteiro	camarero
radice *f*	raiz *f*	raíz *f*
corda	corda	cuerda
rosario	rosário	rosario
rosa	rosa	rosa
marcire	apodrecer	pudrirse

English	*French*	*German*
rotten (decayed) (adj.)	pourri	faul
rouge	rouge *m*	Rouge *n*
rough (harsh)	dur	grob
rough (sea)	agitée	stürmisch
rough (uneven)	rude	rauh
round (adj.)	rond	rund
round trip	voyage *m* d'aller et retour	Hin- und **Rückfahrt** *f*
route	route *f*	**Reiseroute** *f*
row (line)	rang *m*	Reihe *f*
row, to	ramer	rudern
rowboat	bateau *m* à **rames**	Ruderboot *n*
royal	royal	königlich
rub, to	frotter	reiben
rubber	caout**chouc** *m*	Gummi *m*
rubber band	élastique *m*	Gummiband *n*
rubber heels	talons *mpl* en caoutchouc	**Gummiabsätze** *mpl*
rubbers	caout**choucs** *mpl*	**Gummischuhe** *mpl*
ruby	rubis *m*	Rubin *m*
rude (incivil)	impoli	grob
rug	tapis *m*	Teppich *m*
ruins (n.)	ruine *f*	Ruine *f*
rule (govern), to	gouver**ner**	herrschen
rum	rhum *m*	Rum *m*
run (flow), to	couler	fliessen
run (sprint), to	courir	laufen
running water	eau *f* **courante**	fliessendes **Wasser** *n*
runway (plane)	piste *f*	Startbahn *f*
Russia	la Russie	Russland *n*
Russian (adj.)	russe	russisch
rusty	rouillé	rostig
rye bread	pain *m* de **seigle**	Roggenbrot *n*
rye (grain)	seigle *m*	**Roggen** *m*
saboteur	saboteur *m*	Sabo**teur** *m*
sack (bag)	sac *m*	Sack *m*
sad	triste	traurig

Italian	*Portuguese*	*Spanish*
marcio	podre	podrido
rossetto	rouge *m*	colorete *m*
aspro	grosseiro	grosero
agitato	agitado	agitado
ruvido	áspero	áspero
rotondo	redondo	redondo
viaggio d'andata e ritorno	viagem *f* de ida e volta	viaje *m* de ida y vuelta; viaje redondo (Mex.)
itinerario	caminho; rota	ruta
fila	fila	fila
remare	remar	remar
barca a remi	bote *m* de remos	bote *m* de remo
reale; regale	real	real
frizionare	esfregar	frotar
gomma	borracha	caucho; goma
elastico	elástico	elástico; liga de goma (Mex.)
tacchi *mpl* di gomma	tacões *mpl* de borracha	tacones *mpl* de caucho
galosce *mpl*	galochas *fpl*	chanclos *mpl*; zapatos de hule (Mex.)
rubino	rubi *m*	rubí *m*
sgarbato	rude; grosseiro	grosero
tappeto	tapête *m*	alfombra; tapete *m*
rovina	ruínas *fpl*	ruinas *fpl*
governare	governar	gobernar
rum *m*	rum *m*	ron *m*
scorrere	correr	correr
correre	correr	correr
acqua corrente	água corrente	agua corriente
pista (d'atterraggio)	pista	pista (de aterrizaje)
la Russia	a Rússia	Rusia
russo	russo	ruso
rugginoso	enferrujado	oxidado
pane *m* di segala	pão de centeio	pan *m* de centeno
segala	centeio	centeno
sabotatore *m*	sabotador *m*	saboteador *m*
sacco	saco	saco
triste	triste	triste

English	*French*	*German*
saddle (riding)	selle *f*	Sattel *m*
sadness	tristesse *f*	Traurigkeit *f*
safe (no risk)	sûr	sicher
safe (unharmed)	sauf (*f* sauve)	heil
safe (for valuables)	coffre-fort *m*	Geldschrank *m*
safe and sound	sain et sauf	frisch und gesund
safety belt	ceinture *f* de sûreté	Sicherheitsgurt *m*
safety matches	allumettes *fpl* suédoises	Streichhölzer *npl*
safety pin	épingle *f* de sûreté	Sicherheitsnadel *f*
safety razor	rasoir *m* de sûreté	Rasierapparat *m*
said (p.p.)	dit	gesagt
sail (canvas)	voile *f*	Segel *n*
sail (set-), to	partir	abfahren
sailor	marin *m*	Matrose *m*
saint	saint (e) *m, f*	Heilige *m*
salad	salade *f*	Salat *m*
salary	appointements *mpl*	Gehalt *n*
sale	vente *f*	Verkauf *m*
salesman	vendeur *m*	Verkäufer *m*
sales slip	facture *f*	Verkaufszettel *m*
salmon	saumon *m*	Lachs *m*
salt (n.)	sel *m*	Salz *n*
salt shaker	salière *f*	Salzfass *m*
salt water	eau *f* salée	Seewasser *n*
salty	salé	salzig
Salvador (El-)	le Salvador	El Salvador
same	même	derselbe, etc.
same (equal)	égal	gleich
sample (n.)	échantillon *m*	Muster *n*
sand	sable *m*	Sand *m*
sandal	sandale *f*	Sandale *f*
sandpaper	papier *m* de verre	Sandpapier *n*
sandwich	sandwich *m*	Sandwich *n*
sanitary belt	ceinture *f* hygiénique	Bindegürtel *m*

Italian	*Portuguese*	*Spanish*
sella	sela	silla de montar
tristezza	tristeza	tristeza
sicuro	seguro	seguro
salvo	são	salvo
cassetta di sicurezza; cassaforte *f*	cofre *m*; caixa de segurança	cofre *m*; caja fuerte
sano e salvo	são e salvo	sano y salvo
cintura di sicurezza	cinto	cinturón *m*
svedesi *mpl*	fósforos *mpl* de segurança	fósforos *mpl* de seguridad
spillo di sicurezza	alfinête *m* de segurança	imperdible *m*
rasoio di sicurezza	gilete *f*	maquinilla de afeitar
detto	dito	dicho
vela	vela	vela
imbarcarsi	partir	zarpar; salir
marinaio	marinheiro	marinero
santo	santo	santo
insalata	salada	ensalada
stipendio	ordenado; salário	sueldo
vendita	venda	venta; barata (Mex.)
venditore	vendedor *m*	vendedor *m*
scontrino di vendita	recibo de compra	factura
salmone *m*	salmão	salmón *m*
sale *m*	sal *m*	sal *f*
saliera	saleiro	salero
acqua salata	água salgada	agua salada
salato	salgado	salado
il Salvador	o Salvador	el Salvador
stesso	mesmo	mismo
uguale	igual	igual
campione *m*	amostra	muestra
sabbia	areia	arena
sandalo	sandália	sandalia; guarache *m* (Mex.)
cartavetrata	lixa	papel *m* de lija
panino imbottito; sandwich *m*	sanduíche *m*	sandwich *m*
cintura igienica	cintinha	faja sanitaria; cinturón *m* sanitario

English	*French*	*German*
sanitary napkin	serviette *f* hygiénique	Binde *f*
sapphire	saphir *m*	Saphir *m*
sardine	sardine *f*	Sardine *f*
satellite (n.)	satellite *m*	Satellit *m*
satin	satin *m*	Satin *m*
satisfactory	satisfai**sant**	befriedigend
satisfied	satis**fait**	zufrieden
satisfy, to	satis**faire**	befriedigen
Saturday	samedi *m*	Samstag *m*; **Sonnabend** *n.*
sauce	sauce *f*	Sosse *f*
saucepan	casserole *f*	Schmorpfanne *f*
saucer	soucoupe *f*	Untertasse *f*
sauerkraut	choucroute *f*	Sauerkraut *m*
sausage	saucisse *f*	Wurst *f*
save (rescue), to	sauver	retten
save (store up), to	épargner	sparen
savings bank	Caisse *f* d'**épargne**	Sparkasse *f*
saw, to	scier	sägen
saw (tool)	scie *f*	Säge *f*
say, to	dire	sagen
say good-bye, to	faire ses a**dieux**	sich ver**abschieden**
scab	croûte *f*	Schorf *m*
scales (to weigh)	balance *f*	Waage *f*
scar	cicatrice *f*	Narbe *f*
scarce	rare	selten; rar
scarcely	à **peine**	kaum
scare, to	effrayer	erschrecken
scarf (men)	foulard *m*	Halstuch *n*
scarf (women)	écharpe *f*	Schal *m*
scarlet fever	scarlatine *f*	Scharlachfieber *n*
scenery	paysage *m*	Landschaft *f*
scholar (savant)	érudit *m*	Gelehrte *m*
scholarship (grant)	bourse *f*	Stipendium *n*
school	école *f*	Schule *f*
science	science *f*	Wissenschaft *f*
scientific	scientifique	wissenschaftlich
scientist	savant *m*	Wissenschaftler *m*

Italian	*Portuguese*	*Spanish*
pannolino igienico	toalhinha higiênica	toalla sanitaria (higiénica)
zaffiro	safira	zafiro
sardina	sardinha	sardina
satellite *m*	satélite *m*	satélite *m*
raso	cetim *m*	raso
soddisfacente	satisfatório	satisfactorio
soddisfatto	satisfeito	satisfecho
soddisfare	satisfazer	satisfacer
sabato	sábado	sábado
salsa	môlho	salsa
casseruola	caçarola	cacerola
piattino	pires *m*	platillo
crauti *mpl*	chucrute *m*	chucruta
salsiccia	chouriço; lingüiça	salchicha; chorizo
salvare	salvar	salvar
risparmiare	poupar	ahorrar
Cassa di Risparmio	Caixa-econômica	Banco de Ahorros
segare	serrar	serrar
sega	serra	sierra
dire	dizer	decir
dire addio	despedir-se de	despedirse de
crosta	crosta	costra
bilancia	balança	balanza
cicatrice *f*	cicatriz *f*	cicatriz *f*
scarso	escasso	escaso
appena	mal; apenas	apenas
spaventare	espantar	espantar
sciarpa; foulard *m*	cachecol *m*	bufanda
sciarpa	écharpe *f*	chalina; pañuelo
scarlattina	escarlatina	escarlata
paesaggio	paisagem *f*	paisaje *m*
studioso	sábio	sabio
borsa di studio	bôlsa de estudos	beca
scuola	escola	escuela
scienza	ciência	ciencia
scientifico	científico	científico
scienziato	cientista	científico

English	*French*	*German*
scissors	ciseaux *mpl*	Schere *f*
scold, to	gronder	schelten
Scotch (adj.)	écossais	schottisch
Scotch tape	ruban *m* adhésif; Scotch *m*	Klebestreifen *m*
Scotland	l' Écosse *f*	Schottland *n*
scrambled **eggs**	oeufs *mpl* brouillés	Rühreier *npl*
scratch	égratignure *f*	Kratzwunde *f*
scratch, to	gratter	kratzen
scream, to	crier	schreien
screen (movie)	écran *m*	Leinwand *f*
screen (partition)	paravent *m*	Wandschirm *m*
screw (n.)	vis *f*	Schraube *f*
screwdriver	tournevis *m*	Schraubenzieher *m*
scrub, to	frotter	scheuern
sculptor	sculpteur *m*	Bildhauer *m*
sea	mer *f*	See *f*; Meer *n*
seafood	fruits *mpl* de **mer**	Fischgericht *n*
sea level	niveau *m* de la **mer**	Meeresspiegel *m*
seal (animal)	phoque *m*	Seehund *m*
seal (mark)	sceau *m*	Siegel *n*
seal, to	sceller	besiegeln
seam	couture *f*	Naht *f*
search (hunt) (n.)	recherche *f*	Suche *f*
search (for), to	chercher	suchen
seasickness	mal *m* de **mer**	Seekrankheit *f*
season (year)	saison *f*	Jahreszeit *f*
season (theat.)	saison *f*	Saison *f*
season (food), to	assaisonner	würzen
seasoned (food)	assaisonné	gewürzt
seat (in a conveyance)	place *f*	Platz *m*
seat (theat.)	place *f*	Platz *m*
seated (p.p.)	assis	sitzend
second (adj.)	deuxième	der zweite, etc.
second (n.)	seconde *f*	Sekunde *f*
second floor (on the)	au premier	im ersten **Stock**
second-hand (used)	d'occasion	gebraucht
secretary	secrétaire *m, f*	Sekretär *m*: Sekretärin *f*

Italian	*Portuguese*	*Spanish*
forbici *fpl*	tesoura	tijeras *fpl*
rimproverare	ralhar	regañar
scozzese	escocês	escocés
nastro autoadesivo	fita durex	**cin**ta adhe**siva**
la Scozia	a Escócia	Escocia
uova *fpl* strapazzate	ovos *mpl* mexidos	huevos *mpl* revueltos
graffio	arranhão	arañazo; rasguño
graffiare	arranhar	rascar
gridare	gritar	gritar; chillar
schermo	pantalha	pantalla
paravento	biombo	biombo
vite *f*	parafuso	tornillo
cacciavite *m*	**chave** *f* de parafuso	destornilla**dor** *m*
ripulire	esfregar	fregar
scultore *m*	escultor *m*	escultor *m*
mare *m*	mar *m*	mar *m* or *f*
pesce e frutti	mariscos *mpl*	mariscos *mpl*
di mare		
livello del mare	nível *m* do mar	nivel *m* del mar
foca	foca	foca
sigillo	sêlo	sello
suggellare	selar	sellar
cucitura	costura	costura
ricerca	busca	búsqueda
ricercare	procurar; bus**car**	buscar
mal *m* di mare	enjôo *m*	mareo
stagione *f*	estação *f*	estación *f*
stagione *f*	temporada	temporada
condire	temperar	condimentar
condito	temperado	sazonado
posto; sedile *m*	assento	asiento
località; **posto**	localidade *f*	localidad *f*
seduto	sentado	sentado
secondo	segundo	segundo
secondo	segundo	segundo
al primo piano	no primeiro an**dar**	en el primer piso
usato	de segunda mão	de segunda mano
segretario, -a	secretário, -a	secretario, -a

English	*French*	*German*
sedative (n.)	sédatif *m*	Sedativ *n*
see, to	voir	sehen
See you later!	À bientôt!	Auf Wiedersehen!
seed (n.)	graine *f*	Samen *m*
seem, to	sembler	scheinen
seen (p.p.)	vu	gesehen
Seine (river)	la Seine	die Seine
seize, to	saisir	(er)greifen
seldom	rarement	selten
select, to	choisir	wählen
selection	choix *m*	Auswahl *f*
sell, to	vendre	verkaufen
senate	sénat *m*	Senat *m*
senator	sénateur *m*	Senator *m*
send, to	envoyer	schicken; senden
send a telegram, to	envoyer une dépêche	ein Telegramm aufgeben
send back (return), to	renvoyer	zurückgeben
send for, to	faire venir	kommen lassen
Send me...	Envoyez-moi...	Schicken Sie mir...
sender (on mail)	expéditeur *m*	Absender *m*
sensible	sensé	vernünftig
sensitive	sensible	empfindlich
sent (p.p.)	envoyé	geschickt
sentence (gram.)	phrase *f*	Satz *m*
separate, to	séparer	trennen
September	septembre *m*	September *m*
sergeant	sergent *m*	Feldwebel *m*
series	série *f*	Reihe *f*
serious	sérieux, -euse	ernst
sermon	sermon *m*	Predigt *f*
servant (house)	domestique *mf*	Diener *m*
serve, to	servir	dienen (dat.)
service	service *m*	Bedienung *f*
set (hair), to	mettre en plis	einlegen
set (put), to	mettre	setzen
set sail, to	prendre la mer	auslaufen
set the clock, to	régler la pendule	die Uhr stellen

Italian	*Portuguese*	*Spanish*
calmante *m*	sedativo; calmante *m*	sedativo; calmante *m*
vedere	ver	ver
Arrivederci!	Até logo!	¡Hasta luego!
seme *m*	semente *f*	semilla
sembrare	parecer	parecer
visto	visto	visto
la Senna	a Sena	el Sena
afferrare	agarrar; pegar	agarrar
raramente	raramente	rara vez
scegliere	escolher	escoger
selezione *f*	seleção *f*	selección *f*
vendere	vender	vender
senato	senado	senado
senatore *m*	senador *m*	senador *m*
mandare; inviare	mandar	mandar; enviar
mandare un tele-gramma	passar um telegrama	poner un telegrama
rendere	devolver	devolver
mandare a chiamare	mandar chamar	mandar llamar; enviar por
Mi mandi...	Mande-me...	¡Mándeme...!
mittente *m*	remetente *m*	remitente *m*
sensato	sensato	sensato
sensibile	sensível	sensible
mandato	mandado	mandado
frase *f*	frase *f*	frase *f*
separare	separar	separar
settembre *m*	setembro	septiembre *m*
sergente *m*	sargento	sargento
serie *f*	série *f*	serie *f*
serio	sério	serio
sermone *m*	sermão	sermón *m*
domestico, -a	criado, -a; empregado, -a (Br.)	criado, -a
servire	servir	servir
servizio	serviço	servicio
mettere in piega	pentear	marcar
mettere	pôr	poner
salpare	zarpar	zarpar
mettere a punto	acertar o relógio	poner el reloj

English	*French*	*German*
set the table, to	mettre la table	den Tisch decken
seven	sept	sieben
seven hundred	sept cents	siebenhundert
seventeen	dix-sept	siebzehn
seventh	septième	der siebte, etc.
seventy	soixante-dix	siebzig
several	plusieurs	einige; mehrere
several times	plusieurs fois	einige Male
Seville	Séville *f*	Sevilla *n*
sew, to	coudre	nähen
sewer (drain)	égout *m*	Kloake *f*
sewing machine	machine *f* à coudre	Nähmaschine *f*
shade (color)	nuance *f*	Farbton *m*; Nuance *f*
shade (lamp)	abat-jour *m*	Lampenschirm *m*
shade (shadow)	ombre *f*	Schatten *m*
shade (window)	store *m*	Rouleau *n*
shake, to	secouer	schütteln
shake hands, to	donner une poignée de main à	sich die Hände schütteln
shallow	peu profond	seicht
shampoo (n.)	shampooing *m*	Shampoo *n*
shape (n.)	forme *f*	Form *f*
share (part) (n.)	part *f*	Anteil *m*
share (stock)	action *f*	Aktie *f*
share, to	partager	sich teilen
shark	requin *m*	Hai(fisch) *m*
sharp (exactly)	précis	punkt
sharp (not dull)	aigu	scharf
sharp (pain)	cuisant	schneidend
sharpen, to	aiguiser	schärfen
shave (oneself), to	(se) raser	(sich) rasieren
shaving brush	blaireau *m*	Rasierpinsel *m*
shaving cream	crème *f* à raser	Rasierkrem *m*
shaving soap	savon *m* à barbe	Rasierseife *f*
shaving stick	bâton *m* de savon pour la barbe	Rasierseife *f*
shawl	châle *m*	Schal *m*

Italian	*Portuguese*	*Spanish*
apparecchiare la tavola	pôr a mesa	poner la mesa
sette	sete	siete
settecento	setecentos	setecientos
diciassette	dezessete	diez y siete
settimo	sétimo	séptimo
settanta	setenta	setenta
parecchi	vários	varios
molte volte	várias vezes	varias veces
Siviglia	Sevilha	Sevilla
cucire	costurar; coser	coser
fogna	esgôto	albañal *m*; cloaca
macchina da cucire	máquina de costura	máquina de coser
sfumatura	matiz *m*	matiz *m*
paralume *m*	abajur *m*	pantalla de lámpara
ombra	sombra	sombra
tendina	estore *m*	estor *m*
scuotere	sacudir	sacudir
dare la mano	dar um apêrto de mãos	dar la mano
poco profondo	pouco profundo	poco profundo
shampoo *m*	xampu *m*	champú *m*
forma	forma	forma
parte *f*	parte *f*	parte *f*
azione *f*	ação *f*	acción *f*
condividere	compartilhar	compartir
pescecane *m*	tubarão	tiburón *m*
preciso	em ponto	en punto
affilato	afiado	afilado
acuto	agudo	agudo
affilare	afiar	afilar
far (si) la barba; radersi	fazer a barba; barbear (-se)	afeitar (se); rasurar (se) (Mex.)
pennello da barba	pincel *m* de barba	brocha de afeitar
crema per la barba	creme de barbear	crema de afeitar
sapone *m* da barba	sabão de barba	jabón *m* para afeitarse
stick *m* per barba	estique *m* de barbear	jabón *m* de afeitar en barrita
scialle *m*	xale *m*	chal *m*; rebozo (Mex.)

English	*French*	*German*
she	elle	sie
sheep	mouton *m*	Schaf *n*
sheet (bed)	drap *m*	Bettuch *n*
sheet (paper)	feuille *f*	Bogen *m*
shelf	rayon *m*	Regal *n*
shell (n.)	coquille *f*	Schale *f*
shelter (n.)	abri *m*	Schutz *m*
sherbet	sorbet *m*	Sorbett *n*
sherry (wine)	xérès *m*	Sherry *m*
shine (gleam), to	briller	scheinen
shine (shoes), to	cirer	putzen
Shine?	Les souliers, monsieur?	Schuhe putzen?
ship	navire *m*	Schiff *n*
ship, to	expédier	senden; schicken
shipment	envoi *m*	Sendung *f*
shipyard	chantier *m*	Schiffswerft *f*
shirt	chemise *f*	Hemd *n*
shock absorber	amortisseur *m*	Stossdämpfer *m*
shoe	soulier *m*	Schuh *m*
shoehorn	chausse-pied *m*	Schuhlöffel *m*
shoelace	lacet *m*	Schnürsenkel *m*
shoemaker	cordonnier *m*	Schuhmacher *m*
shoe polish	cirage *m*	Schuhkrem *m*
shoe store	magasin *m* de chaussures	Schuhgeschäft *n*
shoe tree	embauchoir *m*	Schuhleisten *m*
shoot (fire at), to	tirer	schiessen
shop (store)	boutique *f*	Geschäft *n*
shop, to	faire des courses *fpl*	einkaufen gehen
shop window	vitrine *f*	Schaufenster *n*
shore (ocean)	bord *m*	Strand *m*
shore (river)	rive *f*	Ufer *n*
short	court	kurz

Italian	*Portuguese*	*Spanish*
lei	ela	ella
pecora	ovelha	oveja
lenzuolo	lençol *m*	sábana
foglio	fôlha	hoja
scaffale *m*; **mensola**	prateleira	estante *m*; anaquel *m*
conchiglia	concha	concha
rifugio	abrigo	abrigo
sorbetto	sorvete *m*	sorbete *m*; nieve *f* (Mex.)
vino di Xeres	vinho de xerez	jerez *m*
brillare	brilhar	brillar
lustrare	engraxar	lustrar
Una lustrata, signore?	Engraxa?	¿Le lustro los zapatos?, ¿Grasa? (Mex.)
vapore *m*	navio	vapor *m*; buque *m*
spedire	expedir	enviar
spedizione *f*	embarque *m*; remessa	envío; embarque *m*
cantiere *m*	estaleiro	astillero
camicia	camisa	camisa
ammortizzatore *m*	amortecedor *m*	amortiguador *m*
scarpa	sapato	zapato
calzatoio	calçadeira	calzador *m*
laccio; **stringa**	atacador *m*; cadarço (Br.)	cordón *m* de zapato; agujeta (Mex.)
calzolaio	sapateiro	zapatero
cera da scarpe	graxa para sapatos	betún *m*
calzoleria	sapataria	zapatería
forma per scarpe	fôrma	horma
tirare (su)	atirar (em)	tirar (a)
negozio	loja	tienda
fare degli acquisti *mpl*	fazer compras	ir de compras; ir de tiendas
vetrina	vitrina	escaparate *m*; vidriera (Amer.)
sponda	beira	orilla
riva	ribeira	ribera
corto	curto	corto

English	*French*	*German*
short (not tall)	petit	klein
short circuit (n.)	court-circuit *m*	Kurzschluss *m*
short cut	raccourci *m*	Kurzweg *m*
shorten, to	raccourcir	kürzen
shorthand	sténographie *f*	Stenographie *f*
shortly	bientôt; sous peu	in kurzem
shorts (underwear)	short *m*; caleçons *mpl*	Shorts *fpl*
short story	conte *m*	Kurzgeschichte *f*
should (vb.)	devoir	sollen
shoulder (anat.)	épaule *f*	Schulter *f*
shout, to	crier	schreien
shovel (n.)	pelle *f*	Schaufel *f*
show (theat.)	pièce *f*; spectacle *m*	Vorstellung *f*
show, to	montrer	zeigen
showcase	vitrine *f*	Schaukasten *m*
Show me...	Montrez-moi...	Zeigen Sie mir...
shower (bath)	douche *f*	Dusche *f*
shower (rain)	averse *f*	Regenschauer *m*
shower curtain	rideau *m* à douches	Brausevorhang *m*
shrimp	crevette *f*	Garnele *f*; Krabbe *f*
shrine	sanctuaire *m*	Schrein *m*
shrink, to	se rétrécir	einlaufen
shut, to	fermer	schliessen; zumachen
shutter (phot.)	obturateur *m*	Verschluss *m*
shutter (window)	volet *m*	Fensterladen *m*
shy (timid)	timide	schüchtern
sick	malade	krank
sickly	maladif	kränklich
sickness	maladie *f*	Krankheit *f*
side (n.)	côté *m*	Seite *f*
sideboard (buffet)	buffet *m*	Büffet *n*
side trip	excursion *f*	Abstecher *m*
sidewalk	trottoir *m*	Bürgersteig *m*
sight (eyesight)	vue *f*	Sehkraft *f*

Italian	*Portuguese*	*Spanish*
basso	baixo	bajo
corto circuito	curto circuito	corto circuito
scorciatoia	atalho	atajo
accorciare	encurtar	acortar
stenografia	taquigrafia	taquigrafía
fra poco	dentro em breve	dentro de poco
mutande *fpl*	cuecas *fpl*; calção *m*	calzoncillos *mpl*
novella	conto	cuento
dovere	dever	deber
spalla	ombro	hombro
gridare	gritar	gritar
pala	pá	pala
spettacolo	espetáculo	función *f*; tanda (Amer.)
mostrare	mostrar	mostrar
vetrina	montra; mostruário (Br.)	vitrina
Mi mostri...	Mostre-me..	Muéstreme...
doccia	banho de chuva; chuveiro (Br.)	ducha; regadera (Mex.)
acquazzone *m*	aguaceiro	aguacero
tenda per la doccia	cortina de chuveiro	cortina de baño
gamberetto	camarão	gamba; camarón *m*
santuario	santuário	santuario
restringersi	encolher	encogerse
chiudere	fechar	cerrar
otturatore *m*	obturador *m*	obturador *m*
imposta; persiana	postigo	persiana
timido	tímido	tímido
ammalato	doente	enfermo
malaticcio	doentio, enfermiço	enfermizo
malattia *f*	doença	enfermedad *f*
lato	lado	lado
credenza	aparador *m*	aparador *m*
escursione *f*	excursão *f*	correría
marciapiede *m*	passeio; calçada (Br.)	acera; vereda (Amer.); banqueta (Mex.)
vista	vista	vista

English	*French*	*German*
sign	écriteau *m*; affiche *f*	Schild *n*
sign, to	signer	unter**schreiben**
signature	signature *f*	Unterschrift *f*
silence	silence *m*	Stille *f*
silent	silen**cieux, -euse**	still
silk	soie *f*	Seide *f*
silver	argent *m*	Silber *n*
silverware	argent**erie** *f*	Besteck *n*
similar	sem**blable**	ähnlich
simple (plain)	simple	einfach
sin	péché *m*	Sünde *f*
sin, to	pécher	sündigen
since (after) (prep.)	depuis	seit
since (ever-) (conj.)	depuis que	seit
since (causal) (conj.)	puisque	da
since then (adv.)	depuis **lors**	seit**her**
sing, to	chanter	singen
singer	chanteur *m*	Sänger *m*
single (not married)	célibataire	ledig
single room	chambre *f* à un lit	Einzelzimmer *n*
sink	évier *m*	Ausguss *m*
sink (go down), to	couler	versinken
sir	monsieur *m*	Mein **Herr**
sirloin	aloyau *m*	Lendenstück *n*
sister	soeur *f*	Schwester *f*
sister-in-law	belle-**soeur** *f*	Schwägerin *f*
sit (be sitting), to	être assis	sitzen
sit down, to	s'asseoir	sich **setzen**
situated, to be	se trouver	liegen
sitz bath	bidet *m*	Bidet *n*
six	six	sechs
sixteen	seize	sechzehn
sixth	sixième	der **sechste**, etc.
sixty	soixante	sechzig
size (hat)	tour *m* de **tête**	Grösse *f*
size (magnitude)	grandeur *f*	Grösse *f*
size (shoe, glove)	pointure *f*	Grösse *f*
size (suit, coat; dress)	taille *f*	Grösse *f*

Italian	*Portuguese*	*Spanish*
insegna	letreiro; anúncio	letrero; aviso
sottoscrivere	assinar	firmar
firma	assinatura	firma
silenzio	silêncio	silencio
silenzioso	silencioso	silencioso
seta	sêda	seda
argento	prata	plata
argenteria	talheres *mpl*	vajilla
simile	semelhante	semejante
semplice	simples	sencillo
peccato	pecado	pecado
peccare	pecar	pecar
da	desde	desde
dacchè	desde que	desde que
siccome	já que	puesto que; ya que
da allora	desde então	desde entonces
cantare	cantar	cantar
cantante *m, f*	cantador *m*	cantador *m*
celibe *m*; nubile *f*	solteiro, -a	soltero, -a
camera a un letto	quarto de solteiro	cuarto para uno
acquaio; lavandino	bacia; pia	lavadero; fregadero
affondare	afundar-se	hundirse
signore *m*	senhor *m*	señor *m*
lombata	lombo de vaca	solomillo
sorella	irmã	hermana
cognata	cunhada	cuñada
sedere	estar sentado	estar sentado
sedersi; accomodarsi	sentar-se	sentarse
trovarsi	estar situado	estar situado
bidet *m*	bidê *m*	bidé *m*
sei	seis	seis
sedici	dezesseis	diez y seis
sesto	sexto	sexto
sessanta	sessenta	sesenta
misura	medida	medida
dimensione *f*	tamanho	tamaño
numero	número	número
misura	medida	talla

English	*French*	*German*
skate (ice), to	patiner	Schlittschuh laufen
ski, to	faire du ski	skilaufen
skid, to	déraper; patiner	schleudern
skim(med) milk	lait *m* écrémé	Magermilch *f*
skin (of animal)	peau *f*	Fell *n*
skin (human)	peau *f*	Haut *f*
skirt	jupe *f*	Rock *m*
skull	crâne *m*	Schädel *m*
sky	ciel *m*	Himmel *m*
skyscraper	gratte-**ciel** *m*	Wolkenkratzer *m*
slack (not tight)	lâche	schlaff
slang	argot *m*	Slang *m*
sled	traîneau *m*	Schlitten *m*
sleep	sommeil *m*	Schlaf *m*
sleep, to	dormir	schlafen
sleeping bag	sac *m* de cou**chage**	Schlafsack *m*
sleeping car	wagon-lit *m*	Schlafwagen *m*; Liegewagen (2nd. cl.)
sleepy, to be	avoir som**meil**	schläfrig sein
sleeve	manche *f*	Ärmel *m*
slender (thin)	maigre	schlank
slice (of bread)	tranche *f*	Stück *n*
slice (of meat)	tranche *f*	Stück *n*
slice, to	couper en **tranches**	schneiden
slide, to	glisser	gleiten
slide (phot.)	diapositive *f*	Diapositiv *n*
sling (med.)	écharpe *f*	(Arm) Schlinge *f*
slip (clothing)	combinai**son** *f*	Unterrock *m*
slipper	pantoufle *f*	Hausschuh *m*
slow (not fast)	lent	langsam
slow, to be (watch)	retarder	nachgehen
slowly	lente**ment**	langsam
small	petit	klein
smaller	plus petit	kleiner
smallpox	variole *f*	Pocken *fpl*
smell (odor)	odeur *f*	Geruch *m*
smell (sense)	odorat *m*	Geruchssinn *m*

Italian	*Portuguese*	*Spanish*
pattinare	patinar	patinar
sciare	esquiar	esquiar
slittare	deslizar; derrapar (Br.)	patinar
latte *m* scremato	leite *m* desnatado	leche *f* desnatada
pelle *f*	pele *f*	piel *f*
pelle *f*	cútis *f*	cutis *m*; piel *f*
gonna	saia	falda
cranio	crânio	cráneo
cielo	céu *m*	cielo
grattacielo	arranha-céu *m*	rascacielos *m*
floscio	frouxo	flojo
gergo	gíria	jerga
slitta	trenó	trineo
sonno	sono	sueño
dormire	dormir	dormir
sacco a pelo	saco forrado	saco para dormir
vagone *m* letto	carruagem-cama *m*; vagão-leito (Br.)	coche *m* dormitorio; vagón *m* cama (Mex.)
aver sonno	ter (estar com) sono	tener sueño
manica	manga	manga
sottile; smilzo	esguio; magro	delgado
fetta	fatia	rebanada
fetta	talhada	tajada
affettare	fatiar; talhar	rebanar; tajar
scivolare	resvalar	deslizarse
diapositiva	transparência	transparencia
fascia	funda	cabestrillo
sottabito	combinação *f*	combinación *f*; (fondo) (Mex.)
pantofola	chinelo; chinela	zapatilla
lento	lento	lento
andare in dietro	estar atrasado	estar atrasado
lentamente	devagar	despacio
piccolo	pequeno	pequeño; chico
più piccolo	mais pequeno	más pequeño
vaiolo	varíola	viruela
odore *m*	cheiro; odor *m*	olor *m*
odorato	olfato	olfato

English	*French*	*German*
smell, to	sentir	riechen
smile	sourire *m*	Lächeln *n*
smile, to	sourire	lächeln
smoke	fumée *f*	Rauch *m*
smoke, to	fumer	rauchen
smoking car	compartiment *m* fumeur	Raucher abteil *m*
smooth (flat)	lisse	glatt
snack	casse-croûte *m*	Imbiss *m*
snail	escargot *m*	Schnecke *f*
snake	serpent *m*	Schlange *f*
snapshot	instantané *m*	Aufnahme *f*
sneeze, to	éternuer	niesen
snore, to	ronfler	schnarchen
snow	neige *f*	Schnee *m*
snow, to	neiger	schneien
snuff	tabac *m* à priser	Schnupftabak *m*
so (therefore)	donc	also
so (thus)	ainsi	so
so (to such a degree)	si	so
So long!	À bientôt!	Auf Wiedersehen!
so many	tant de	so viele
so much	tant de	so viel
So so (fair)	Comme ci, comme ça	So so
so that (in order that)	pour que	damit
so that (result)	de sorte que	so dass
soak, to	tremper	durchnässen; einweichen
soap	savon *m*	Seife *f*
soccer	football *m*	Fussball *m*
sock (n.)	chaussette *f*	Socke *f*
socket (in wall)	douille *f*	Steckdose *f*
soda (bicarb.)	bicarbonate *m*	Soda *n*
soda water	eau *f* gazeuse; soda *m*	Sodawasser *n*
soft (not hard)	mou, molle	weich
soft (not loud)	doux; douce	leise

Italian	Portuguese	Spanish
odorare	cheirar	oler
sorriso	sorriso	sonrisa
sorridere	sorrir	sonreír
fumo	fumo; fumaça (Br.)	humo
fumare	fumar	fumar
vettura per fuma-tori	fumador *m*	coche *m* fumador
liscio	liso	liso
spuntino	merenda; lanche *m*	bocadillo; tentempié *m*
lumaca	caracol *m*	caracol *m*
serpente *m*	cobra	culebra
istantanea	instantâneo	instantánea
starnutire	espirrar	estornudar
russare	roncar	roncar
neve *f*	neve *f*	nieve *f*
nevicare	nevar	nevar
tabacco da fiuto	rapé *m*	rapé *m*
dunque	por isso	por lo tanto
così	assim	así
così	tão	tan
A presto!; Ciao!	Até logo!; Chau!	¡Hasta luego!
tanti	tantos	tantos
tanto	tanto	tanto
Così, così	Assim, assim	Así, así
acciocché; affinché	para que	para que
così che	de modo que	de modo que
mettere in bagno; bagnare	remolhar	remojar; poner en remojo
sapone *m*	sabão; sabonete *m*	jabón *m*
calcio	futebol *m*	fútbol *m*
calzino	peúga; meia (Br.)	calcetín *m*
presa (elettrica)	tomada; soquête *m* (Br.)	enchufe *m*
soda	soda	sosa; soda
acqua gassosa	água gasosa	agua gaseosa
soffice	brando; mole	blando
sommesso	quedo	quedo

English	*French*	*German*
soft (to touch)	doux; lisse	weich
soft boiled	à la coque	weichgekocht
soft drink	boisson *f* gazeuse	Erfrischungs-getränk *n*
soil (make dirty), to	souiller	beschmutzen
sold (p.p.)	vendu	verkauft
solder, to.)	souder	löten
soldier	soldat *m*	Soldat *m*
sole (fish)	sole *f*	Seezunge *f*
sole (foot)	plante *f*	Sohle *f*
sole (only)	seul	einzig
sole (shoe)	semelle *f*	Schuhsohle *f*
solid (compact)	solide	fest
some (a few)	quelques	einige
some (certain)	certains	manche
somebody	quelqu'un	jemand
somehow	d'une façon ou d'autre	irgendwie
someone	quelqu'un	jemand
something	quelque chose	etwas
something better	quelque chose de meilleur	etwas Besseres
something cheaper	quelque chose de moins cher	etwas Billigeres
something else	autre chose	sonst noch etwas
sometimes	quelquefois	manchmal
somewhat (quite)	quelque peu	etwas
somewhere	quelque part	irgendwo
son	fils *m*	Sohn *m*
son-in-law	gendre *m*	Schwiegersohn *m*
song	chanson *f*	Lied *n*
soon (early)	tôt	früh
soon (shortly)	bientôt	bald
sooner	plus tôt	früher
sooner or later	tôt ou tard	früher oder später
sore (hurting)	douloureux, -euse	wund
sore throat	mal *m* à la gorge	Halsweh *n*
sorry, to be	regretter	bedauern

Italian	*Portuguese*	*Spanish*
morbido	macio	suave
alla coque	quente	pasado por agua; tibio (Mex.)
(bibita) gassosa	gasosa; refrêsco; refrigerante *m* (Br.)	refresco; gaseosa
sporcare	sujar	ensuciar
venduto	vendido	vendido
saldare	soldar	soldar
soldato	soldado	soldado
sogliola	linguado	lenguado
pianta	planta do pé	planta del pie
solo	único	único
suola	sola; solado (Br.)	suela
solido	sólido	sólido
alcuni	alguns	algunos
certi	alguns	algunos
qualcuno	alguém	alguien
in qualche modo	de algum modo	de algún modo
qualcuno	alguém	alguien
qualche cosa	alguma coisa; algo	algo
qualcosa di migliore	alguma coisa melhor	algo mejor
qualcosa di meno caro	alguma coisa mais barato	algo más barato
qualcosa d'altro	outra coisa	otra cosa
qualche volta	algumas vezes	algunas veces
un poco	um pouco	algo
in qualche luogo	em algum lugar	en alguna parte
figlio	filho	hijo
genero	genro	yerno
canzone *f*	canto	canción *f*
presto	cedo	temprano
tra poco	em breve	pronto; en breve
più presto	mais a tempo	más temprano
prima o poi	mais cedo ou mais tarde	tarde o temprano
dolente	dolorido	dolorido
mal *m* di gola	dor *f* de garganta	dolor *m* de garganta
dispiacere	sentir	sentir

English	*French*	*German*
soul	âme *f*	Seele *f*
sound (noise)	son *m*	Laut *m*
soundproof	insonore	schalldicht
soup	soupe *f*; potage *m*	Suppe *f*
soup plate	assiette *f* à soupe	Suppenteller *m*
sour	aigre	sauer
south (n.)	sud *m*	Süden *m*
South America	l'Amérique du Sud	Südamerika *n*
southern	méridional	südlich
souvenir	souvenir *m*	Reiseandenken *n*
Soviet (adj.)	soviétique	Sowjetisch
Soviet (n.)	soviet *m*	Sowjet *m*
sow, to	semer	säen
space (area)	espace *m*	Raum *m*
space ship	astronef *m*	Raumschiff *n*
Spain	l'Espagne *f*	Spanien *n*
Spanish (adj.)	espagnol	spanisch
spare parts	pièces *fpl* de rechange	Ersatzteile *mpl*
spare tire	pneu *m* de rechange	Reservereifen *m*
spark plug	bougie *f*	Zündkerze *f*
speak, to	parler	sprechen
Speak slower, please!	Parlez plus lentement, s'il vous plaît!	Bitte, sprechen Sie langsamer!
special (adj.)	spécial	besonder-
special (on menu)	plat *m* du jour	Tagesgericht *n*
special delivery	exprès	per Eilpost
speed (n.)	vitesse *f*	Geschwindigkeit *f*
speed limit	vitesse *f* maxima	Höchstgeschwindigkeit *f*
speedometer	compteur *m*	Tachometer *n*
spell, to	épeler	buchstabieren
spend (money), to	dépenser	ausgeben
spend (time), to	passer	verbringen
spent (p.p.)	dépensé	ausgegeben
spice	épice *f*	Gewürz *n*
spider	araignée *f*	Spinne *f*
spill, to	renverser	verschütten
spinach	épinards *mpl*	Spinat *m*
spine (anat.)	épine *f* dorsale	Rückgrat *n*

Italian	*Portuguese*	*Spanish*
anima	alma	alma
suono	som *m*	sonido
antisonoro	à prova de **som**	antisonoro
minestra	sopa	sopa
scodella	prato fundo	plato sopero
agro	azedo	agrio
sud *m*	sul *m*	sur *m*
l'America del **Sud**	a América do **Sul**	la América del **Sur**
meridionale	meridional; do **sul**	meridional; del **sur**
ricordo	lembrança	recuerdo
sovietico	soviético	soviético
soviet *m*	soviete *m*	Soviet *m*
seminare	semear	sembrar
spazio	espaço	espacio
astronave *f*	astronave *f*	nave *f* del espacio
la Spagna	a Espanha	España
spagnolo	espanhol	español
pezzi *mpl* di ricambio	peças *fpl* sobressalentes	piezas *fpl* de repuesto
gomma di ricambio	pneu *m* sobressalente	neumático (llanta) de repuesto
candela	vela	bujía
parlare	falar	hablar
Parli più lentamente, per favore!	Faça favor de falar mais devagar!	¡Favor de hablar más despacio!
speciale	especial	especial
piatto del giorno	especialidade *f* do dia	plato del día
per espresso	entrega rápida	de entrega inmediata
velocità	velocidade *f*	velocidad *f*
velocità **massima**	velocidade *f* máxima	velocidad *f* máxima
tachimetro	velocímetro	velocímetro
scrivere	soletrar	deletrear
spendere	gastar	gastar
passare	passar	pasar
speso	gasto	gastado
spezia	especiaria	especia
ragno	aranha	araña
versare	derramar	derramar
spinaci *mpl*	espinafre *m*	espinacas *fpl*
spina dorsale	espinha dorsal	espina dorsal

English	*French*	*German*
spit, to	cracher	spucken
splint (med.) (n.)	éclisse *f*	Schiene *f*
spoil (a child), to	gâter	verziehen
spoil (go bad), to	se gâter	verderben
spoiled	gâté	verdorben
spoken (p.p.)	parlé	gesprochen
sponge (n.)	éponge *f*	Schwamm *m*
spoon	cuiller *f*	Löffel *m*
spoonful	cuillerée *f*	ein Löffel voll
spot (place)	endroit *m*	Stelle *f*
spot (stain)	tache *f*	Fleck *m*
spot remover	détachant *m*	Entfleckungsmittel *n*
sport (game)	sport *m*	Sport *m*
sprain	entorse *f*	Verrenkung *f*
sprain, to	se donner une entorse à	verrenken
spray, to	arroser	besprengen
spread, to	répandre	verbreiten
spring (coil) (n.)	ressort *m*	Feder *f*
spring (season)	printemps *m*	Frühling *m*
spring (water)	source *f*	Quelle *f*
sprinkle (rain), to	bruiner	rieseln
spy (n.)	espion *m*	Spion *m*
square (adj.)	carré	viereckig
square (plaza)	place *f*	Platz *m*
squash (vegetable)	courge *f*	Kürbis *m*
squeeze, to	serrer	drücken
squeeze (out), to	presser	ausdrücken
stable (barn)	écurie *f*; étable *f*	Stall *m*
stadium	stade *m*	Stadion *n*
stage (theat.)	scène *f*	Bühne *f*
stain (spot)	tache *f*	Fleck *m*
stain, to	tacher	beflecken
stainless steel	acier *m* inoxydable	rostfreier Stahl
stained-glass window	vitrail *m* (*pl.* vitraux)	gemaltes Fenster
stairs, stairway	escalier *m*	Treppe *f*
stale	rassis	altbacken
stall (stop going), to	caler	stehenbleiben
stammer, to	bégayer	stammeln

Italian	*Portuguese*	*Spanish*
sputare	cuspir	escupir
stecca	tala	tablilla
viziare	mimar	mimar
guastarsi	apodrecer	echarse a perder
guasto	apodrecido	echado a perder
parlato	falado	hablado
spugna	esponja	esponja
cucchiaio	colher *f*	cuchara
cucchiaiata	colherada	cucharada
luogo	lugar *m*	sitio
macchia	mancha	mancha
smacchiatore *m*	tira-manchas *m*	quitamanchas *m*
sport *m*	esporte *m*	deporte *m*
storta	torcedura	torcedura
storcersi	torcer	torcer
spruzzare	pulverizar; borrifar	rociar; pulverizar
spargere	esparzir	esparcir
molla	mola	muelle *m* (*f* in Mex.)
primavera	primavera	primavera
fonte *f*	fonte *f*	manantial *m*
piovigginare	chuviscar	lloviznar
spia	espião *m*	espía *m*
quadrato	quadrado	cuadrado
piazza	praça; largo	plaza
zucca	abóbora	calabaza
stringere	apertar	apretar
spremere	espremer	exprimir
stalla	estábulo	establo
stadio	estádio	estadio
scena; palcoscenico	palco	escena
macchia	mancha	mancha
macchiare	manchar	manchar
acciaio inossidabile	aço inoxidável	acero inoxidable
vetrata istoriata	vitral *m*	vidriera
scala	escada	escalera
stantio	velho	viejo
arrestarsi	parar	parar
balbettare	gaguejar	tartamudear

English	*French*	*German*
stamp (postage)	timbre *m*	**Briefmarke** *f*
stand (be upright)	être debout	stehen
stand (tolerate), to	supporter	ertragen
stand in line, to	faire la queue	sich **anstellen**, **Schlange** stehen
standing room only	debout seulement	Stehplatz *m*
stand up, to	se lever	aufstehen
stapler (tool)	agrafeuse *f*	Heftmaschine *f*
star (n.)	étoile *f*	Stern *m*
starboard (ship's right side)	tribord *m*	Steuerbord *m*
starch	amidon *m*; fécule *f* (food)	Stärke *f*; Stärkemehl *n* (food)
starch, to	empeser	stärken
start (n.)	commencement *m*	Anfang *m*
start (begin), to	commencer	anfangen
start (a car), to	mettre en **marche**	anlassen
start (to do something), to	se mettre à	anfangen
starter (auto)	démarreur *m*	Anlasser *m*
start out, to	se mettre en **route**	losgehen
starve, to	mourir de **faim**	verhungern
state (nation)	état *m*	Staat *m*
stateroom	cabine *f*	Kabine *f*
stateroom plan	plan *m* du **navire**	Schiffsplan *m*
stationmaster (R.R.)	chef *m* de **gare**	Stationsvorsteher *m*
station (R.R.)	gare *f*	Bahnhof *m*
station wagon	familiale *f*	Kombiwagen *m*
stationery	papier *m* à **lettres**	Schreibpapier *n*
stationery store	papeterie *f*	Papiergeschäft *n*
statue	statue *f*	Bildsäule *f*
stay (remain), to	rester	bleiben
stay (visit) (n.)	séjour *m*	Aufenthalt *m*
stay in bed, to	garder le **lit**	das Bett hüten; im Bett bleiben

Italian	*Portuguese*	*Spanish*
francobollo	selo	sello de correo; estampilla; timbre *m* (Mex.)
stare in piedi	estar (ficar) de pé	estar de pie
tollerare	agüentar	aguantar
fare la coda	ficar em linha; estar na fila	hacer cola; ponerse en fila; formarse (Mex.)
posti *mpl* in piedi	lugares *mpl* de pé	localidades *fpl* de pie
levarsi	pôr-se de pé	ponerse de pie; pararse (Mex.)
cucitrice *m*	grampeador *m*	engrapador *m*
stella	estrêla	estrella; astro
tribordo	estibordo	estribor *m*
amido; fecola (food)	amido; fécula (food)	almidón *m*; fécula (food)
inamidare	engomar	almidonar
principio	princípio	comienzo
cominciare	começar	empezar; comenzar
mettere in marcia	pôr em marcha; acionar	arrancar; poner en marcha
mettersi a	pôr-se a	ponerse a
starter *m*	arranque *m*	arranque *m*
avviarsi	pôr-se a caminho	ponerse en camino
morire di fame	morrer de fome	morirse de hambre
stato	estado	estado
cabina	camarote *m*; cabina	camarote *m*
pianta delle cabine	plano das acomodações	plano de acomodaciones
capostazione *m*	chefe *m* de estação	jefe *m* de estación
stazione *f*	estação *f*	estación *f* de ferrocarril
giardinetta	caminhonete *m*	camioneta
carta da lettere	papel *m* de escrever	papel *m* de escribir
cartoleria	papelaria	papelería
statua	estátua	estatua
restare	ficar; estar	quedarse
soggiorno	estada	estancia
stare a letto	guardar o leito; ficar de cama	guardar cama

English	*French*	*German*
steak	bifteck *m*	Beefsteak *n*
steal, to	voler	stehlen
steam	vapeur *f*	Dampf *m*
steamer rug	couverture *f* de voyage	Reisedecke *f*
steamer trunk	malle *f* de cabine	Kabinenkoffer *m*
steam heat	chauffage *m* à la vapeur	Dampfheizung *f*
steamship	vapeur *m*	Dampfer *m*
steel	acier *m*	Stahl *m*
steep (adj.)	raide	steil
steer, to	conduire	steuern
steering wheel	volant *m*	Steuerrad *n*
stencil (n.)	stencil *m*	Matrize *f*
stenographer	sténographe *f*	Stenografin *f*
step (stair)	marche *f*	Stufe *f*
step (stride)	pas *m*	Schritt *m*
step, to	faire un **pas**	treten
stepdaughter	belle-fille *f*	Stieftochter *f*
stepfather	beau-père *m*	Stiefvater *m*
stepmother	belle-mère *f*	Stiefmutter *f*
stepson	beau-fils *m*	Stiefsohn *m*
sterilize, to	stériliser	sterilisieren
stern (ship)	poupe *f*	Heck *n*
stern (strict)	sévère	streng
stew (n.)	ragoût *m*	Ragout *n*
steward (boat, air)	steward *m*	Steward *m*
stewardess (air)	hôtesse *f*	Stewardess *f*
stewed fruit	compote *f*	Kompott *n*
stick (branch)	bâton *m*; **rameau** *m*	Stock *m*
stick (adhere to), to	se coller	kleben
sticky	gluant	klebrig
stiff	raide	steif
still (nevertheless)	cependant	jedoch
still (quiet)	tranquille	still
still (yet)	toujours	noch
stimulant	stimulant *m*	Reizmittel *n*
sting, to	piquer	stechen

Italian	*Portuguese*	*Spanish*
bistecca	bife *m*	biftec *m*
rubare	roubar	robar
vapore *m*	vapor *m*	vapor *m*
coperta da viaggio	manta de viagem	manta de viaje
baule *m* da cabina	mala de cabine	baúl *m* de camarote
riscaldamento a vapore	calefação *f* a vapor	calefacción *f* por vapor
piroscafo	vapor *m*	vapor *m*; buque *m*
acciaio	aço	acero
erto	escarpado	escarpado
guidare	guiar	conducir
volante *m*	volante *m*	volante *m*
stampino	papel *m* estêncil	esténcil *m*
stenografa	estenógrafa	estenógrafa
gradino; scalino	degrau *m*	escalón *m*; peldaño
passo	passo	paso
fare un passo	dar um passo	dar un paso
figliastra	enteada	hijastra
padrigno	padrasto	padrastro
matrigna	madrasta	madrastra
figliastro	enteado	hijastro
sterilizzare	esterilizar	esterilizar
poppa	pôpa	popa
severo	severo	severo
stufato	guisado	guisado; estofado
cameriere *m* di bordo	criado de bordo	camarero
hostess *f*	hospedeira; aeromoça (Br.)	azafata; aeromoza (Amer.)
composta di frutta	compota de fruta	compota de frutas
stecco; ramo	pau *m*	palo
aderire	colar-se	pegarse
attaccaticcio	pegajoso	pegajoso
rigido	têso	tieso
eppure	contudo	sin embargo
tranquillo	tranqüilo	tranquilo
tuttavia	ainda	todavía; aun; aún
stimolante *m*	estimulante *m*	estimulante *m*
pungere	picar	picar

English	*French*	*German*
stingy (miserly)	chiche	geizig
stink, to	puer	stinken
stir (mix), to	remuer	rühren
stitch	point *m*	Stich *m*
stitch, to	faire un point à	nähen
stock (goods) (n.)	assortiment *m*; stock *m*	Auswahl *m*
stock (shares)	actions *fpl*	Aktien *fpl*
Stockholm	Stockholm *m*	Stockholm *n*
stocking	bas *m*	Strumpf *m*
stock market	Bourse *f*	Börse *f*
stomach	estomac *m*	Magen *m*
stomach ache	mal *m* d'estomac	Magenschmerzen *mpl*
stone (rock)	pierre *f*	Stein *m*
stool (seat)	escabeau *m*	Schemel *m*
Stop!	Arrêtez!	Halt!
stop (bus, car) (n.)	arrêt *m*	Haltestelle *f*
stop (cease), to	cesser	aufhören
stop (make halt), to	arrêter	aufhalten
stop (come to a standstill), to	s'arrêter	anhalten
stop at (hotel), to	descendre dans un hôtel	in einem Hotel absteigen
stop light	feu *m* (stop)	Verkehrsampel *f*
stop over, to	s'arrêter	übernachten
store (shop)	magasin *m*	Laden *m*; Geschäft *n*
storeroom (closet)	cagibi *m*	Abstellkammer *f*
storm (n.)	orage *m*	Sturm *m*
stormy	orageux, -euse	stürmisch
story (floor)	étage *m*	Stock *m*; Stockwerk *n*
story (tale)	histoire *f*	Geschichte *f*
stout (corpulent)	corpulent	stark
stout (strong)	fort	stark
stove (cooking)	fourneau *m*; cuisinière *f*	Herd *m*
stove (heating)	poêle *m*	Ofen *m*
straight (not crooked)	droit	gerade
straight ahead	tout droit	geradeaus
straight razor	rasoir *m* à main	Rasiermesser *n*

Italian	*Portuguese*	*Spanish*
tirchio	mesquinho	mezquino; tacaño
puzzare	cheirar mal	apestar
mescolare	mexer	mezclar; revolver
punto	ponto	puntada
dar dei punti	pespontar	dar puntos
assortimento	existência; estoque *m* (Br.)	surtido; existencias
azioni *fpl*	ações *fpl*	acciones *fpl*
Stoccolma *f*	Estocolmo	Estocolmo
calza	meia	media
Borsa (Valori)	Bôlsa	Bolsa
stomaco	estômago	estómago
mal *m* di stomaco	dor *f* de estômago	dolor *m* de estómago
pietra	pedra	piedra
sgabello	tamborete *m*	taburete *m*
Ferma!	Pare!	¡Pare!
fermata	paragem *f*; ponto (Br.)	parada
cessare	cessar	cesar
fermare	deter	detener
fermarsi	parar	pararse
scendere ad un albergo	hospedar-se em um hotel	alojarse en un hotel
semaforo	semáforo	semáforo
fermarsi	parar de passagem	hacer una parada intermedia; hacer escala
negozio	loja; armazém *m*	tienda
sgabuzzino	depósito	depósito; bodega
tempesta	tempestade *f*	tempestad *f*
tempestoso	tempestuoso	tempestuoso
piano	andar *m*	piso
storia	história	historia
corpulento	corpulento	corpulento
robusto	forte	fuerte
fornello	fogão	estufa
stufa	estufa	estufa
diritto	direito	derecho
sempre diritto	sempre em frente	todo derecho
rasoio (con manico mobile)	navalha de barba	navaja de afeitar

English	*French*	*German*
strain (filter), to	filtrer	durchseihen
strainer	passoire *f*	Sieb *m*
strait (passage)	détroit *m*	Meerenge *f*
strange (odd)	étrange	seltsam
stranger	étranger *m*; -ère *f*	Fremde *m, f*
strap (n.)	courroie *f*	Riemen *m*
straw	paille *f*	Stroh *n*
straw (drinking)	paille *f*	Strohhalm *m*
strawberry	fraise *f*	Erdbeere *f*
straw hat	chapeau *m* de **paille**	Strohhut *m*
stream (rivulet)	ruisseau *m*	Bach *m*
street	rue *f*	Strasse *f*
streetcar	tramway *m*	Strassenbahn *f*
stretcher (for the sick)	civière *f*	Tragbahre *f*
strict (severe)	sévère	streng
strike (hit), to	frapper	schlagen
strike (work stoppage)	grève *f*	Streik *m*
string (cord)	ficelle *f*	Schnur *f*
string beans	haricots *mpl* **verts**	Schnittbohnen *fpl*
stroke (med.)	attaque *f*	Schlaganfall *m*
stroll, to	se prom**en**er	schlendern
strong	fort	stark
strong coffee	café *m* fort	starker Kaffee
strop (razor) (n.)	cuir *m* à ra**soir**	Streichriemen *m*
struggle, to	lutter	kämpfen
stubborn	obstiné	hartnäckig
student	étudiant(e) *m, f*	Student *m*, Studentin *f*
study, to	étudier	studieren
stuff (fill), to	bourrer	stopfen
stuffed (with stuffing)	farci	gefüllt
stumble, to	trébucher	stolpern
stupid	stupide	dumm
style (fashion)	mode *f*	Mode *f*
style (manner)	style *m*	Stil *m*
styptic pencil	crayon *m* hémo-statique	Alaunstift *m*
subject (citizen)	sujet *m*	Untertan *m*

Italian	*Portuguese*	*Spanish*
passare; colare	coar	colar
colino	coador *m*	colador *m*
stretto	estreito	estrecho
strano	estranho; esquisito	extraño
forestiero	estranho; forasteiro	forastero
correggia	correia	correa
paglia	palha	paja
cannuccia (da bere)	canudinho	pajita; popote *m* (Mex.)
fragola	morango	fresa; frutilla (Amer.)
cappello di paglia	chapéu *m* de palha	sombrero de paja
ruscello	arroio; riacho (Br.)	arroyo
strada	rua	calle *f*
tram *m*	(carro)elétrico; bonde *m* (Br.)	tranvía *m*; tren *m* (Mex.)
barella	maca	camilla
severo	severo	severo
colpire	golpear	golpear; pegar
sciopero	greve *f*	huelga
spago	fio; barbante *m*	cuerda
fagiolini *mpl*	feijões *mpl* verdes; vagens *fpl* (Br.)	habichuelas *fpl*; ejotes *mpl* (Mex.)
colpo; attacco	ataque *m*; acesso	ataque *m*
passeggiare	passear	pasearse
forte	forte	fuerte
caffè *m* carico	café *m* forte	café *m* cargado
coramella; cuoio per rasoio	assentador *m* de navalha	suavizador *m*; asentador *m*
lottare	lutar	luchar
testardo	teimoso	terco
studente *m, f*	estudante *m, f*	estudiante *m, f*
studiare	estudar	estudiar
riempire	estofar	rellenar
ripieno	estofado	relleno
inciampare	tropeçar	tropezar
stupido	estúpido	estúpido
moda	moda	moda
stile *m*	estilo	estilo
matita emostatica	lápis *m* estíptico	lápiz *m* estíptico
suddito	súbdito	súbdito

English	*French*	*German*
subject (topic)	sujet *m*	Gegenstand *m*
submarine	sous-marin *m*	Unterseeboot *n*
submit (offer), to	offrir	vorlegen
suburbs	banlieue *f*	Umgebung *f*
subway	métro *m*	Untergrundbahn *f*
succeed in, to	réussir à	Erfolg haben
success	succès *m*	Erfolg *m*
successful	heureux, -euse	erfolgreich
such a	(un) tel	solch ein
suck, to	sucer	saugen
suckling pig	cochon *m* de lait	Spanferkel *n*
sudden	soudain	plötzlich
suddenly	subitement	plötzlich
sue, to	intenter (un procès)	verklagen
suede (n.)	suède *m*	Wildleder *n*
suffer, to	souffrir	erleiden
sufficient	assez	genügend
sugar	sucre *m*	Zucker *m*
sugar bowl	sucrier *m*	Zuckerdose *f*
suggest (bring to mind), to	suggérer	nahelegen
suggest (recommend)	proposer	vorschlagen
suit (at law)	procès *m*	Prozess *m*
suit (man's)	complet *m*	Anzug *m*
suit (woman's)	tailleur *m*	Kostüm *n*
suit (fit), to	convenir	passen
suitable	convenable	passend
suitcase	valise *f*	Handkoffer *m*
sulfur	soufre *m*	Schwefel *m*
summer	été *m*	Sommer *m*
summer vacation	grandes vacances *fpl*	Sommerferien *pl*
summit	sommet *m*	Gipfel *m*
sun	soleil *m*	Sonne *f*
sunburned	brûlé par le soleil	sonnenverbrannt
Sunday	dimanche *m*	Sonntag *m*
sun glasses	lunettes *fpl* de soleil	Sonnenbrille *f*

Italian	*Portuguese*	*Spanish*
tema *m*	assunto	asunto
sottomarino	submarino	submarino
sottoporre	submeter	someter
dintorni *mpl*	arredores *mpl*; subúrbios *mpl*	afueras *fpl*
metropolitana	metrô	metro (Madrid); **subte** *m* (Buenos Aires)
riuscire à	lograr	lograr
successo	êxito; sucesso (Br.)	éxito
fortunato	afortunado	próspero
tale	tal	tal
succhiare	chupar	chupar
maialino di latte	leitão	lechoncillo
improvviso	súbito	súbito
improvvisamente	de repente	de repente
citare in giudizio	demandar	demandar
pelle *f* scamosciata	camurça	ante *m*
soffrire	sofrer	sufrir
bastante	bastante	bastante
zucchero	açúcar *m*	azúcar *m*
zuccheriera	açucareiro	azucarero
suggerire	sugerir	sugerir
suggerire	sugerir	sugerir
causa; processo	processo	pleito
abito	fato; terno (Br.)	traje *m*; terno
vestito	costume *m*; tailleur *m*	traje *m* sastre
andare bene	assentar	caer bien
conveniente	conveniente	conveniente
valigia	mala; valise *f*	maleta; velís *m* (Amer.)
zolfo	enxôfre *m*	azufre *m*
estate *f*	verão	verano
vacanze *fpl* estive	grandes férias *fpl*	vacaciones *fpl* de verano
cima	cimo	cumbre *f*
sole *m*	sol *m*	sol *m*
bruciato dal sole	queimado do sol	quemado por el sol
domenica	domingo	domingo
occhiali *mpl* da sole	óculos *mpl* escuros	gafas *fpl* de sol

English	*French*	*German*
sunny	ensoleillé	sonnig
sunrise	lever *m* de soleil	Sonnenaufgang *m*
sunset	coucher *m* de soleil	Sonnenuntergang *m*
sunshine	soleil *m*	Sonnenschein *m*
sunstroke	coup *m* de soleil	Sonnenstich *m*
sun tan lotion	huile *f* de soleil	Sonnenschutzkrem *m*
sun-visor	pare-soleil *m*	Sonnenblende *f*
supper	souper *m*	Abendessen *n*
supply (provide), to	fournir	versehen
suppose, to	supposer	vermuten
sure	sûr	sicher
surgeon	chirurgien *m*	Chirurg *m*
surname	nom *m* de famille	Zuname *m*
surprise	surprise *f*	Überraschung *f*
surprise (astonish), to	surprendre	überraschen
surrender (oneself), to	se rendre	sich ergeben
surround, to	entourer	umgeben
survive (remain alive)	survivre	am Leben bleiben
suspenders	bretelles *fpl*	Hosenträger *mpl*
swallow, to	avaler	verschlucken
swamp (n.)	marais *m*	Sumpf *m*
swan	cygne *m*	Schwan *m*
swear (curse), to	jurer	fluchen
swear (vow), to	jurer	schwören
sweat (n.)	sueur *f*	Schweiss *m*
sweater	chandail *m*; sweater *m*	Pullover *m*; Sweater
Sweden	la Suède	Schweden *n*
Swedish (adj.)	suédois	schwedisch
sweep, to	balayer	fegen
sweet	doux, douce	süss
sweetbreads	ris *m*	Bröschen *n*
sweetheart	bien-aimé(e)	Liebchen *n*
sweet potato	patate *f*	süsse Kartoffel *f*; Batate *f*
sweet wine	vin *m* doux	Süsswein *m*⟩
swell, to	s'enfler	(an) schwellen
Swell!	Épatant!	Prima!

Italian	*Portuguese*	*Spanish*
soleggiato	ensolarado	de sol; asoleado
levata del sole	nascer *m* do sol	salida del sol
tramonto	pôr *m* do sol	puesta del sol
sole *m*	luz *f* do sol	luz *f* del sol
colpo di sole	insolação *f*	insolación *f*
olio abbronzante	loção *f* para bronzear	loción *f* para quemadura de sol
parasole *m*	viseira	visera
cena	jantar *m*; ceia	cena
provvedere	prover; fornecer	proveer
supporre	supor	suponer
sicuro	seguro	seguro
chirurgo	cirurgião	cirujano
cognome *m*	sobrenome *m*; apelido	apellido
sorpresa	surprêsa	sorpresa
sorprendere	surpreender	sorprender
arrendersi	entregar-se	rendirse; entregarse
circondare	rodear	rodear
sopravvivere	sobreviver	sobrevivir
bretelle *fpl*	suspensórios *mpl*	tirantes *mpl*
inghiottire	tragar; engolir	tragar
palude *f*	pântano; paul *m* (Br.)	pantano
cigno	cisne *m*	cisne *m*
bestemmiare	blasfemar	blasfemar
giurare	jurar	jurar
sudore *m*	suor *m*	sudor *m*
golfetto; maglione *m*	suéter *m*, malha	suéter *m*; jersey *m*
la Svezia	a Suécia	Suecia
svedese	sueco	sueco
spazzare, scopare	varrer	barrer
dolce	doce	dulce
animelle *fpl*	moela	lechecillas *fpl*; mollejas *fpl*; menudo (Mex.)
fidanzato, -a	namorado, -a	novio, -a
patata americana	batata doce	batata; camote *m* (Mex.)
vino dolce	vinho doce	vino dulce
gonfiarsi	inchar	hincharse
Benissimo!	Magnífico!	¡Magnífico!

English	*French*	*German*
swift	rapide	geschwind
swim, to	nager	schwimmen
swimming pool	piscine *f*	Schwimmbad *n*
swine	cochon *m*	Schwein *n*
Swiss (adj.)	suisse	schweizerisch
switch (elect.)	interrupteur *m*	Schalter *m*
Switzerland	la Suisse	die Schweiz
swollen	enflé	geschwollen
sword	épée *f*	Schwert *n*
syllable	syllabe *f*	Silbe *f*
symphony	symphonie *f*	Symphonie *f*
symptom	symptôme *m*	Symptom *n*
synagogue	synagogue *m*	Synagoge *f*
syringe	seringue *f*	Spritze *f*
syrup	sirop *m*	Sirup *m*
table	table *f*	Tisch *m*
tablecloth	nappe *f*	Tischtuch *n*
table d'hote	table d'hôte *f*	Table d'hote *f*
table linen	linge *m* de table	Tischzeug *n*
tablespoon	cuillèr *f* à soupe	Esslöffel *m*
tablet (pill)	comprimé *m*	Tablette *f*
Tagus (river)	le Tage	der Tajo
tail	queue *f*	Schwanz *m*
tail light (auto)	feu *m* arrière	Rücklicht *n*
tailor	tailleur *m*	Schneider *m*
tailor shop	tailleur *m*	Schneiderei *f*
take, to	prendre	nehmen
take a bath, to	se baigner	baden
take advantage of, to	profiter de	benutzen
take a nap, to	faire la sieste	ein Schläfchen halten
take an exam, to	passer un examen	eine Prüfung machen
take (a person), to	amener	mitbringen
take a picture, to	prendre une photo	eine Aufnahme machen

Italian	*Portuguese*	*Spanish*
rapido	**rá**pido	**rá**pido
nuotare	na**dar**	na**dar**
piscina	piscina	piscina; alberca (Amer.)
maiale *m*; **porco**	**porco**	marrano
svizzero	suíço	suizo
interruttore *m*	interruptor *m*	interruptor *m*
la Svizzera	a Suíça	Suiza
gonfiato	inchado	hinchado
spada	espada	espada
sillaba	sílaba	sílaba
sinfonia	sinfonia	sinfonía
sintomo	sintoma *m*	síntoma *m*
sinagoga	sinagoga	sinagoga
siringa	seringa	jeringa
sciroppo	xarope *m*	almíbar *m*; jarabe *m*
tavola	mesa	mesa
tovaglia	toalha de **mesa**; mantel *m*	mantel *m*
pranzo a prezzo fisso	refeição a **preço fixo**	comida a la orden; comida corrida (Mex.)
biancheria da **tavola**	roupa de mesa	mantelería
cucchiaio	colher *f* de **sopa**	cuchara
pastiglia; **pasticca**	comprimido	pastilla
il Tago	o Tejo	el Tajo
coda	cabo	cola
luce *f* posteriore	luz *f* traseira	farol *m* trasero
sarto	alfaiate *m*	sastre *m*
sartoria	alfaiataria	sastrería
prendere	apanhar; **tomar**	tomar
fare il **bagno**	banhar-se; **tomar** banho	bañarse
approfittare	aproveitar	aprovechar
fare un sonnellino	tirar uma soneca	dormir la siesta
fare un esame	fazer um exame	sufrir un examen; examinarse
condurre	tomar; conduzir	llevar
fare una foto	tirar uma fotografia	sacar una fotografía

English	*French*	*German*
take a ride, to	aller en voiture	spazierenfahren
take a seat, to	s'asseoir	Platz nehmen
take a trip, to	faire un voyage	eine Reise machen
take a walk, to	faire une promenade	spazierengehen
take care of, to	soigner	besorgen
take leave of, to	prendre congé de	Abschied nehmen
Take me to...	Voulez-vous bien me conduire à...	Bitte, bringen Sie mich nach...
take-off (plane)	décollage *m*	Start *m*
take off (clothes), to	ôter	ausziehen; abnehmen (Hut)
take off (plane), to	décoller	starten
take place, to	avoir lieu	stattfinden
taken (occupied)	occupé	besetzt; belegt
talcum powder	(poudre *f* de) talc *m*	Talkumpuder *m*
talk, to	parler	reden
tall (high)	haut	hoch
tall (vs. short)	grand	gross
tame	domestiqué	zahm
tampon	tampon *m*	Tampon *m*
tangerine	mandarine *f*	Mandarine *f*
tank (container)	réservoir *m*	Tank *m*
tank (mil.)	char *m*	Panzer *m*
tape measure	mètre-ruban *m*	Bandmass *n*
tape recorder	magnétophone *m*	Tonbandgerät *n*
tapestry	tapisserie *f*	Tapete *f*
task	tâche *f*	Aufgabe *f*
taste (sense)	goût *m*	Geschmack *m*
taste, to	goûter	kosten
taste like, to	avoir un goût de	schmecken nach
tasty	savoureux, -euse	schmackhaft
tax (n.)	impôt *m*	Steuer *f*
taxi	taxi *m*	Taxi *n*
taxi fare	prix *m* de la course	Fahrpreis *m*
taxi stand	station *f* de taxis	Droschkenplatz *m*
tea	thé *m*	Tee *m*
teach, to	enseigner	lehren

Italian	*Portuguese*	*Spanish*
fare una corsa in auto	passear de (trem, bonde)	pasearse en coche
sedersi; accomodarsi	sentar-se	tomar asiento
fare un viaggio	fazer uma viagem	hacer un viaje
passeggiare	dar um passeio	dar un paseo
curarsi di	cuidar de	cuidar de
pigliar congedo da	despedir-se de	despedirse de
Per favore, mi porti a...	Faça o favor de levar-me a...	¡Lléveme a...por favor!
decollo	decolagem *f*	despegue *m*
togliersi	despirse	quitarse
decollare	levantar vôo; decolar (Br.)	despegar
aver luogo	ter lugar	tener lugar
occupato	ocupado	ocupado
(polvere *m* di) talco	(pó *m* de) talco	(polvos *mpl* de) talco
parlare	falar	hablar
alto	alto	alto
alto	alto	alto
domestico	manso	manso
tampone *m*	tampão	tapón *m*
mandarino	tangerina	tangerina
serbatoio	tanque *m*	tanque *m*
carro armato	tanque *m*	tanque *m*
metro (a nastro)	fita métrica	cinta métrica
registratore *m*	gravador *m* magnético	grabador *m* de cinta
tappezzeria	tapête *m*	tapicería
compito	tarefa	tarea
gusto	sabor *m*; gôsto	gusto
assaporare	saborear	saborear
sapere di	saber a	saber a
gustoso; saporito	saboroso	sabroso
tassa; imposta	taxa; impôsto	impuesto
tassì *m*	táxi *m*	taxi *m*; libre *m* (Mex.)
prezzo della corsa	preço de passagem	tarifa de taxi
stazione *f*	ponto de táxi	estación *f* de taxis; sitio (Mex.)
tè *m*	chá *m*	té *m*
insegnare	ensinar	enseñar

English	*French*	*German*
teacher	instituteur *m*	Lehrer *m*
teacup	tasse *f* à thé	Teetasse *f*
team (sports)	équipe *f*	Mannschaft *f*
teapot	théière *f*	Teekanne *f*
tear (-drop)	larme *f*	Träne *f*
tear (rip), to	déchirer	(zer) reissen
tease, to	taquiner	necken
teaspoon	cuiller *f* à thé	Teelöffel *m*
telegram	télégramme *m*; dépêche *f*	Telegramm *n*
telegraph, to	télégraphier	telegraphieren
telephone	téléphone *m*	Telefon *n*
telephone, to	téléphoner	anrufen
telephone book	annuaire *m* du téléphone	Telefonbuch *n*
telephone booth	cabine *f* téléphonique	Telefonzelle *f*
telephone message	communication *f* par téléphone	Telefonnachricht *f*
television	télévision *f*	Fernsehen *n*
television set	téléviseur *m*	Fernsehapparat *m*
tell (narrate), to	raconter	erzählen
tell (say to), to	dire	sagen
Tell me...	Dites-moi...	Sagen Sie mir...
temperature	température *f*	Temperatur *f*
temple (anat.)	tempe *f*	Schläfe *f*
temple (bldg.)	temple *m*	Tempel *m*
temporary	provisoire	vorläufig
tempt, to	tenter	versuchen
ten	dix	zehn
tenant	locataire *m, f*	Mieter *m*
tender (loving)	tendre	zärtlich
tender (well done)	tendre	weich
tenderloin	filet *m*	Filet *n*
tent	tente *f*	Zelt *n*
tenth (adj.)	dixième	der zehnte, etc.
terrace	terrasse *f*	Terrasse *f*
terminal (bus, plane)	terminus *m*	Endstation *f*
terrible	terrible	furchtbar

Italian	*Portuguese*	*Spanish*
maestro	professor *m*	maestro
tazza da tè	chávena	taza para té
squadra	equipe *f*; time *m* (Br.)	equipo
teiera	bule *m* de chá	tetera
lagrima	lágrima	lágrima
strappare	rasgar	rasgar
stuzzicare	arreliar	embromar
cucchiaino	colher *f* de chá	cucharita
telegramma *m*	telegrama *m*	telegrama *m*
telegrafare	telegrafar	telegrafiar
telefono	telefone *m*	teléfono
telefonare	telefonar	telefonear
elenco telefonico	lista telefônica	guía telefónica
cabina telefonica	pôsto de telefone	cabina telefónica
chiamata; telefonata	chamada; telefonema *m* (Br.)	recado telefónico; telefonema (Mex.)
televisione *f*	televisão *f*	televisión *f*
televisore *m*	televisor *m*	televisor *m*
raccontare	contar	contar
dire	dizer	decir
Mi dica...	Diga-me...	¡Dígame...!
temperatura	temperatura	temperatura
tempia	têmpora; fonte *f*	sien *f*
tempio	templo	templo
provvisorio	provisório	provisional
tentare	tentar	tentar
dieci	dez	diez
inquilino	inquilino; locatário	inquilino
tenero	tenro	tierno
tenero	bem passado	tierno
filetto	filé *m*	filete *m*
tenda	tenda	tienda
decimo	décimo	décimo
terrazza	terraço *m*	terraza
capolinea *m*; stazione *f* terminale	término; estação *f* final (Br.)	estación *f* terminal
terribile	terrível	terrible

English	*French*	*German*
test (exam) (n.)	examen *m*	Prüfung *f*
test (trial) (n.)	épreuve *f*	Probe *f*
test (try), to	éprouver	probieren
testify, to	témoigner	bezeugen
tetanus	tétanos *m*	Tetanus *m*
textbook	manuel *m*	Lehrbuch *n*
textile (n.)	textile *m*	Textilien *fpl*
Thailand	Thaïlande *f*	Thailand *n*
Thames (river)	la Tamise	die Themse
than	que	als
thank, to	remercier	danken
Thank you (very much)!	Merci (beaucoup)!	Danke (schön)!
thanks to...	grâce à...	dank (gen.)...
that (conj.)	que; qui	dass
that (dem. adj.)	ce, cet, cette	jener, jene, jenes
that (dem. pron.)	cela, ça	das
that (rel. pron.)	que	der, die, das
that depends	ça dépend	das kommt darauf an
that is (to say)	c'est-à-dire	nämlich
that way (to)	par là	in jene(r) Richtung
That's enough	Cela suffit	Das genügt
thaw, to	dégeler	tauen
the (with *f* noun)	la, l'	die
the (with *m* noun)	le, l'	der
the (with *n* noun)	—	das
the (with *pl* noun)	les	die
The pleasure is mine!	Enchanté!	Es ist meine Freude!
The same to you!	Vous aussi!	Gleichfalls!
theatre	théâtre *m*	Theater *n*
their	leur	ihr
theirs	le leur, etc.	ihr, ihrer, ihre; der ihrige, etc.
them (dir. obj.)	les	sie
them (ind. obj.)	leur	ihnen
then (at that time)	à ce temps-là; alors	damals

Italian	*Portuguese*	*Spanish*
esame *m*	exame *m*	examen *m*
prova	**prova**	**prueba**
provare	**provar**	**probar**
testimoniare	testemunhar	atestiguar
tetano	tétano	tétanos *m*
libro di **testo**	manual *m*	libro de **texto**
tessuto	tecido	textil *m*; tejido
Tailandia	Tailândia	Tailandia
il Tamigi	a Tâmisa	el Támesis
di; che	que; do que	que; de lo que
ringraziare	agradecer	agradecer; dar las gracias
(Molte) Grazie!	(Muito) Obrigado!; Obrigada! *f*	¡(Muchas) **Gracias!**
grazie a...	graças a...	gracias a...
che	que	que
codesto, -a; quel, -la, -lo	esse, essa; aquele, aquela	ese, esa; **aquel**, etc.
quello	isso	eso; aquello
che	que	que
ciò dipende	isso depende	eso depende
cioè (a dire)	isto é	**es decir**
di là	por ali	por allí
Basta (così)	**Chega**	Eso basta
sgelarsi	degelar	deshelarse
la	a	la
il, lo	o	el
—	—	—
i, gli, le	os (*m*); as (*f*)	los (*m*); las (*f*)
Il piacere è **mio!**	O prazer é todo meu!	¡El **gusto** es **mío!**
Altrettanto!	Igualmente!	¡Igualmente!
teatro	teatro	teatro
loro	seu, sua, seus, suas	su, sus
(il) loro, etc.	(o)seu, etc.	(el)suyo, etc.
le, li	os, as	los, las
loro	lhes	les
allora	então	entonces

English	*French*	*German*
then (in that case)	donc	dann
then (next)	puis	dann
there	là	dort; da
therefore	par conséquent	deshalb
there is, there are	il y a	es gibt
there was (were)	il y avait	es gab; es waren
thermometer	thermomètre *m*	Thermometer *n*
thermos jug	thermos *f*	Thermosflasche *f*
these (dem. adj.)	ces	diese
they	ils, elles	sie
they are	ils (elles) sont	sie sind
they say (it is said)	on dit	man sagt
thick (bulky)	épais	dick
thick (dense)	dense	dicht
thick soup	potage *m*	Suppe *f*
thief	voleur *m*	Dieb *m*
Thief!	Au voleur!	Haltet den Dieb!
thigh	cuisse *f*	Schenkel *m*
thimble	dé *m* à coudre	Fingerhut *m*
thin (not fat)	maigre	dünn; mager
thin (not thick)	mince	dünn
thing	chose *f*	Ding *n*
think, to	penser	meinen; denken
third (adj.)	troisième	der dritte, etc.
thirsty, to be	avoir soif	Durst haben
thirteen	treize	dreizehn
thirty	trente	dreissig
this (dem. adj.)	ce, cet, cette	dieser, etc.
this (pron.)	ceci	dies
this afternoon	cet après-midi	heute nachmittag
This does not work	Ceci ne marche pas	Dies funktioniert nicht
this evening	ce soir	heute abend
this is...	c'est...	dies ist...
This is not mine	Ceci ne m'appartient pas	Dies gehört mir nicht
This is not what I want	Ce n'est pas ce que je veux	Das ist nicht, was ich wünsche
this morning	ce matin	heute morgen

Italian	*Portuguese*	*Spanish*
allora; dunque	nesse caso	en tal caso
poi	depois	luego
là; li	aí; ali; lá	ahí; allí; allá
perciò; quindi	por isso; portanto	por eso; por lo tanto
c'è, ci sono	há	hay
c'era(no)	havia	había
termometro	termômetro	termómetro
termos *m*	termo	termo
questi, queste	estes, estas	estos, estas
essi, esse, loro	eles, elas	ellos, ellas
essi (esse, loro) sono	(eles, elas) são; estão	(ellos, ellas) son; están
si dice	dizem	se dice
spesso	grosso; espêsso	espeso
spesso	espêsso	espeso
minestrone *m*	potagem *f*	potaje *m*
ladro	ladrão	ladrón *m*
Al ladro!	Ladrão!	¡Ladrón!
coscia	coxa	muslo
ditale *m*	dedal *m*	dedal *m*
magro	magro	delgado; flaco
sottile	delgado	delgado
cosa	cousa; coisa (Br.)	cosa
pensare	pensar; achar	pensar
terzo	terceiro	tercero
aver sete	ter sêde	tener sed
tredici	treze	trece
trenta	trinta	treinta
questo, -a	êste, esta	este, -a
questo	isto	esto
questo pomeriggio	hoje à tarde	esta tarde
Questo non funziona	Isto não funciona	Esto no funciona
stasera	esta tarde	esta tarde
questo è...	isto é...	esto es...
Questo non è mio	Isto não é meu	Esto no es mío
Questo non é ciò che voglio	Isto não é o que eu desejo	Esto no es lo que deseo
stamani	esta manhã	esta mañana

English	*French*	*German*
this time	cette fois	diesmal
this way (to)	par ici	in diese **Richtung**
those (dem. adj.)	ces	jene
thousand	mille	tausend
thread (n.)	fil *m*	Faden *m*
threaten, to	mena**cer**	drohen
three	trois	drei
throat	gorge *f*	Hals *m*
throne	trône *m*	Thron *m*
through (prep.)	à travers	durch
through coach	voiture *f* directe	Kurswagen *m*
throw, to	jeter	werfen
thumb	pouce *m*	Daumen *m*
thumbtack	punaise *f*	Reisszwecke *f*
thunder	tonnerre *m*	Donner *m*
thunder, to	tonner	donnern
Thursday	jeudi *m*	Donnerstag *m*
thus (in this way)	ainsi	so
thus (therefore)	donc	also
ticket (R.R.)	billet *m*	Fahrkarte *f*
ticket (theat.)	billet *m*	Eintrittskarte *f*
ticket window	guichet *m*	Schalter *m*
tickle, to	chatouiller	kitzeln
tide (high)	marée *f* haute	Flut *f*
tide (low)	marée *f* basse	Ebbe *f*
tie (fasten), to	lier	binden
tie clip	pince *f* à cravate	Krawattenklipp *m*
tiger	tigre *m*	Tiger *m*
tight (not loose)	serré	eng
tighten, to	resserrer	anziehen
tile (n.)	tuile *f*	Kachel *f*
till (time)	jusqu' à	bis
time (general)	temps *m*	Zeit *f*
time (a series)	fois *f*	Mal *n*
time (of day)	heure *f*	Uhr *f*
times (math.)	fois; par	mal
timetable	horaire *m*	Fahrplan *m*

Italian	*Portuguese*	*Spanish*
questa volta	esta vez	esta vez
di qui	por aqui	por aquí
quei, quelli, quelle	esses, essas; aqueles, aquelas	esos, esas; aquellos, aquellas
mille	mil	mil
filo	linha; fio	hilo
minacciare	ameaçar	amenazar
tre	três	tres
gola	garganta	garganta
trono	trono	trono
attraverso; per	através; por	a través de; por
vettura diretta	vagão direto	vagón *m* directo
gettare	jogar; atirar	echar
pollice *m*	polegar *m*	pulgar *m*
cimice *f*	percevejo	chinche *m* or *f*
tuono	trovão	trueno
tuonare	trovejar	tronar
giovedì *m*	quinta-feira	jueves *m*
così	assim	así
così; perciò	por isso	por eso
biglietto	bilhete *m*; passagem *f* (Br.)	billete *m*; boleto (Amer.)
biglietto d'ingresso	entrada *f*	entrada
sportello dei biglietti	guichê *m*	ventanilla
solleticare	fazer cócegas	hacer cosquillas
alta marea	maré cheia	marea alta
bassa marea	maré baixa	marea baja
legare	atar	atar
fermacravatta	prendedor *m* de gravata	sujetador *m* de corbata
tigre *f*	tigre *m*	tigre *m*
stretto	apertado	apretado
stringere	apertar	apretar
mattonella	telha; ladrilho	azulejo
fino a	até	hasta
tempo	tempo	tiempo
volta	vez *f*	vez *f*
ora	hora	hora
per	vezes	por
orario	horário	horario

English	*French*	*German*
tin	étain *m*	Zinn *n*; Blech *n*
tint (hair), to	teindre	tönen
tiny	tout petit	winzig
tip (gratuity)	pourboire *m*	Trinkgeld *n*
tip (point)	bout *m*	Spitze *f*
tire (auto)	pneu *m*	Reifen *m*
tire (become weary)	se fatiguer	müde werden
tire (make weary)	fatiguer	ermüden
tired (be), to	(être) fatigué	müde (sein)
tissue paper	papier *m* de soie	Zellstofftuch *n*
to (a place)	à; en	zu; nach
to (in order to)	pour	um zu
To be sure!	Bien entendu!	Freilich!
to the left	à gauche	links
to the right	à droite	rechts
To whom?	À qui?	Wem?
toast (bread) (n.)	pain *m* grillé	Toast *m*
toast (drink)	toast *m*	Trinkspruch *m*
toaster	grille-pain *m*	Toaster *m*
tobacco	tabac *m*	Tabak *m*
tobacco pouch	blague *f*	Tabakbeutel *m*
tobacco shop	bureau *m* de tabac	Zigarrenladen *m*
today	aujourd'hui	heute
toe	doigt *m* du pied	Zehe *f*
together	ensemble	zusammen
toilet	cabinet *m*; W.C. *m*	Toilette *f*; Klosett *n*
toilet paper	papier *m* hygiénique	Klosettpapier *n*
toilet soap	savon *m* de toilette	Toilettenseife *f*
token (bus, phone)	jeton *m*	Zeichenmünze *f*
Tokyo	Tokyo *m*	Tokio *n*
tomato	tomate *f*	Tomate *f*
tomb	tombe *f*	Grab *n*; Gruft *f*
tomorrow	demain	morgen
tomorrow afternoon	demain après-midi	morgen nachmittag
tomorrow morning	demain matin	morgen früh
tomorrow night	demain soir	morgen abend
ton	tonne *f*	Tonne *f*
tone	ton *m*	Ton *m*

Italian	*Portuguese*	*Spanish*
stagno	estanho	estaño
tingere	tingir	teñir; matizar
piccolino	pequenino	chiquito
mancia	gorjeta	propina
punta	ponta	punta
gomma; pneumatico	pneu *m*	neumático; cubierta; llanta (Mex.)
stancarsi	cansar-se	cansarse
stancare	cansar	cansar
(essere) stanco	(estar) cansado	(estar) cansado
carta velina	papel *m* de sêda	papel *m* de seda
a; in	a; para	a; hasta
per	para	para
Certamente!	Certamente!	¡Claro!
a sinistra	à esquerda	a la izquierda
a destra	à direita	a la derecha
A chi?	A quem?	¿A quién?
pane *m* tostato	torradas	tostadas *fpl*; pan *m* tostado
brindisi *m*	brinde *m*; saúde *f*	brindis *m*
tostapane *m*	torradeira	tostador *m*
tabacco	tabaco; fumo (Br.)	tabaco
borsa da tabacco	bôlsa de tabaco	petaca
tabaccheria	tabacaria	estanco; tabaquería
oggi	hoje	hoy
dito del piede	dedo do pé	dedo del pie
insieme	juntos	juntos
gabinetto; W.C. *m*	toilete *f*; lavatório	retrete *m*; excusado
carta igienica	papel *m* higiênico	papel *m* higiénico
sapone *m* da toletta	sabonete *m*	jabón *m* de tocador
gettone *m*	ficha; senha	ficha
Tokio *f*	Tóquio	Tokio
pomodoro	tomate *m*	tomate *m*; jitomate *m* (Mex.)
tomba	tumba	tumba
domani	amanhã	mañana
domani pomeriggio	amanhã de tarde	mañana por la tarde
domattina	amanhã de manhã	mañana por la mañana
domani sera	amanhã à noite	mañana por la noche
tonnellata	tonelada	tonelada
tono	tom *m*	tono

English	*French*	*German*
tongue	langue *f*	Zunge *f*
tonight	ce soir	heute abend
tonsil	amygdale *f*	Mandel *f*
tonsillitis	amygdalite *f*	Mandelentzündung *f*
too (also)	aussi	auch
too (overly)	trop	zu
Too bad!	C'est dommage!	Schade!
too expensive	trop cher	zu teuer
too large	trop grand	zu gross
too late	trop tard	zu spät
too much, many	trop de	zu viel(e)
too raw	trop cru	zu roh
too small	trop petit	zu klein
too sour	trop aigre	zu sauer
too sweet	trop sucré	zu süss
too tough	trop dur	zu zäh
tool	outil *m*	Werkzeug *n*
tooth	dent *f*	Zahn *m*
toothache	mal *m* aux dents	Zahnweh *n*
toothbrush	brosse *f* à dents	Zahnbürste *f*
tooth paste	pâte *f* dentifrice	Zahnpasta *f*
toothpick	cure-dents *m*	Zahnstocher *m*
tooth powder	poudre *f* dentifrice	Zahnpulver *n*
top (auto)	capote *f*	Verdeck *n*
top (highest) (adj.)	plus haut	höchst
top (summit)	sommet *m*	Gipfel *m*
top (upper surface)	dessus *m*	obere Seite *f*
topcoat	pardessus *m*	Überzieher *m*
tortoise shell	écaille *f* de tortue	Schildpatt *n*
total (sum)	total *m*	Gesamtbetrag *m*
touch (sense of)	toucher *m*	Gefühl *n*
touch, to	toucher	berühren
tough (resistant)	dur	zäh
tour (n.)	tour *m*; circuit *m*	Reise *f*; Tour *f*
tourist	touriste *m, f*	Tourist *m*
tourniquet (med.)	tourniquet *m*	Aderpresse *f*; Tourniquet *n*

Italian	*Portuguese*	*Spanish*
lingua	língua	lengua
questa notte; stanotte	hoje à noite; esta noite	esta noche
tonsilla	amígdala	amígdala; tonsila
tonsillite *f*	amigdalite *f*	amigdalitis *f*
anche	também	también
troppo	...demais	demasiado
Che peccato!	É pena!	¡Es lástima!
troppo caro	caro demais	demasiado caro
troppo grande	grande demais	demasiado grande
troppo tardi	tarde demais	demasiado tarde
troppo, troppi	...demais	demasiado(s)
troppo crudo	cru demais	demasiado crudo
troppo piccolo	pequeno demais	demasiado pequeño
troppo acido	azêdo demais	demasiado agrio
troppo dolce	doce demais	demasiado dulce
troppo duro	duro demais	demasiado duro
utensile *m*	ferramenta	herramienta
dente *m*	dente *m*	diente *m*
mal *m* di denti	dor *m* de dentes	dolor *m* de muelas
spazzolino da denti	escôva de dentes	cepillo de dientes
pasta dentifricia	pasta dentifrícia	pasta dentífrica
stecchino; stuzzicadenti *m*	palito	palillo; mondadientes *m*
polvere *f* dentifricia	pós *mpl* dentrifícios	polvos *mpl* dentífricos
capote *f*; capotta	capota	capota
più alto	mais alto	más alto
cima	cume *m*	cumbre *f*
superficie *f*	cimo	superficie *f*
soprabito	sobretudo (leve)	abrigo; sobretodo
guscio di tartaruga	tartaruga	carey *m*
totale *m*	total *m*	total *m*
tatto	tato	tacto
toccare	tocar	tocar
resistente	duro	duro
giro; gita turistica	giro; excursão *f*	jira; excursión *f*
turista *m, f*	turista *m, f*	turista *m, f*
pinza emostatica	torniquete *m*	torniquete *m*

English	*French*	*German*
tow, to	remorquer	schleppen
toward	vers	nach
towel	serviette *f*	Handtuch *n*
towel rack	porte-serviettes *m*	Handtuchständer *m*
tower	tour *f*	Turm *m*
tow line	câble *m* de remorque	Schleppseil *n*
town	ville *f*	Stadt *f*
town hall	Hôtel *m* de Ville; mairie *f*	Rathaus *n*
toy	jouet *m*; joujou *m*	Spielzeug *n*
track (rails)	voie *f*	Gleis *n*
tractor	tracteur *m*	Traktor *m*
trademark	marque *f* déposée	Handelsmarke *f*
traffic	circulation *f*	Verkehr *m*
traffic light	feu *m* de circulation	Verkehrsampel *f*
trail (path)	piste *f*	Pfad *m*
trailer (goods)	remorque *f*	Anhänger *m*
trailer (house)	caravane *f*	Wohnwagen *m*
train (R.R.)	train *m*	Zug *m*
transfer	billet *m* de correspondance	Umsteigebillet *n*
transfer, to	transborder	umsteigen
translate, to	traduire	übersetzen
translation	traduction *f*	Übersetzung *f*
transmission (auto)	transmission *f*	Transmission *f*
transport, to	transporter	befördern; transportieren
transportation	transport *m*	Beförderung *f*
trash	ordures *fpl*	Abfall *m*
travel, to	voyager	reisen
travel agency	agence *f* de voyages	Reisebüro *n*
traveler	voyageur *m*	Reisende *m, f*
traveler's check	chèque *m* de voyage	Reisescheck *m*
traveling companion	compagnon *m* de voyage	Reisegefährte *m, f*
traveling salesman	commis *m* voyageur	Handelsreisende *m*
travel insurance	assurance *f* de voyage	Reiseversicherung *f*

Italian	*Portuguese*	*Spanish*
rimorchiare	rebocar	remolcar
verso	para	hacia
asciugamano	toalha	toalla
porta-asciugamani *m*	toalheiro	toallero
torre *f*	tôrre *f*	torre *f*
cavo da rimorchio	cabo de reboque	cable *m* de remolque
città	cidade *f*	pueblo
municipio	município	ayuntamiento
giocattolo	brinquedo	juguete *m*
binario	carril *m*; trilho	vía
trattore *m*	trator *m*	tractor *m*
marca di fabbrica	marca de fábrica	marca de fábrica
traffico	tráfego	tráfico
semaforo	semáforo; sinal *m*	semáforo
pista	senda	sendero
rimorchio	reboque *m*	remolque *m*
casa mobile; roulotte *f*	carro-reboque *m*	coche-habitación *m*; coche-vivienda
treno	combóio; trem *m* (Br.)	tren *m*
trasferta	transferência	transbordo
trasferire	transferir	transbordar
tradurre	traduzir	traducir
traduzione *f*	tradução *f*	traducción *f*
trasmissione *f*	transmissão *f*	transmisión *f*
trasportare	transportar	transportar
trasporto	transporte *m*	transporte *m*
rifiuti *mpl*	lixo	basura
viaggiare	viajar	viajar
agenzia di viaggi	agência de viagens	agencia de viajes
viaggiatore *m*	viajante *m*	viajero
assegno di viaggio	cheque de viajante	cheque *m* de viajeros
compagno di viaggio	companheiro de viagem	compañero de viaje
commesso viaggiatore	caixeiro viajante	viajante *m* de comercio
assicurazione *f* di viaggio	seguro de viagem	seguro de viaje

English	*French*	*German*
tray	plateau *m*	Tablett *n*
treasure (n.)	trésor *m*	Schatz *m*
treasurer	trésorier *m*	Schatzmeister *m*
treasury	trésorerie *f*	Schatz *m*
treat (medically), to	traiter	behandeln
treat (pay), to	offrir	spendieren
treatment (med.)	traitement *m*	Behandlung *f*
treaty	traité *m*	Vertrag *m*
tree	arbre *m*	Baum *m*
tremble, to	trembler	zittern
trench (mil.)	tranchée *f*	Graben *m*
tribe	tribu *f*	Stamm *m*
trick (ruse)	tour *m*	Trick *m*
trim, to	tailler	abschneiden
trip (n.)	voyage *m*	Reise *f*
trip (stumble), to	trébucher	stolpern
tripe	tripe *f*	Kaldaunen *pl*
tripod (phot.)	trépied *m*	Stativ *n*
trolley bus	trolleybus *m*	Oberleitungsbus *m*
troops (mil.)	troupes *fpl*	Truppen *fpl*
tropical	tropique	tropisch
Tropics (the)	les Tropiques *fpl*	die Tropen *fpl*
trouble (be in), to	avoir des ennuis	in Not sein
trouble, to	déranger	belästigen
trousers	pantalon *m*	Hose *f*
trout	truite *f*	Forelle *f*
truce (mil.)	trêve *f*	Waffenstillstand *m*
truck (auto)	camion *m*	Lastwagen *m*
true (real)	vrai	wahr
true? (is it-)	n'est-ce pas?	nicht wahr?
truffle	truffe *f*	Trüffel *f*
trunk (auto)	malle-arrière *f*; coffre *m*	Kofferraum *m*
trunk (luggage)	malle *f*	Koffer *m*
truss (to wear)	bandage *m* herniaire	Bruchband *n*
trust (rely on), to	se fier à	vertrauen auf
truth	vérité *f*	Wahrheit *f*

Italian	*Portuguese*	*Spanish*
vassoio	bandeja; tabuleiro	bandeja; charola (Amer.)
tesoro	tesouro	tesoro
tesoriere	tesoureiro	tesorero
tesoro	tesouraria	tesorería
trattare	tratar	tratar
offrire	obsequiar	obsequiar
cura	tratamento	tratamiento
trattato	tratado	tratado
albero	árvore *f*	árbol *m*
tremare	tremer	temblar
trincea	trincheira	trinchera
tribù *f*	tribo *f*	tribu *f*
trucco	truque *m*	truco
tagliare; cimare	aparar	recortar
viaggio	viagem *f*	viaje *m*
inciampare	tropeçar	tropezar
trippa	dobradinha	callos *mpl*; mondongo
tripode *m*	tripé *m*; trípode *f*	trípode *m*
filobus *m*	trólebus *m*	trolebús *m*
truppe *fpl*	tropas *fpl*	tropas *fpl*
tropicale	tropical	tropical
i tropici *mpl*	os trópicos *mpl*	los trópicos *mpl*
trovarsi nei guai	estar em dificuldades	tener dificultades
incomodare	incomodar	molestar
pantaloni *mpl*	calças *fpl*	pantalones *mpl*
trota	truta	trucha
tregua	trégua	tregua
autocarro; camion *m*	camião; caminhão	camión *m*; camioneta (Mex.)
vero	verdadeiro	verdadero
non è vero?	não é?	¿verdad?
tartufo	trufa	trufa
portabagagli *m*	porta-malas *m*	portaequipaje *m*; cajuela (Mex.)
baule *m*	baú *m*; mala	baúl *m*; petaca (Mex.)
cinto erniario	bragueiro; funda	braguero
fidarsi di	confiar em	confiar en
verità	verdade *f*	verdad *f*

English	*French*	*German*
try (attempt), to	essayer	versuchen
try on, to	essayer	anprobieren
try (test), to	éprouver	prüfen
tub (bath-)	baignoire *f*	Wanne *f*
tube (inner-)	chambre *f* à air	Schlauch *m*
tube (pipe)	tube *m*; tuyau *m*	Rohr *n*
tube (radio-)	lampe *f*	Röhre *f*
Tuesday	mardi *m*	Dienstag *m*
tuition	frais *m* d'inscription	Schulgeld *n*
tulip	tulipe *f*	Tulpe *f*
tumor	tumeur *f*	Geschwulst *f*
tuna fish	thon *m*	Thunfisch *m*
tune (melody)	air *m*	Melodie *f*
tunnel (n.)	tunnel *m*	Tunnel *m*
turkey	dindon *m*	Truthahn *m*
Turkey	la Turquie	die Türkei
Turkish (adj.)	turc	türkisch
turn (n.)	virage *m*	Wendung *f*
turn (face about), to	se retourner	sich umdrehen
turn off (light), to	éteindre	ausschalten
turn off (radio), to	fermer	abstellen
turn on (light), to	allumer	anschalten
turn on (radio), to	ouvrir	anstellen
turn signal (auto)	clignotant *m*	Blinker *m*
turn (something), to	tourner	wenden
turnip	navet *m*	Rübe *f*
turnpike	autoroute *f*	Autobahn *f*
turquoise	turquoise *f*	Türkis *m*
turtle	tortue *f*	Schildkröte *f*
tutor (instructor)	précepteur *m*	Privatlehrer *m*
tuxedo	smoking *m*	Frack *m*; **Smoking** *m*
tweezers	pincettes *fpl*	Pinzette *f*
twelve	douze	zwölf
twenty	vingt	zwanzig
twice	deux fois	zweimal

Italian	*Portuguese*	*Spanish*
cercare di	tentar; procurar	tratar de
provarsi	provar; experimentar	probarse
provare	experimentar	probar
vasca	banheira	bañera; baño; tina (Mex.)
camera d'aria	câmara de ar	cámara de aire
tubo	tubo	tubo
valvola	válvula; lâmpada de rádio	válvula
martedì *m*	terça-feira	martes *m*
tasse *fpl* scolastiche	custo de ensino	derechos *mpl* académicos
tulipano	tulipa	tulipán *m*
tumore *m*	tumor *m*	tumor *m*
tonno	atum *m*	atún *m*
aria	ária	tonada
galleria; tunnel *m*	túnel *m*	túnel *m*
tacchino	peru *m*	pavo; guajolote *m* (Mex.)
la Turchia	a Turquia	Turquía
turco	turco	turco
giro; voltata	volta	vuelta
voltarsi	voltar-se	volverse
spegnere	desligar	apagar
spegnere	desligar	quitar
accendere	ligar	encender; prender
accendere	ligar	poner
lampeggiatore *m*	seta de direção	indicador *m* de dirección
girare	voltar; virar	dar la vuelta a
rapa	nabo	nabo
autostrada	autostrada	autopista
turchese *m*	turquesa	turquesa
tartaruga	tartaruga	tortuga
precettore *m*	professor *m* particular	maestro particular
smoking *m*	smoking *m*	smoking *m*
pinzette *fpl*	pinças *fpl*	pinzas *fpl*
dodici	doze	doce
venti	vinte	veinte
due volte	duas vezes	dos veces

English	*French*	*German*
twin (n.)	jumeau *m*; jumelle *f*	Zwilling *m*
twin beds	lits *mpl* jumeaux	Doppelbett *n*
twist, to	tordre	winden
two	deux	zwei
type, to	taper à la machine	tippen
typewriter	machine *f* à écrire	Schreibmaschine *f*
typewriter ribbon	ruban *m* de machine à écrire	Farbband *n*
typhoid fever	fièvre *f* typhoïde	Unterleibstyphus *m*
typist	dactylographe *m, f*	Maschinenschreiber *m*
ugly	laid	hässlich
ulcer	ulcère *m*	Geschwür *n*
umbrella	parapluie *m*	Regenschirm *m*
unbutton, to	déboutonner	aufknöpfen
uncle	oncle *m*	Onkel *m*
uncomfortable	incommode	unbequem
unconscious	sans connaissance	bewusstlos
under (prep.)	sous	unter
underneath (prep.)	au-dessous de	unter
undershirt	tricot *m*	Unterhemd *n*
understand, to	comprendre	verstehen
undertake (attempt), to	entreprendre	unternehmen
undertaker (mortician)	entrepreneur *m* de pompes funèbres	Leichenbestatter *m*
underwear	sous-vêtements *mpl*	Unterwäsche *f*
undress (oneself), to	se déshabiller	sich ausziehen
undress (someone)	déshabiller	ausziehen
undressed (naked)	nu	nackt
uneasy (anxious)	inquiet	unruhig
unequal	inégal	ungleich
unexpected	inattendu	unerwartet
unfair	injuste	ungerecht
unfortunate	malheureux, -euse	unglücklich
unfortunately	malheureusement	leider
unfurnished	non meublé	unmöbliert
ungrateful	ingrat	undankbar
unhappy	malheureux, -euse	unglücklich

Italian	*Portuguese*	*Spanish*
gemello	gêmeo	gemelo; cuate *m* (Mex.)
letti *mpl* gemelli	camas *fpl* separadas	camas *fpl* gemelas
torcere	torcer	torcer
due	dois (*f* duas)	dos
scrivere a macchina	escrever à máquina	escribir a máquina
macchina da scrivere	máquina de escrever	máquina de escribir
nastro per macchina da scrivere	fita para máquina de escrever	cinta para máquina de escribir
febbre *f* tifoidea	febre *f* tifóide	fiebre *f* tifoidea
dattilografo, -a	dactilógrafo, -a	mecanógrafo, -a
brutto	feio	feo
ulcera	úlcera	úlcera
ombrello	guarda-chuva *m*; chapéu *m* de chuva	paraguas *m*
sbottonare	desabotoar	desabotonar
zio	tio	tío
scomodo	incômodo	incómodo
privo di sensi	inconsciente	inconsciente
sotto	debaixo de; sob	bajo
disotto	em baixo de	debajo de
camiciola	camiseta; camisa de meia	camiseta; camisola
capire	compreender; entender	entender; comprender
intraprendere	intentar	intentar
impresario di pompe funebri	empresário fúnebre	empresario de pompas fúnebres
biancheria	roupa de baixo	ropa interior
svestirsi; spogliarsi	despir-se	desvestirse
svestire	despir	desvestir
nudo	nu (*f* nua)	desnudo
inquieto	inquieto	inquieto
ineguale	desigual	desigual
imprevisto	inesperado	inesperado
ingiusto	injusto	injusto
sfortunato; disgraziato	infortunado	desventurado
purtroppo; sfortunatamente	infelizmente	desgraciadamente
non ammobiliato	desmobilado	desamueblado
ingrato	ingrato	ingrato
infelice	infeliz	infeliz; desgraciado

English	*French*	*German*
unhealthy	malsain	ungesund
unite, to	unir	vereinigen
United Nations	les Nations Unies; O.N.U. *f*	die Vereinten Nationen
United States	les États-Unis	die Vereinigten Staaten
university	université *f*	Universität *f*
unknown	inconnu	unbekannt
unless (conj.)	à moins que	wenn nicht
unload, to	décharger	abladen
unlucky	malchanceux, -euse	unglücklich
unnecessary	inutile	unnötig
unoccupied	libre	frei
unpack, to	déballer	auspacken
unpaid	impayé	unbezahlt
unpleasant	désagréable	unangenehm
untie, to	détacher; délier	aufmachen; aufbinden
until (conj.)	jusqu'à ce que	bis
until (up to the time of) (prep.)	jusqu'à	bis
Until tomorrow!	À demain!	Bis morgen!
Until we meet again!	Au revoir!	Auf Wiedersehen!
untrue	faux, fausse	falsch; unwahr
unusual	insolite	ungewöhnlich
unwillingly	à contre-coeur	widerwillig
unwise	malavisé	unklug
unwrap, to	défaire	auswickeln
up (adv.)	(en) haut	oben
up to now	jusqu'à présent	bisher
upon (prep.)	sur	auf
upper (adj.)	supérieur	ober
upper berth	couchette *f* supérieure	Oberbett *n*
upset (overturn), to	renverser	umstürzen
upstairs	en haut	oben; die Treppe hinauf
urge, to	exhorter	zureden; drängen

Italian	Portuguese	Spanish
malsano	malsão	malsano
unire	unir	unir
le Nazioni Unite	as Nações Unidas	las Naciones Unidas
gli Stati Uniti	os Estados Unidos	los Estados Unidos
università	universidade *f*	universidad *f*
sconosciuto	desconhecido	desconocido
a meno che	a menos que	a menos que
scaricare	descarregar	descargar
sfortunato	desventurado	desgraciado
inutile	desnecessário	innecesario
libero	livre	desocupado
disfare le valigie	desfazer; desarrumar	deshacer
non pagato	não pago	no pagado
spiacevole	desagradável	desagradable
sciogliere	desatar	desatar
fino a che	até que	hasta que
fino a	até	hasta
A domani!	Até amanhã!	¡Hasta mañana!
Arrivederci!	Até a vista!	¡Hasta la vista!
falso	falso	falso
insólito	insólito	insólito
malvolentieri	de má vontade	sin querer; de mala gana
imprudente; insensato	imprudente	mal aconsejado
scartocciare	desembrulhar	desenvolver
su	acima; arriba	arriba
fino ad ora	até agora	hasta ahora
sopra	sôbre	sobre
superiore	superior; de cima	superior; alto
cuccetta superiore	cama de cima; leito superior (Br.)	cama alta
capovolgere; rovesciare	derrubar	volcar
sopra; al piano superiore	(lá) em cima	arriba; hacia arriba
sollecitare; esortare	instar	instar

English	*French*	*German*
urgent	urgent	dringend
urinate, to	uriner	harnen
Uruguay	l'Uruguay *m*	Uruguay *n*
Uruguayan (adj.)	uruguayen	uruguayisch
us	nous	uns
use (-fulness)	utilité *f*	Nützlichkiet *f*
use (utilization)	usage *m*	Gebrauch *m*
use, to	employer	benutzen; gebrauchen
useful	utile	nützlich; brauchbar
useless	inutile	nutzlos
usher (n.)	ouvreuse *f*	Platzanweiser *m*
usual	usuel; habituel	gewöhnlich
usually	d'habitude	gewöhnlich
vacant (on doors)	libre	frei
vacation (n.)	vacances *fpl*	Ferien *pl*
vaccinate, to	vacciner	impfen
vaccination	vaccination *f*	Impfung *f*
vaccination certificate	certificat *m* de vaccination	Impfschein *m*
vaccine	vaccin *m*	Impfstoff *m*
vacuum cleaner	aspirateur *m*	Staubsauger *m*
Valencia	Valence *f*	Valencia *n*
valid until	valable jusqu'à	gültig bis zum
valise	valise *f*	Handkoffer *m*
valley	vallée *f*	Tal *n*
valuable	de valeur	wertvoll
valuables	objets *mpl* de valeur	Wertsachen *fpl*
value (worth)	valeur *f*	Wert *m*
valve	soupape *f*	Ventil *n*
van (vehicle)	fourgon *m*	Lieferwagen *m*
vanilla	vanille *f*	Vanille *f*
vanity (dressing table)	coiffeuse *f*	Toilettentisch *m*
variety (assortment)	assortiment *m*	Auswahl *m*
variety (diversity)	variété *f*	Mannigfaltigkeit *f*
various	varié; divers	verschieden
varnish	vernis *m*	Firnis *m*
varnish, to	vernir	firnissen

Italian	*Portuguese*	*Spanish*
urgente	urgente	urgente
orinare	urinar	orinar
l'Uruguay *m*	o Uruguai	el Uruguay
uruguaiano	uruguaio	uruguayo
ci; noi	nos	nos
utilità	utilidade *f*	utilidad *f*
uso	uso	uso
usare	usar	usar
utile	útil	útil
inutile	inútil	inútil
maschera	vaga-lume *m*; porteiro (Br.)	acomodador *m*
solito; abituale	de costume	de costumbre
di solito	usualmente	usualmente
libero	livre	desocupado
vacanze *fpl*	férias *fpl*	vacaciones *fpl*
vaccinare	vacinar	vacunar
vaccinazione *f*	vacinação *f*	vacunación *f*
certificato di vaccinazione	atestado de vacina	certificado de vacuna
vaccino	vacina	vacuna
aspirapolvere *m*	aspirador *m* (de pó)	aspirador *m* de polvo
Valenza	Valença	Valencia
valido fino a	válido até	válido hasta
valigetta	maleta; valise *f*	maleta; velís *m* (Amer.)
vallata; valle *f*	vale *m*	valle *m*
di valore	de valor	valioso; de valor
oggetti *mpl* di valore	objetos *mpl* de valor	objetos *mpl* de valor
valore *m*	valor *m*	valor *m*
valvola	válvula	válvula
carro; furgone *m*	carro	camión *m*
vaniglia	baunilha	vainilla
toeletta	mesa de toilete; toucador *m* (Br.)	tocador *m*; coqueta
assortimento	sortimento	surtido
varietà	variedade *f*	variedad *f*
diverso	vários	varios
vernice *f*	verniz *m*	barniz *m*
verniciare	envernizar	barnizar

English	*French*	*German*
vase	vase *m*	Vase *f*
vaudeville	vaudeville *m*	Varieté *n*
veal	veau *m*	Kalbfleisch *n*
veal cutlet	côtelette *f* de **veau**	Kalbskotelett *n*
vegetable	légume *m*	Gemüse *n*
vegetable **garden**	jardin *m* **potager**	Gemüsegarten *m*
veil (n.)	voile *m*	Schleier *m*
vein (anat.)	veine *f*	Ader *f*
velvet (n.)	velours *m*	Samt *m*
Venetian blind	jalousie *f*	Jalousie *f*
Venezuela	le Venezuela	Venezuela *n*
Venezuelan (adj.)	vénézuélien	venezuelisch
Venice	Venise *f*	Venedig *n*
venison	venaison *f*	Wildbret *n*
verb	verbe *m*	Verb *n*
vertical	vertical	senkrecht
very	très	sehr
vessel (ship)	vaisseau *m*	Schiff *n*
vest	gilet *m*	Weste *f*
veterinarian	vétérinaire *m*	Tierarzt *m*
via (by way of)	par	über
vicinity	voisinage *m*	Nähe *f*
victim	victime *f*	Opfer *n*
Vienna	Vienne *f*	Wien *n*
Viet Nam	le Viêt-**Nam** *m*	Vietnam *n*
view (opinion)	vue *f*; avis *m*	Ansicht *f*
view (scene)	vue *f*	Aussicht *f*
village	village *m*	Dorf *n*
vine	vigne *f*	Weinstock *m*
vinegar	vinaigre *m*	Essig *m*
vineyard	vignoble *m*	Weinberg *m*
violence	violence *f*	Gewalt *f*
violent	violent	gewaltsam
violet (flower)	violette *f*	Veilchen *n*
violin	violon *m*	Geige *f*
virgin (n.)	vierge *f*	Jungfrau *f*

Italian	*Portuguese*	*Spanish*
vaso	vaso	vaso; jarrón *m*
rivista; varietà	revista; variedades *fpl*	variedades *fpl*
vitello	vitela	ternera
costoletta di vitello	costeleta de vitela	chuleta de ternera
legume *m*	legume *m*	legumbre *f*; verduras (Mex.)
orto	horta	huerta; huerto
velo	véu *m*	velo
vena	veia	vena
velluto	veludo	terciopelo
tapparella	persiana; veneziana	persiana de tiro
il Venezuela	a Venezuela	Venezuela
venezueliano	venezuelano	venezolano
Venezia	Veneza	Venecia
cacciagione *f*	carne *f* de veado	carne *f* de venado
verbo	verbo	verbo
verticale	vertical	vertical
molto	muito	muy
nave *f*; vascello	navio	barco
panciotto; gilè *m*	colête *m*	chaleco
veterinario	veterinário	veterinario
per; via	por	por
vicinanza; vicinato	vizinhança	vecindad *f*
vittima	vítima	víctima
Vienna	Viena	Viena
Vietnam *m*	o Vietname *m*	Viet-Nam *m*
opinione *f*	parecer *m*	parecer *m*
veduta	vista	vista
villaggio	aldeia	aldea
vite *f*	videira	vid *f*
aceto	vinagre *m*	vinagre *m*
vigna; vigneto	vinha	viña
violenza	violência	violencia
violento	violento	violento
violetta	violeta	violeta
violino	violino	violín *m*
vergine *f*	virgem *f*	virgen *f*

English	*French*	*German*
visa (n.)	visa *m*	Visum *n*
visible	visible	sichtbar
vision (eyesight)	vision *f*	Sehkraft *f*
vision (foresight)	prévoyance *f*	Einsicht *f*
visit (a call)	visite *f*	Besuch *m*
visit (a stay)	séjour *m*	Besuch *m*
visit (call on), **to**	rendre visite *f* à	besuchen
visitor	visiteur *m*	Besucher *m*
vitamin	vitamine *f*	Vitamin *n*
vivid	vif, vive	lebhaft
voice	voix *f*	Stimme *f*
volcano	volcan *m*	Vulkan *m*
volt (elect.)	volt *m*	Volt *n*
volume (book)	volume *m*	Band *m*
volume (quantity)	volume *m*	Volumen *n*; **Menge** *f*
volume (space)	volume *m*	Rauminhalt *m*
vomit, **to**	vomir	sich erbrechen
vote	vote *m*	Stimme *f*
vote, **to**	voter	stimmen
voter	électeur *m*	Wähler *m*
vow (n.)	voeu *m*	Gelübde *n*
voyage (n.)	voyage *m*	Reise *f*
vulgar (ill-bred)	grossier	gemein
vulgar (dirty)	grossier	pöbelhaft
wade, **to**	patauger	waten
waffle	gaufre *f*	Waffel *f*
wages (pay)	salaire *m*	Lohn *m*
waist	taille *f*	Taille *f*
Wait a moment, please!	Voulez-vous attendre un moment?	Warten Sie bitte einen Augenblick!
wait for, **to**	attendre	warten auf (acc.)
wait on, **to**	servir	bedienen
waiter	garçon *m*	Kellner *m*
waiting room	salle *f* d'attente	Wartesaal *m*
waitress	serveuse *f*	Kellnerin *f*; **Fräulein** *n*
wake up (someone)	réveiller	wecken
wake up (rouse oneself), **to**	s'éveiller	erwachen

Italian	*Portuguese*	*Spanish*
visto	visto	visa
visibile	visível	visible
vista	visão *f*	vista
previdenza	previsão *f*	previsión *f*
visita	visita	visita
soggiorno	visita	visita
visitare	visitar	hacer una visita; visitar
visitatore *m*	visitante *m*	visita *m, f*
vitamina	vitamina	vitamina
vivido	vívido	vívido
voce *f*	voz *f*	voz *f*
vulcano	vulcão	volcán *m*
volta	volt *m*	voltio
volume *m*	volume *m*; **tomo**	volumen *m*; **tomo**
volume *m*; quantità	quantidade *f*	cantidad *f*
volume *m*	volume *m*	volumen *m*
vomitare	vomitar	vomitar
voto	voto	voto
votare	votar	votar
elettore	votante *m, f*	votante *m, f*
voto	voto	voto
viaggio	viagem *f*	viaje *m*
volgare	grosseiro	grosero
volgare; grossolano	chulo; baixo	vulgar
guadare	vadear	vadear
cialda	waffle *m*	barquillo; **wafle** *m*
salario	salário	salario
vita; cintola	cintura	cintura
Vuole attendere un momento?	Faça favor de esperar um momento?	¡Favor de esperar un momento!
aspettare	esperar	esperar
servire	atender	atender
cameriere *m*	môço; garção *m* (Br.)	camarero; **mesero** (Mex.)
sala d'aspetto	sala de espera	sala de espera
cameriera	garçonete *f*	moza; mesera (Mex.)
svegliare	acordar	despertar
svegliarsi	acordar-se	despertarse

English	*French*	*German*
Wales	le Pays de **Galles**	Wales *n*
walk (a stroll)	prome**nade** *f*	Spaziergang *m*
walk, to	mar**cher**	gehen
wall (inside)	mur *m*	Wand *f*
wall (outside)	mur *m*	Mauer *f*
wallet	porte**feuille** *m*	Brieftasche *f*
wallpaper	papier *m* **peint**	Tapete *f*
walnut (to eat)	noix *f*	Walnuss *f*
wander, to	errer	wandern
want (desire), to	vouloir	wollen
war (n.)	guerre *f*	Krieg *m*
wardrobe (closet)	garde-**robe** *f*	Kleiderschrank *m*
wardrobe trunk	malle-**armoire** *f*	Schrankkoffer *m*
warehouse	entrepôt *m*	Lagerhaus *n*
warm	chaud	warm
warm, to	chauffer	wärmen
warmth	chaleur *f*	Wärme *f*
warn, to	avertir	warnen
warning	avertisse**ment** *m*	Warnung *f*
warp, to	se déjeter	sich werfen
Warsaw	Varsovie *f*	Warschau *n*
wart	verrue *f*	Warze *f*
washable	lavable	waschbar
washbasin	cuvette *f*	Waschbecken *n*
washer (for bolt)	rondelle *f*	Scheibe *f*
washing machine	machine *f* à la**ver**	Waschmaschine *f*
wash oneself, to	se la**ver**	sich waschen
washroom	lavabo *m*	Waschzimmer *n*
wash (something), to	laver	waschen
washstand	lavabo *m*	Waschtisch *m*
waste (squandering)	gaspill**age** *m*	Verschwendung *f*
waste (squander), to	gaspiller	verschwenden
waste (time), to	perdre	Zeit verschwenden
wastebasket	corbeille *f* à **papier**	Papierkorb *m*
watch (pocket-)	montre *f*	Taschenuhr *f*
watch (guard), to	veiller	bewachen

Italian	*Portuguese*	*Spanish*
Galles *m*	Gales *m*	Gales *m*
passeggiata	passeio	paseo
camminare	andar	andar
parete *f*	parede *f*	pared *f*
muro	muro	muro
portafogli *m*	carteira	cartera
carta da parati	papel *m* de parede	papel *m* tapiz
noce *f*	noz *f*	nuez *m* de nogal
vagare; errare	vaguear; vagar	vagar
volere	desejar	desear
guerra	guerra	guerra
armadio	armário	armario
baule *m* armadio	mala - armário	baúl *m* ropero
magazzino; deposito	armazém *m*	almacén *m*
caldo	quente	caliente
riscaldare	aquecer	calentar
calore *m*	calor *m*	calor *m*
avvertire	prevenir; avisar	avisar; advertir
avvertimento;	aviso;	aviso;
avvertenza	advertência	advertencia
deformarsi	empenar-se	combarse; pandearse
Varsavia	Varsóvia	Varsovia
verruca	verruga	verruga
lavabile	lavável	lavable
lavabo; catinella	bacia	lavamanos *m*
rondella	arruela	arandela
macchina da lavare;	máquina de lavar;	máquina de lavar;
lavatrice *f*	lavadora	lavadora
lavarsi	lavar-se	lavarse
gabinetto; bagno	lavabo	lavabo;
(in home)		gabinete *m* de aseo
lavare	lavar	lavar
lavabo	lavabo	lavabo
sciupio; sperpero	perda	derroche *m*
sciupare; sperperare	dissipar	derrochar; malgastar
guastare	gastar	perder
cestino (per rifiuti)	cesta de papéis	cesto para papeles
orologio	relógio (de bôlso)	reloj *m* (de bolsillo)
vigilare	vigiar	vigilar

English	French	German
watch-band	bracelet *m*	Uhrband *n*
watch (observe), to	regarder	beobachten
Watch out!	Attention!	Passen Sie **auf**!
water (n.)	eau *f*	Wasser *n*
water cress	cresson *m*	Brunnenkresse *f*
waterfall	chute *f* d'eau	Wasserfall *m*
water heater	chauffe-eau *m*	Badeofen *m*
watermelon	melon *m* d'eau; pastèque *f*	Wassermelone *f*
water pitcher	carafe *f*	Wasserkrug *m*
waterproof	imperméable	wasserdicht
water pump	pompe *f* à l'eau	Wasserpumpe *f*
wave (ocean)	vague *f*	Welle *f*
wax	cire *f*	Wachs *n*
wax (apply-), to	cirer	bohnern
way (manner)	façon *f*	Weise *f*
way (route)	chemin *m*	Weg *m*
we	nous	wir
we are	nous sommes	wir sind
weak	faible	schwach
weaken, to	affaiblir	schwächen
weakness	faiblesse *f*	Schwäche *f*
wealth	richesse *f*	Reichtum *m*
wealthy	riche	vermögend
wean, to	sevrer	entwöhnen
weapon	arme *f*	Waffe *f*
wear (have on), to	porter	tragen
weary (adj.)	las, -se	müde
weather	temps *m*	Wetter *n*
weave, to	tisser	weben
wedding	mariage *m*	Hochzeit *f*
Wednesday	mercredi *m*	Mittwoch *m*
weed (n.)	mauvaise herbe *f*	Unkraut *n*
week	semaine *f*	Woche *f*
weekend	week-end *m*	Wochenende *n*
weekly (adj.)	hebdomadaire	wöchentlich
weep, to	pleurer	weinen

Italian	*Portuguese*	*Spanish*
cinturino d'orologio	pulseira	pulsera
stare a guardare	observar	observar
Attenzione!	Cuidado!	¡Cuidado!
acqua	água	agua
crescione *m*	agrião *m*	berro
cascata	queda d'água; cascata	caída de agua; cascada; catarata
scaldabagno *m*	aquecedor *m* d'água	calentador *m* de agua
cocomero	melancia	sandía; patilla (Amer.)
brocca dell'acqua; caraffa	jarro	jarro; cántaro
impermeabile	impermeável	impermeable
pompa d'acqua	bomba de água	bomba de agua
onda	onda	ola
cera	cêra	cera
dare la cera	encerar	encerar
maniera; modo	maneira; modo	manera; modo
via	caminho	camino; ruta
noi	nós; a gente	nosotros, -as
(noi) siamo	(nós) somos; estamos	(nosotros) somos; estamos
debole; fiacco	débil; fraco	débil; flaco
indebolire	debilitar	debilitar
debolezza	debilidade *f*	debilidad *f*
ricchezza	riqueza	riqueza
ricco	rico	rico
svezzare	desmamar	destetar
arma	arma	arma
portare	vestir	llevar; vestir
spossato; stanco	cansado	cansado
tempo	tempo	tiempo
tessere	tecer	tejer
nozze *fpl*	casamento; matrimônio	boda
mercoledì *m*	quarta-feira	miércoles *m*
erbaccia	erva daninha	mala hierba
settimana	semana	semana
fine *f* di settimana	fim *m* de semana	fin *m* de semana
settimanale	semanal	semanal
piangere	chorar	llorar

English	*French*	*German*
weigh, to	peser	wiegen
weight	poids *m*	Gewicht *n*
welcome	accueil *m*	Willkommen *n*
Welcome!	Bienvenu!	Willkommen!
welcome, to	souhaiter la bienvenue à	begrüssen
well (in fine shape)	bien	gut; wohl
well (in health)	bien portant	gesund
Well! (is that so!)	Tiens!	Was Sie nicht sagen!
well (for water)	puits *m*	Brunnen *m*
well done (food)	bien cuit	gut durchgebraten
well-known	bien connu	bekannt
well (-then)	alors	nun; also
well-to-do	à son aise; aisé	wohlhabend
Welsh (adj.)	gallois	walisisch
west (n.)	ouest *m*	Westen *m*
western	occidental	westlich
West Indies	les Indes Occidentales	Westindien *n*
wet (adj.)	mouillé	nass
wet, to	mouiller	nass machen
whale	baleine *f*	Wal *m*
wharf	quai *m*	Kai *m*
What?	Qu'est-ce qui . . . ?	Was . . . ?
what (that which)	ce qui, ce que	was
What a...!	Quel...!	Was für ein...!
What a pity!	Quel dommage!	Schade!
What can I do for you?	Est-ce que je puis vous servir?	Womit kann ich Ihnen dienen?
What did you say? (pardon?)	Comment?; Plaît-il?	Wie bitte?
What do you call this?	Comment appelle-t-on ceci?	Wie nennt man das?
What do you mean?	Que voulez-vous dire?	Was meinen Sie?
What do you want?	Que désirez-vous?	Was wünschen Sie?
What does—mean?	Que veut dire...?	Was bedeutet...?
whatever (adj.)	quelque...que (qui)	welch, etc....auch
whatever (pron.)	tout ce qui (que)	was auch
What is it made of?	De quoi est-ce fait?	Woraus ist es?

Italian	*Portuguese*	*Spanish*
pesare	pesar	pesar
peso	pêso	peso
accoglienza	boas-vindas *fpl*	bienvenida
Benvenuto!	Bem-vindo!	¡Bienvenido!
dare il benvenuto	dar as boas vindas	dar la bienvenida
bene	bem	bien
sano	bem de saúde	bien de salud
Ah, è così!	Então!	¡No me diga!
pozzo	poço	pozo
ben cotto	bem-passado	bien asado (cocido)
ben conosciuto (noto)	conhecido	bien conocido
ebbene	pois bem	pues bien
ricco	abastado	acomodado
gallese	galês	galés
ovest *m*	oeste *m*	oeste *m*
occidentale	ocidental	occidental
le Indie occidentali	as Antilhas	las Antillas
bagnato	molhado	mojado
bagnare	molhar	mojar
balena	baleia	ballena
scalo; molo	cais *m*	muelle *m*
Che (cosa) . . . ?	(O) que . . . ?	¿Qué . . . ?
ciò che	o que	lo que
Che. . .!	Que. . .!	¡Qué. . .!
Peccato!	Que pena!	¡Qué lástima!
In che posso servirla?	Em que posso servi-lo?	¿En qué puedo servirle?
Come, prego?	Como?	¿Cómo?; ¿Mande?
Come si chiama questo?	Como se chama isto?	¿Cómo se llama esto?
Che cosa intende dire?	Que quer dizer?	¿Qué quiere decir?
Che cosa desidera?	Que quer o senhor?	¿Qué quiere Ud.?
Che vuol dire. . .?	Que quer dizer. . .?	¿Qué quiere decir. . .?
qualunque	qualquer	cual(es)quier(a)
qualsiasi cosa	qualquer coisa que	cualquier cosa que
Di che cosa è fatto?	De que é feito?	¿De qué es?

English	*French*	*German*
What is that?	Qu'est-ce que c'est que cela?	Was ist **das**?
What is that in (language)?	Comment dit-on cela en...?	Wie heisst das auf...?
What is the date?	Quelle est la **date**?	Den wievielten haben wir heute?
What is the fare to...?	Quel est le prix du billet pour...?	Wieviel kostet die Fahrkarte nach...?
What is the matter?	Qu'y a-t-il?	Was ist los?
What is the matter with you?	Qu'avez-**vous**?	Was haben Sie?
What is the rate of exchange?	Quel est le cours du **change**?	Wie ist der **Kurs**?
What is the weather like?	Quel temps fait-il?	Wie ist das **Wetter**?
What is this?	Qu'est-ce que c'est que ceci?	Was ist **das**?
What is this for?	A quoi sert ceci?	Wozu gebraucht man das?
What is your address?	Quelle est votre adresse?	Was ist Ihre **Adresse**?
What is your name?	Comment vous appelez-**vous**?	Wie heissen Sie?
What kind of a...?	Quelle **sorte** de...?	Was für ein (etc.)...?
What time does it start?	A quelle heure est-ce que cela commen**ce**?	Wann fängt es **an**?
What time is it?	Quelle heure est-il?	Wieviel Uhr ist es?
What will you **have** (to drink)?	Qu'est-ce que vous voulez?	Was möchten Sie?
What's new?	Quoi de **neuf**?	Was gibt es **Neues**?
wheat	blé *m*	Weizen *m*
wheel	roue *f*	Rad *n*
wheel chair	fauteuil *m* **roulant**	Rollstuhl *m*
when (at the time that)	lorsque	als
When? (at what time)	Quand?	Wann?
When does it let out? (finish)	A quelle heure sort-on?	Wann ist es **aus**?
When does the (train) leave?	A quelle heure part (le train)?	Um wieviel **Uhr** fährt (der Zug) ab?
When is it open?	Quand est-ce ouvert?	Wann wird es geöffnet?
When shall I come back?	Quand de**vrai**-je revenir?	Wann soll ich zurückkommen?

Italian	*Portuguese*	*Spanish*
Che cosa è quello?	Que é isso?	¿Qué es eso?
Come si chiama quello in...?	O que é isso em ...?	¿Cómo se llama eso en...?
Quanti ne abbiamo?	Quantos são?	¿A cuántos estamos?
Quanto costa il biglietto per...?	Quanto custa a passagem para...?	¿Cuánto vale el pasaje a...?
Che cosa c'è?	Que há?	¿Qué hay?
Che cosa ha?	Que é que o senhor tem?	¿Qué tiene Ud.?
Qual' è il cambio?	Qual é o câmbio?	¿A cuánto está el cambio?
Che tempo fa?	Que tempo faz?	¿Qué tiempo hace?
Che cosa è questo?	O que é isto?	¿Qué es esto?
A che serve questo?	Para que é isto?	¿Para qué sirve esto?
Qual' è il Suo indirizzo?	Qual é o seu enderêço?	¿Cuáles son sus señas?
Come si chiama?	Como se chama?	¿Cómo se llama?
Che genere di...?	Que tipo de...?	¿Qué clase de...?
A che ora incomincia?	Quando começa?	¿Cuándo empieza?
Che ora è?	Que horas são?	¿Qué hora es?
Che cosa prende?	Que quer?	¿Qué quiere Ud. tomar?
Che c'è di nuovo?	Que há de nôvo?	¿Qué hay de nuevo?
grano; frumento	trigo	trigo
ruota	roda	rueda
poltrona a rotelle	cadeira de rodas	silla de ruedas
quando	quando	cuando
Quando?	Quando?	¿Cuándo?
A che ora finisce?	A que horas acaba?	¿Cuándo termina?
A che ora parte (il treno)?	Quando sai (o trem)?	¿Cuándo sale (el tren)?
Quando è aperto?	Quando é aberto?	¿Cuándo se abre?
Quando devo ritornare?	Quando devo voltar?	¿Cuándo debo volver?

English	*French*	*German*
When were you born?	Quand êtes-vous **né?**	Wann sind Sie geboren?
When will it be ready?	Quand sera-t-il **prêt?**	Wann wird es **fertig** sein?
whenever	chaque fois que	so oft
Where? (in what place?)	Où?	**Wo?**
Where? (to what place?)	Où?	**Wohin?**
Where are...?	Où sont...?	Wo sind...?
Where are you from?	D'où venez-**vous?**	Woher **stammen** Sie?
Where are you going?	Où allez-**vous?**	Wohin gehen Sie?
Where can I find...?	Où puis-je trou**ver...?**	Wo kann ich... finden?
Where can I mail...?	Où puis-je mettre... à la **poste?**	Wo kann ich dies-... aufgeben?
Where can I send...?	Où puis-je envoyer...?	Wo kann ich... schicken?
Where do I pay?	Où dois-je payer?	Wo bezahlt man?
Where do you live?	Où demeurez-**vous?**	Wo wohnen Sie?
Where is (the nearest)?	Où se trouve... le plus **proche?**	Wo ist der (etc.) nächste...?
Where to?	Où?	**Wohin?**
Where were you born?	Où êtes-vous **né?**	Wo sind Sie geboren?
wherever (no matter where)	n'importe **où**	wo **immer**
whether (either)	soit	ob
whether (if)	si	ob
Which?	Lequel?	**Welcher, etc.**
Which is the way to...?	Comment arrive-t-on à...?	Wie kommt man nach (zum)...?
whichever (adj.)	n'importe quel...	welcher, etc.
while (during the time that) (conj.)	pendant **que**	**während**
while (short time)	temps *m*	Weile *f*
whip (flog), to	fouetter	peitschen
whipped cream	crème *f* fouet**tée**	Schlagsahne *f*
whisk broom	balayette *f*	Handfeger *m*
whisky	whisky *m*	Whisky *m*
whisper, to	chuchoter	flüstern

Italian	*Portuguese*	*Spanish*
Quando è nato?	**Quando nasceu?**	**¿Cuándo nació?**
Quando sarà pronto?	**Quando ficará (estará) pronto?**	**¿Cuándo estará listo?**
ogni volta che	sempre que	siempre que
Dove?	**Onde?**	**¿Dónde?**
Dove?	**Para onde?**	**¿A dónde?**
Dove si trovano...?	**Onde estão...?**	**¿Dónde están...?**
Di dov' è Lei?	**De onde é?**	**¿De dónde es Ud.?**
Dove va Lei?	**Para onde vai?**	**¿A dónde va Ud.?**
Dove potrei trovare...?	**Onde posso obter...?**	**¿Dónde puedo conseguir...?**
Dove posso impostare...?	**Onde posso pôr no correio...?**	**¿Dónde puedo echar al correo...?**
Dove posso spedire...?	**Onde posso mandar...?**	**¿Dónde puedo enviar...?**
Dove pago?	**Onde pago?**	**¿Dónde pago?**
Dove abita?	**Onde mora?**	**¿Dónde vive?**
Dov' è (il)... più vicino?	**Onde fica (o)... mais cercano?**	**¿Dónde está (el)... más cercano?**
Dove?	**Para onde?**	**¿A dónde?**
Dov' è nato?	**Onde nasceu?**	**¿Dónde nació?**
non importa dove	onde quer que	dondequiera que
sia	quer ... quer	sea que...o que
se	se	si
Quale?	**Qual?**	**¿Cuál?**
Qual è la strada che porta a...?	**Por onde é...?**	**¿Por dónde se va a...?**
qualunque	qualquer que	cual (es) quiera (que)
mentre	enquanto; ao passo que	mientras (que)
breve tempo	espaço de tempo	rato
frustare	açoitar	azotar
panna montata	creme *m* batido	nata batida
scopetta	vassourinha; escôva	escobilla
whisky *m*	whisky *m*; uísque *m*	whisky *m*
bisbigliare	cochichar	cuchichear

English	*French*	*German*
whistle, to	siffler	pfeifen
white	blanc, blanche	weiss
white wine	vin *m* blanc	Weisswein *m*
Who?	Qui (est-ce qui)?	Wer?
who (rel.)	qui	der, die, das
Who is it?	Qui est-ce?	Wer ist es?
Who is knocking?	Qui frappe?	Wer klopft?
Who knows?	Qui sait?	Wer weiss?
whoever (any person who)	quiconque	wer auch immer
whole (adj.)	entier (*f* entière)	ganz
wholesale	en gros	Engros...
Whom?	Qui (est-ce que)?	Wen?
whom (rel.)	que	den, die, das, die
whooping cough	coqueluche *f*	Keuchhusten *m*
Whose?	À qui?	Wessen?
whose (rel.)	dont	dessen; deren
Why?	Pourquoi?	Warum?
Why not?	Pourquoi pas?	Warum nicht?
wick (lighter-)	mèche *f*	Docht *m*
wide (not narrow)	large	breit; weit
widow	veuve *f*	Witwe *f*
widower	veuf *m*	Witwer *m*
width	largeur *f*	Breite *f*; Weite *f*
wife	femme *f*	Frau *f*
wild (not tame)	sauvage	wild
wild boar	sanglier *m*	Wildschwein *n*
wilderness	désert *m*	Wildnis *f*
will (document)	testament *m*	Testament *n*
Will there be...?	Y aura-t-il...?	Wird (werden)... sein (geben)?
willing, to be	vouloir bien	bereitwillig sein
willingly	de bon gré	gern
wilt, to	se flétrir	welken
win, to	gagner	gewinnen
wind (a timepiece)	remonter	aufziehen
wind (breeze)	vent *m*	Wind *m*
window	fenêtre *f*	Fenster *n*

Italian	*Portuguese*	*Spanish*
fischiare	assobiar; silvar	silbar
bianco	branco	blanco
vino bianco	vinho branco	vino blanco
Chi?	Quem?	¿Quién?
che	que	que
Chi è?	Quem é?	¿Quién es?
Chi bussa?	Quem chama?	¿Quién llama?
Chi sa?	Quem sabe?	¿Quién sabe?
chiunque	quem quer que	quienquiera que
intero	inteiro	entero
all' ingrosso	por atacado	al por mayor
Chi?	Quem?	¿A quién?
che, cui	que	que, a quien (es)
pertosse *f*	tosse *f* comprida	tos *f* ferina
Di chi?	De quem?	¿De quién?
il cui	cujo	cuyo
Perchè?	Por que?	¿Por qué?
Perchè no?	Por que não?	¿Por qué no?
stoppino	pavio; mecha	mecha
largo	largo	ancho
vedova	viúva	viuda
vedovo	viúvo	viudo
larghezza	largura; largo	anchura
moglie *f*	mulher *f*; espôsa	esposa; mujer *f*
selvaggio	selvagem	salvaje
cinghiale *m*	javali *m*	jabalí *m*
deserto	êrmo; sertão	yermo
testamento	testamento	testamento
Ci sará...?	Haverá...?	¿Habrá...?
essere disposto a	estar disposto a	estar deseoso a
volentieri	de bom grado	de buena gana
avvizzire	murchar	marchitarse
vincere	vencer; ganhar	vencer; ganar
caricare	dar corda a	dar cuerda a
vento	vento	viento
finestra	janela	ventana

English	*French*	*German*
window (in vehicle)	fenêtre *f*; glace *f*	Wagenfenster *n*
windshield	pare-brise *m*	Windschutzscheibe *f*
windshield wiper	essuie-**glace** *m*	Scheibenwischer *m*
wine	vin *m*	Wein *m*
wine glass	verre *m* à **vin**	Weinglas *n*
wine list	carte *f* des **vins**	Weinkarte *f*
wing (anat.)	aile *f*	Flügel *m*
wing (theat.)	coulisse *f*	Kulisse *f*
winter	hiver *m*	Winter *m*
wipe (-clean or -off)	nettoyer	reinigen
wipe (dry), to	essuyer	wischen
wire (metal)	fil *m*	Draht *m*
wisdom (being wise)	sagesse *f*	Weisheit *f*
wisdom (judgment)	jugement *m*	Weisheit *f*
wise	sage	weise; klug
wish	désir *m*; souhait *m*	Wunsch *m*
wish for, to	désirer	wünschen
wit (humor)	esprit *m*	Witz *m*
with	avec	mit
with bath	avec salle de **bain**	mit **Bad**
with me	avec **moi**	mit **mir**
with pleasure	avec **plaisir**	sehr gerne
with us	avec **nous**	mit uns
with what (where-with)	avec **quoi**	womit
with your permission	permettez-**moi**	mit Ihrer Erlaubnis
within (inside) (adv.)	à l'intérieur	drinnen
within (prep.)	dans	innerhalb (gen.)
without (conj.)	sans **que**	ohne **dass**
without (prep.)	sans	ohne
without bath	sans salle *f* de **bain**	ohne **Bad**
without doubt	sans **doute**	ohne Zweifel
without fail	sans **faute**	unfehlbar
witness (n.)	témoin *m*	Zeuge *m*
wolf	loup *m*	Wolf *m*
woman	femme *f*	Frau *f*

Italian	*Portuguese*	*Spanish*
finestrino	janelinha	ventanilla
parabrezza *m*	pára-brisa *m*	parabrisas *m*
tergicristallo	limpador *m* de pára-brisa	limpiaparabrisas *m*
vino	vinho	vino
bicchiere *m* da vino	copo para vinho	copa
lista dei vini	lista de vinhos	lista de vinos
ala	asa	ala
quinta	bastidores *mpl*	bastidor *m*
inverno	inverno	invierno
pulire	limpar	limpiar
asciugare	secar	secar
filo metallico	arame *m*	alambre *m*
saggezza	sabedoria	sabiduría
giudizio	juízo	juicio
saggio	sábio	sabio
desiderio	desejo	deseo
desiderare	desejar	desear
spirito	espírito; graça	humor *m*; ingenio
con	com	con
con bagno	com banho	con baño
meco; con me	comigo	conmigo
con piacere	com muito prazer	con mucho gusto
con noi	conosco	con nosotros
con che	com que	con qué
con permesso	com licença	con permiso
all' interno	dentro	dentro
dentro	dentro de	dentro de
senza che	sem que	sin que
senza	sem	sin
senza bagno	sem banheiro	sin baño
senza dubbio	sem dúvida	sin duda
senza meno; senza fallo	sem falta	sin falta
testimone *m*	testigo	testigo
lupo	lôbo	lobo
donna	mulher *f*	mujer *f*

English	*French*	*German*
wonder (ask oneself)	se demander	sich fragen
wonderful!	magnifique!	wunderbar!
wood (lumber)	bois *m*	Holz *n*
wooden (of wood)	de bois	hölzern; aus **Holz**
wood(s) (forest)	bois *m*	Wald *m*
wool (cloth)	laine *f*	Wolle *f*
woolen (of wool)	de laine	wollen
word	mot *m*; pa**role** *f*	Wort *n*
work (labor) (n.)	travail *m*	Arbeit *f*
work (opus)	oeuvre *f*	Werk *n*
work, to	travailler	arbeiten
worker	ouvrier *m*	Arbeiter *m*
workshop	atelier *m*	Werkstätte *f*
world	monde *m*	Welt *f*
worm	ver *m*	Wurm *m*
worried	préoccupé	besorgt
worry, to	se tourmenter	sich sorgen
worse (adj.)	pire	schlimmer
worse (adv.)	pis	schlimmer
worst (adj.)	(le) pire	schlimmst
worth (n.)	valeur *f*	Wert *m*
worth, to be	valoir	wert sein; **gelten**
worth while, to be	valoir la **peine**	sich lohnen
worthless	sans valeur	wertlos
worthy	digne	würdig; wert
wound	bles**sure** *f*	Wunde *f*
wound, to	blesser	verwunden
wounded (p.p.)	bles**sé**	verwundet
wrap up, to	envelopper	einpacken
wrapping paper	papier *m* d'emballage	**Packpapier** *n*
wreath	couronne *f*	Kranz *m*
wrecker (auto)	dépanneuse *f*	Abschleppwagen *m*
wrench (tool)	clef *f* an**glaise**	**Schrauben-**schlüssel *m*
wrestle, to	lutter	ringen
wring, to	tordre	drehen
wrinkle (in clothes)	pli *m*	Falte *f*

Italian	*Portuguese*	*Spanish*
domandarsi	perguntar-se	preguntarse
magnifico!	formidável!	¡magnífico!
legno	madeira	madera
di legno	de madeira	de madera
bosco	bosque *m*; mata	bosque *m*
lana	lã	lana
di lana	de lã	de lana
parola	palavra	palabra
lavoro	trabalho	trabajo
lavoro; opera	obra	obra
lavorare	trabalhar	trabajar
operaio	trabalhador *m*	trabajador *m*
officina	oficina	taller *m*
mondo	mundo	mundo
verme *m*	verme *m*	gusano
preoccupato	preocupado	preocupado
preoccuparsi	preocupar-se	preocuparse
peggiore	pior	peor
peggio	pior	peor
(il) peggiore	(o) pior	(el) peor
valore *m*	valor *m*	valor *m*
valere	valer	valer
valere la pena	valer a pena	valer la pena
senza valore	sem valor	sin valor
degno	digno	digno
ferita	ferida	herida
ferire	ferir	herir
ferito	ferido	herido
avvolgere	embrulhar	envolver
carta da pacchi	papel *m* de embrulho	papel *m* de envolver
corona	coroa	guirnalda; corona
rimorchiatore *m*	carro-socorro	camión *m* de auxilio
chiave *f* inglese	chave *f* inglêsa	llave *f* inglesa
lottare	lutar corpo a corpo	luchar a brazo partido
torcere; strizzare	torcer; espremer	retorcer; exprimir
grinza	ruga	arruga

English	*French*	*German*
wrinkle (in skin)	ride *f*	Runzel *f*
wrist	poignet *m*	Handgelenk *n*
wrist watch	montre-bracelet *f*	Armbanduhr *f*
write, to	écrire	schreiben
Write it down, please	Veuillez l'écrire	Bitte, schreiben Sie es auf
writer (author)	écrivain *m*	Schriftsteller *m*
writing desk	bureau *m*	Schreibtisch *m*
writing paper	papier *m* à lettres	Schreibpapier *n*
written (p.p.)	écrit	geschrieben
wrong (incorrect)	erroné	falsch
wrong (unjust)	injuste	unrecht
wrong, to be	avoir tort	Unrecht haben
X-ray(s)	rayons X *mpl*	Röntgenstrahlen *mpl*
X-ray picture	radiographie *f*	Röntgenaufnahme *f*
X-ray, to	radiographier	durchleuchten
yard (court)	cour *f*	Hof *m*
yarn (fiber)	fil *m*	Garn *n*
yawn, to	bâiller	gähnen
year	an *m*; année *f*	Jahr *n*
yearly (adj.)	annuel	jährlich
yeast	levure *f*	Hefe *f*
yell, to	hurler	schreien; brüllen
yellow	jaune	gelb
yellow fever	fièvre *f* jaune	gelbes Fieber *n*
yes	oui	ja
Yes indeed!	Mais oui!	Jawohl!
Yes, thank you!	Oui, merci!	Bitte!
yesterday	hier	gestern
yet (however)	cependant	dennoch
yet (until now)	encore	noch
yield (give in), to	céder	nachgeben
you (dir. obj.)	vous	Sie
you (ind. obj.)	vous	Ihnen
you (subject, familiar)	tu	du
you (subject, polite)	vous	Sie
you are	vous êtes	Sie sind
You are mistaken	Vous vous trompez	Sie irren sich

Italian	*Portuguese*	*Spanish*
ruga	**ruga**	arruga
polso	**pulso**	muñeca
orologio da **polso**	relógio-pulseira	reloj *m* de pulsera
scrivere	escrever	escribir
Per favore, me lo **scriva**	Faça favor de escrevê-lo	¡Favor de escribirlo!
scrittore *m*	escritor *m*	escritor *m*
scrivania	escrivaninha; secretária	escritorio
carta da **scrivere**	**papel** *m* de escrever	papel *m* de escribir
scritto	escrito	escrito
sbagliato; errato	errado	equivocado
ingiusto	injusto	injusto
aver torto	não ter razão	no tener razón
raggi X *mpl*	raios X	rayos X
radiografia	radiografia	radiografía
radiografare	radiografar	radiografiar
cortile *m*	pátio; quintal *m*	patio; cercado
filato; filo	fio	hilado
sbadigliare	bocejar	bostezar
anno	ano	año
annuale	anual	anual
lievito	levedura	levadura
gridare	gritar	gritar
giallo	amarelo	amarillo
febbre *f* gialla	febre *f* amarela	fiebre *f* amarilla
sì	sim	sí
Sì, certo!	Claro que **sim!**	¡Claro que **sí!**
Sì, per piacere!	Sim, faça o favor!	¡Sí, gracias!
ieri	ontem	ayer
nondimeno; tuttavia	contudo; porém	sin embargo
ancora	ainda	todavía
cedere	ceder	ceder
La	o, a, os, as	le, la, les
Le	lhe, lhes	le, les
tu	tu; você	tú
Lei	o senhor, a senhora	Usted(es); Ud(s).
Lei è	o senhor é; está	Usted es; Usted está
Lei si **sbaglia**	O senhor se enganou	Usted se equivoca

English	*French*	*German*
You are very kind	Vous êtes très **aimable!**	Das ist sehr **freundlich** von Ihnen!
You don't say!	Pas possible!	Was Sie nicht **sagen!**
You're welcome!	Je vous en **prie!;** De **rien!**	Bitte (schön)!
You can...	Vous **pouvez...**	Sie können...
young (adj.)	jeune	jung
younger	plus **jeune**	jünger
youngest	le plus **jeune**	jüngste
youngster (kid)	gosse *m, f*	Kind *n*
your	votre, vos	Ihr
yours	le vôtre, etc.	der Ihre, etc.
youth (period)	jeunesse *f*	Jugend *f*
youth (young man)	jeune **homme** *m*	Jüngling *m*; der Junge Mann
youth hostel	auberge *f* de la Jeunesse	Jugendherberge *f*
Zaragoza	Saragosse	Saragossa *n*
zero	zéro *m*	Null *f*
zinc	zinc *m*	Zink *n*
zipper	fermeture *f* **éclair**	Reissverschluss *m*
zone (n.)	zone *f*	Zone *f*
zoo	jardin *m* zoologique	Zoo (logische **Garten**) *m*
Zurich	Zurich	Zürich *n*